THE EARLIER STONE AGE SETTLEMENT
OF SCANDINAVIA

To Scandinavian colleagues

THE EARLIER
STONE AGE SETTLEMENT
OF SCANDINAVIA

GRAHAME CLARK

MASTER OF PETERHOUSE AND
DISNEY PROFESSOR OF ARCHAEOLOGY IN
THE UNIVERSITY OF CAMBRIDGE

CAMBRIDGE UNIVERSITY PRESS

Published by the Syndics of the Cambridge University Press
Bentley House, 200 Euston Road, London NW1 2DB
American Branch: 32 East 57th Street, New York, N.Y.10022

© Cambridge University Press 1975

Library of Congress Catalogue Card Number: 73-94358

ISBN: 0 521 20446 1

First published 1975

Printed in Great Britain
at the University Printing House, Cambridge
(Euan Phillips, University Printer)

CONTENTS

v

CONTENTS

TABLES

TABLES

MAPS

MAPS

FIGURES

FIGURES

FIGURES

PLATES

PREFACE

The occasion for writing this book was an invitation from the Cambridge University Press to revise the text for reprinting *The Mesolithic Settlement of Northern Europe*. The proposal was a flattering one since that book had been published as long ago as 1936 and had never been reprinted, still less revised. Where frequent editions are called for it may often be possible to maintain the life of a standard work by injecting fresh information and eradicating or modifying conclusions shown to have been erroneous. Even so the time comes when old books can no longer absorb new information, for it is not only facts that change but the concepts that give them meaning. There is a generational tide in ideas and interests that frequently cuts across academic disciplines and renders stale what may once have been novel and exciting. When a book is thirty-eight years old, especially when it has received no intermediate editions, it is unlikely to be a useful vehicle for new information. I decided therefore instead to write a new book.

The time is past for another work introducing English readers to the bare sequence of Scandinavian Stone Age archaeology or even to the context of its various phases in the history of environmental change. The present work will be concerned with a specific theme, the manner in which Scandinavia was first colonised since the time when by far the greater part of it first became available for settlement. The reasons why I chose this region as a geographical frame of reference are stated further on in this Preface. In the meantime it needs to be stated which of the several definitions of Scandinavia is followed in this book. I shall use it to embrace the Fennoscandian shield, comprising Finland, much the greater part of Sweden and the whole of Norway, and south Scandinavia, in which I include Denmark and southernmost Sweden, much of which formed part of the Danish dominions down to 1658. I intend to concentrate on my chosen area because I am concerned above all with the process of settlement and with the means by which patterns of social life were maintained over long periods of time by exploiting the natural resources of specific territories in particular ways. At the same time, since the first people to colonise Scandinavia must have come from territories south and east of the Baltic basin, it is no less evident that some attention must be paid to the archaeology of the tract of territory extending from north Germany, Poland, the east Baltic states and northern Russia as far east as the Ural mountains. Again, despite the emphasis on continuity of settlement, on the tenacity with which people, once possessed of territory, tend to hold and exploit it, the fact remains that the social changes reflected in the archaeological data were to a significant degree affected or precipitated by contacts from without. In this connection one should not forget that Jutland and to begin with the rest of south Scandinavia formed a north-ward extension of the north European plain and that Finland and to a remoter degree northern Scandinavia as a whole was a western extension of the northern taiga reaching as far east as the Ural moun-tains; again, one should remember that the enclosed waters of the Baltic formed a common hunting and fishing ground and could easily have been crossed by primitive craft or, when frozen, on foot.

For a number of reasons, some practical, others reflecting the current state of research and publication, it has proved convenient to present this study of the Scandinavian Stone Age in two volumes. The present one covers the older Stone Age, that is the period from the Late-glacial to the end of the Atlantic period dealt with in 1936 from another point of view in *The Mesolithic Settlement of Northern Europe*. The second, now in preparation, is concerned on the one hand with the development of agriculture and peasant communities and on the other with the quite remarkable and sophisticated economies based on a variety of forms of catching and foraging in territories where these were the most economical methods of harvesting natural resources. Although directed to the same basic theme as the second, the first and present volume has been so constructed as to form an independent work with its own index and list of references.

My reasons for choosing Scandinavia as a theatre are in part the same as those which led me to this region first in my study of Meso-lithic settlement and later for the several articles concerned with basic subsistence activities of prehistoric hunter-gatherers written in prepara-tion for *Prehistoric Europe: the economic basis*. These include: (1) the wealth of evidence relating to prehistoric settlement in the area, a wealth accounted for in part by natural conditions which at least in south Scandinavia have favoured the survival of organic traces vital to a reconstruction of subsistence patterns and crucial also to an appreciation of the technical equipment available to the early inhabitants of the region, (2) the long tradition of systematic archaeological research and the relatively full knowledge of temporal and spatial patterns in the cultural material, (3) the magnitude of changes in the habitat and biosphere that have taken place during the period of human occupation and the clarity with which such changes have been charted, notably in respect of the progressive contraction of the Scandinavian ice-sheet, and in regard to land and sea levels, climate, vegetation and animal life, (4) the abundance and reliability of geochronological indices, the product of intensive application of radiocarbon analysis both directly to organic traces from archaeological occupation layers and indirectly to sequential changes in the biosphere and habitat established by Quaternary research and not least (5) the admirable school of Northern Ethnography and the rich documentation of the kind of activities responsible for much of the material of prehistoric archaeology, a documentation rendered possible by the relative tardiness of industrialisation and the fact that farming has normally been carried on there, sometimes down to modern times, in association with a variety of the catching and gathering activities.

Another good reason for returning to Scandinavia is that knowledge of any region and of the institutions and personalities concerned with its archaeology, history, ethnography and Quaternary environment is of its nature cumulative. It seemed better to cultivate and intensify my understanding of Scandinavia as a region and as a field of archaeological research, than to start up in a new field even if one could have been found as suitable as this for the purpose in hand.

ACKNOWLEDGEMENTS

My knowledge of the Scandinavian terrain as it exists today as well as of the key archaeological sites and of the museums in which the small finds are stored and to some extent displayed extends over more than forty years. My first experiences were confined to the collections of Copenhagen, Lund and Stockholm and to the countryside of Scania, but in 1936 our honeymoon took us further afield to the rock-engravings of Jämtland, the Trøndelag and east Norway and the collections at Trondheim, Oslo and Bergen. Before the war interrupted travel we managed to explore Schleswig-Holstein and acquire some understanding, with the help of Albrecht Rust, Gustav Schwantes and Karl Kersten of the Late-glacial and early Post-glacial archaeology of this key region, to visit sites and more particularly Iron Age settlements in northern Jutland in the stimulating company of Gudmund Hatt and to take in Fünen, Langeland and Zealand. In 1947 the opportunity came to see something of the more northerly parts of Scandinavia when the Trustees of the Leverhulme Foundation made possible the extended travel that proved so valuable as a stimulus to the production of *Prehistoric Europe*. My round journey began with a memorable expedition from Bergen to Hespriholm and Bømlo off the west coast in the company of J. Bøe, Johannes Brøndsted and Knut Fægri and thence by sea up to the west coast of Norway stopping off at various points on the route to Tromsø and its rich collections from the far north. I then traversed Swedish Lappland and rounded the head of the Gulf of Bothnia before heading south through Finland to Helsingfors where I was introduced by C. A. Nordman to the rich archaeological collections, and by T. I. Itkonen to the no less rich and indeed unique ethnographic data. Crossing to Stockholm the experience of viewing the phenomenon of human adaptation to a common (even though rapidly changing) environment was carried further when I was able to complement study in the State Historical Museum by an introduction under the tutelage of Gösta Berg to the riches of the Nordiska Museum. An exciting archaeological experience was a flying visit to Gotland where I was able among other things to visit Mårten Stenberger's excavations at Vallhager. A family vacation in 1955 gave the opportunity to traverse the mixed-forest zone between Göteborg and Stockholm, to cross the southern part of the coniferous zone of Dalarna and to experience the southernmost outlier in Sweden of the *fjäll*–reindeer–Lapp zone in the neighbourhood of Grövelsjön. The journey was rounded off by passing through the Hamardal to Oslo and down the Bohuslän coast, taking in the rock-engravings of Tanum. Other visits that stand out in memory include attendance at the 1954 Radio-Carbon Conference at Copenhagen and at the Lund meeting of the Permanent Council of the International Conference of Pre- and Protohistoric Sciences, each of which presented opportunities of fruitful contacts with colleagues as well as for museum study.

The decision to write the present book called for additional travel and contact with colleagues and material. In 1971 we decided to fill gaps in our knowledge of southern Norway and northernmost Jutland. Entering Norway by way of Christiansand we passed through the archaeologically rich area of Jæren stopping at Stavanger Museum and visiting the classic cave site of Viste excavated first by Haakon Shetelig and later by H. E. Lund, whose wife most kindly accompanied us to the site. At Bergen we were made welcome in the library of the Archaeological Institute of the University, thanks to the good offices of Professor Anders Hagen, and we owe much to Dr Egil Bakke who went to the greatest trouble to show us the terrain of the west Norwegian 'dwelling-place culture', as well as the locations of individual sites, including those investigated by himself, as well as such 'classic' ones at Ruskenesset and Skippshelleren. Our stay in Bergen was further enriched by discussions with Professor Fægri. On the way to Oslo we spent a few days with Aarne Johansen's Hardangervidda Project at Halne where we had a renewed opportunity of experiencing a reindeer habitat and had the chance of discussing the problem of the earliest settlement by man in this region. From Oslo we crossed the Skagerrak to Frederikshavn, a route followed in each direction during the Stone Age, in order to explore Vendsyssel and Thy, including the Late-glacial cliffs of Nørre Lyngby, the Litorina shore-lines of the Limfjord as well as field monuments and museums. Before returning home, by way of Esjberg, we traversed the landscape of Therkel Mathiassen's so-called 'Gudenaa culture' to Aahrus where we stayed briefly at the University Institute of Prehistoric Archaeology at Møsgaard, a visit made memorable by the new museum as well as by fruitful conversations with Paul Kjærum and Søren Andersen.

A main gap in my experience of Sweden was that apart from Dalarna and Jämtland I had very little knowledge of the huge territory of Norrland comprising nearly two-thirds of the country and only a cursory experience of the territories immediately adjacent to Lake Mälar. The opportunity to remedy this as well as to indulge in a long period of reading and museum study came in 1972 when I held a Visiting Professorship at Uppsala University under a scheme sponsored by the Trustees of the Leverhulme Foundation and administered by the British Academy. I am immensely grateful to both these institutions for making this possible as well as to Uppsala University. More particularly I am indebted to the Institute for Nordic and Comparative

Archaeology whose seminar and splendid library are housed appropriately in the Gustavianum, a former palace of the Archbishops, later the headquarters of the Royal University and now the headquarters of three departments concerned with the culture of antiquity. I would like to acknowledge the help given me in the course of discussion and in many practical ways especially by Professor Bertil Almgren, Director of the Institute, by Docent Ulf Hagberg, Dr Hans Christiansson and Lic. Bo Gräslund. I also benefited greatly from discussions with Professor Sten Florin and Professor Lars König-Königsson the present director of the University's Institute of Quaternary Research as well as from the use of the Institute's excellent library. Residence at Uppsala also made it practicable to examine at leisure the landscape on either side of Lake Mälar, more particularly in north Södermanland and Uppland. A day's excursion led by Ingvar Jansson of the Uppsala Seminar round the Stone Age sites first explored by Ekholm half a century ago in western Uppland stands out with particular clarity and it was a special privilege to be taken by Bertil Almgren on another occasion round some of the recently discovered Bronze Age rock-engravings of the region.

Uppsala was also exceptionally well placed in relation to Stockholm, where the staff of the State Historical Museum and in particular Dr Evert Baudou and Dr Louise Cederschiöld showed great forbearance. The Gustavianum also proved a fine centre from which to make expeditions to Finland and Norrland. I am particularly grateful to Dr Torsten Edgren, Coordinator of Archaeological Research for Finland, who most kindly took us to see Suomusjärvi and Comb Ware sites between Turku and Helsingfors and gave most valuable assistance with the literature, as well as in gaining access to material in the National Museum. Although on vacation at the time, Professor Meinander went out of his way to welcome us and allow us the use of the library of his Institute.

In respect of Norrland we began by revisiting Dalarna as guests of Dr and Mrs Gösta Berg than whom there could have been no better guides to the traditional background of the peasant culture of the region; but our main objectives lay further north in the territories affected by modern hydro-electric schemes designed to harness the great rivers flowing down from the Caledonian *fjäll* country through the coniferous forest zone and the coastal tract to the Gulf of Bothnia. Preliminary reports of a generalised nature and exhibits in the State Historical Museum had made it clear that rescue and survey operations in advance of flooding had opened a new dimension in the prehistory of Sweden. We are extremely grateful to Dr Evert Baudou, head of the prehistoric section of the State Historical Museum, who has charge of the scientific publications of the discoveries made by N.T.B. (Norrlands Tidlig Bebyggelse or Norrlands Early Settlement) Project, for showing us something of Ångermanland and its early archaeology. In his company we gained a vivid impression of the magnitude of geographic change resulting from isostatic recovery of land during the period of human settlement, in a territory with a maximum vertical displacement of over 280 m. The rapidity of land recovery was vividly illustrated by the Bronze Age cairns distributed along the coast at successive levels between 30 and 50 m above modern sea-level. Moving upstream we had the opportunity to examine the rock-engravings among the rapids of the Ångerman river, a concentration first scientifically surveyed and recorded by Gustav Hallström, who had received us while on our honeymoon in Stockholm and in the years before the First World War had accompanied our old teacher Miles Burkitt to this same site. The abundance of traces of settlement along the rivers and lakes of the interior testified to the wide-ranging activities of Stone Age man in the north, and the heights above sea-level of the oldest ones again bore witness to the scale and rapidity of geographical change. We next moved further north into Västerbotten, the territory of the Norrlands Arkeologie Project led by Dr Hans Christiansson and centred locally on the museums at Umeå and Skellefteå. We were unfortunately deprived by circumstances of Dr Christiansson's company, but we are most grateful to him for many enlightening talks and for ensuring that we were well looked after, as well as to Mr and Mrs Neil Broadbent of the Uppsala Seminar, Dr Eric Westerlund of Skellefteå Museum and Lenart Sundqvist of Bjurselet for demonstrating sites and discussing their problems on the ground.

When the time came to return home we visited the strangely neglected site of Alvastra close to the north-east shore of Lake Vättern, just as on the way out we had gained a useful impression of the mega-lithic passage-graves concentrated on the Falbygden. A brief visit to the Archaeological Museum at Göteborg gave us some impression of the difficulty of the research being carried out there on the Stone Age settlement of west Sweden due in part to a peculiarly complex history of change in the levels of land and sea.

While still conscious of some omissions of particular interest in respect of their archaeology – notably Finnmark and the islands of Bornholm and Öland – we have been fortunate to gain some first hand impression of most of the varied landscapes of Scandinavia as well as to visit many of their outstanding prehistoric sites and archaeological museums. In the course of this we have met with uniform helpfulness and cooperation. A word of particular gratitude is due to museum staffs. As I well know, directly from personal experience and vicariously from the complaints of research students, it is not everywhere that one finds museums staffed by men and women well qualified by training and willing to make their collections and their knowledge freely available to those who wish to use them. The excellence of the photographic work done in Scandinavian museums is also a subject for grateful comment.

In writing a book of this kind an author owes more than he can realise to the work of others and to their willingness to communicate. I have benefited from countless conversations and bibliographical clues, many of which are only tacitly recognised. Where scholars have published their discoveries and their ideas acknowledgement has been made in the usual way by citing their works, many of which are listed at the end of this book. No attempt has been made to prepare even a restricted bibliography, nor has every work consulted been listed. My aim has been to make it possible for readers to check information by reference to detailed papers or monographs, as far as possible ones likely to be available in a good archaeological library. Where I have been able to cite relatively accessible works provided with full references I have often felt justified in omitting references to local or ephemeral publications.

Where so many differing views have been expressed on particular topics, it is hardly possible for an author to agree with all his authorities. On the other hand I have avoided the kind of polemical writing occasionally suitable in the periodicals. When I cite an article or monograph this only means that I have consulted it, not necessarily that I concur with an author's conclusions. In writing this book I have of necessity gone beyond what can be demonstrated with precision. What I have aimed to do – and that is all any author is surely entitled to do in discussing a subject about which so little is known – is to present hypotheses in the light of explicit theory and in terms of systematically acquired data. One of the main results of such a study is to bring out even more clearly the deficiencies in our data, the need not merely for more research, but for research devoted to specific questions and supported with adequate means.

PREFACE

Amid the banalities of the consumer society and the business of science in ministering to physical needs, the chances of attracting sufficient resources to the study of men as human beings might appear small. Yet there are encouraging signs, not least among professional scientists, of an increasing recognition of the value and relevance of the humanities and of the need to give much greater financial support for studying the history of the beings for whose welfare all other activities including the pursuit of the natural sciences are supposedly carried on. It has given me immense encouragement to be associated, if only symbolically, and in an honorary capacity, with some of the leading academic institutions in Scandinavia dedicated to the advance of knowledge in this sphere, notably the Royal Society of Denmark (Hist. Phil. Class), the Society of Northern Antiquaries of Copenhagen, the Jutland Archaeological Society, the Royal Scientific Society of Uppsala (Hist. Phil. Class), the Gustav Adolf Academy, Stockholm, and the Finnish Archaeological Society.

Last but far from least it is a pleasure to acknowledge the huge advantages I have enjoyed in my home environment. No familiarity can lessen the stimulus to long sustained scholarly endeavour bestowed by association with my College, Peterhouse, or again with the British Academy and in particular with its Archaeology Section. Again, I have been fortunate to work in the Faculty of Archaeology and Anthropology at Cambridge, the only one in Europe to enjoy the advantage so widely shared in the New World of combining in an intimate and organic way the study of technologically simple societies in both living and fossil forms. As one engaged since 1946 in studying the economic aspects of prehistory, I have found it logical to approach Scandinavian prehistory in the way I have done in this book, but I would like to acknowledge the stimulus received particularly in respect of territory from association with Eric Higgs and his colleagues working for the British Academy's Major Research Project on the Early History of Agriculture. In conclusion, let me add that I owe more than I can say to the help and forbearance of my wife, my companion on nearly all my travels and one who has helped by drawing specimens, criticising my text and generally putting up with the trials of having a perennial author in the house. Above all she has learned to accept that the launching of one book serves only to clear my study for another.

Peterhouse, Cambridge   GRAHAME CLARK

1973

I

Some basic concepts

It is important at the outset to emphasise that the basic theme of this book, the colonisation and exploitation of Scandinavia by prehistoric man, is one about which extremely little is known. Paradoxically it is only when the initial stages in archaeological research have been carried out as well as they have been in Scandinavia that it becomes easier to see how much remains to be learned about the proper subject of concern, the social life of prehistoric man. It follows that a book of this kind ought to concern itself as much with defining areas of ignorance as with displaying what is known, since it is only by giving direction to research that we can hope to learn more about the way in which the communities represented in the archaeological record in fact lived.

I have already hinted at the difficulty of the subject, a difficulty of which I had little idea when as a younger man I addressed myself to the early settlement of northern Europe (Clark 1936). One reason why we know so little is that by comparison with the large and disciplined resources brought to bear on the natural sciences those directed to the early history of man have been relatively puny and haphazard. Yet no increase in material means can alter the difficulties inherent in the subject. These arise at bottom from the number and complexity of the variables and contingencies of which account needs to be taken when studying human affairs, more especially when these have to be studied indirectly through the medium of vestigial material data. By comparison the study of other animals, of plants or of rocks is of an altogether lower level of complexity, a warning if one were needed that methods and approaches adequate for the natural sciences are seldom appropriate to prehistory except for answering specific kinds of question. I nevertheless remain convinced, as I have been for many years (since Clark 1949, 188), that to extract the most from archaeological data we need to view them in both ecological and social terms.

The ecological approach. Both archaeology and anthropology have had to free themselves from dogmatic formulations that stemmed from evolutionary ideas prematurely applied before they could establish themselves as serious disciplines. Social anthropology could only emerge as an effective study after its exponents had repudiated an outlook dominated at bottom by a crude concept of unilinear evolution and an ineffable sense of superiority. When A. C. Haddon took his team to the Torres Straits in 1898 he made a clean break with the past by treating the indigenous peoples of New Guinea as worthy of study in their own right rather than as fossils of a bygone state of society. As H. J. Fleure so admirably phrased it in his obituary notice for the Royal Society in 1940 (453), Haddon 'was too sagacious to fall into the ancient error which supposed that all humanity was struggling up different rungs of one and the same ladder'. The mere act of leaving his study and going out to record the customs and technology of remote non-literate people in a particular region was all the more striking in that James Frazer was still ensconced in his study enlarging *The Golden Bough* with twigs and branches plucked from a thousand contexts in a wide range of cultures active at many periods of time. From one point of view Haddon's example pointed the way all the more effectively that he was content to act without striking a self-conscious theoretical posture. Yet a general advance in fact waited on a more analytical approach and specifically on the formulation of theories bearing on how primitive societies functioned. The publication in 1922 of the monographs of A. Radcliffe-Brown on *The Andaman Islanders* and by B. Malinowski on *Argonauts of the Pacific* marked an important advance precisely because each concentrated on trying to discover how primitive societies worked and how they were structured to perform the tasks which had to be performed if life was to be maintained and succeeding generations raised. Anthropologists in fact were beginning to view human societies as functioning systems in much the same way as under the inspiration of A. G. Tansley (1911) botanists had been learning to study plants in ecological terms as components of communities occupying specific habitats in association and competition with other forms of life. And there was more to it than mere analogy. The next great break-through in the study of primitive societies came when social systems were analysed in the context of the ecosystems in which they operated, to which they were adjusted and of which in a certain sense they even formed a part. The pioneer studies by D. F. Thomson (1939) on the Wik-Monkan people of Cape York peninsula and by E. Evans-Pritchard (1940) on the Nuer of the Upper Nile were concerned among other things to trace the effect of seasonal rhythms on economic and social life. The effect of these and the many studies stimulated by them has been to bring out the manner in which social systems and ways of life were so to say intermeshed with natural systems.

Archaeologists have for some time been learning to study their data in similar fashion. Instead of concentrating on a restricted range of data and using this exclusively as a means of defining periods and cultural assemblages, archaeologists have widened the scope of their evidence. Success in further expanding the evidential base must depend in the first instance on concentrating excavation on sites where the maximum range of primary data may be expected to survive, that is sites retaining organic materials, the materials on which men lived and on which in primitive society they depend very largely for their equipment. Aims and strategies go together. So long as archaeologists concentrated, as in the initial stages of research in any area they had to, on defining cultural assemblages, their genesis, contacts and chronology, there was even an advantage in concentrating on limited categories of the least perishable materials like flint, stone, metal and fired clay, since these could be relied upon to survive in most circumstances. On the other hand, once it was admitted that the time had come to discover how people in fact lived, then it followed that extra efforts had to be made to find and excavate sites where organic materials were most likely to survive. The very possibility of bioarchaeology, the archaeology concerned first and foremost with life, depends on obtaining the most adequate samples of these materials from archaeological levels. It was for instance the wealth of organic data contained in the settlement mounds (terpen) of north Holland, data ranging from farmsteads to food refuse, that led van Giffen to want to explore them systematically; and it was this concept that underlay his creation of the Biological–Archaeological Institute at Groningen. To take an example from my own experience the excavations at Star Carr (1949–51) were undertaken for the express purpose of recovering the organic components of an archaeological assemblage previously represented by lithic assemblages and isolated objects of antler or bone: recovery of animal and plant remains made it possible not merely to obtain a much fuller picture of the material equipment of a Maglemosian group, but also to gain some

3

insight into its scale, its basis of subsistence and its seasonal round (Clark *et al.* 1954; Clark 1972*a*).

When I wrote *Prehistoric Europe: the economic basis* I did so partly as an act of propaganda to illustrate how much information bearing on economic life during prehistoric times already existed and by implication how rich a harvest might be expected if research could be turned in this direction. Economic life was chosen partly because evidence for this, however unsystematic, was nevertheless most ready to hand, but partly also for a theoretical reason: I was interested in the conjunction of human society and natural environment implicit in the fact that men could live only by utilising their habitat and eating components of the biome. The economy practised by a prehistoric community had to represent 'a more or less perfect adjustment between social appetites, technical capacity and organisation' and the available natural resources (Clark 1952, 7). The concern was made explicit again in 'The Economic Approach to Prehistory' in which I defined my main theme as 'the interplay between culture, habitat and biome' (Clark 1953, 218).

In both these publications I was at pains to emphasise three closely related points: first that the economic arrangements made by prehistoric communities were not conditioned by but rather were adjusted to available natural resources; second that the nature of this adjustment underwent major changes in time, changes which served to define the periodisation of conventional archaeology; and thirdly, if not perhaps so explicitly, that economic life cannot be understood out of its social context. My approach was broadly ecological, but I was careful to emphasise the difference in the level of complexity of ecosystems that comprehended human societies and those that did not.

Uniqueness of human society. The study of animal behaviour is capable of yielding valuable insights into human behaviour only in so far as the basic distinction between them is kept in mind. Indeed, as anthropologists have recently been emphasising, the main result of applying the principles of animal behaviour to human societies is to highlight their differences. In a recent reconsideration of the results of the Star Carr investigation I made the point explicitly that models of thought 'appropriate to biology are insufficiently sophisticated to cope without qualification with all the complexities of human society' (Clark 1972*a*, 15) and pointed to the qualitative difference that exists between 'communities whose members subscribed to socially transmitted and

4

consciously held values' and those of animals whose behaviour was not so conditioned. Again in *Aspects of Prehistory* (Clark 1970, 145) I emphasised that one can only usefully study human behaviour by remembering that in the course of the last two or three million years man has emerged as a very special kind of animal, an animal whose 'most basic biological functions – such as eating, sheltering, pairing and breeding, fighting and dying – are performed in idioms acquired by belonging to historically and locally defined cultural groups', groups 'whose patterns of behaviour are conditioned by particular sets of values'. It follows that in considering the environment of early man one needs to take account of the web of social, cultural and historical relations that bind societies together and help men to conform to patterns, maintain their identity and survive. In more theoretical terms one could say that bioarchaeology needs to be studied within the framework of social archaeology: the former is concerned with the process by which human societies acquire what they need to sustain life, whereas social archaeology is concerned with the kind of life chosen by communities within the constraints imposed by their environments and their socio-cultural inheritances. If in practice most of this book is concerned with the former, this is due not to choice but to the exigencies of the surviving data. Where evidence of cultural patterning can be discerned, the opportunity has been taken to use this as a means of defining social territories, a level in the hierarchy of territory which can hardly be ignored without distorting the outcome of bioarchaeological research.

The case for an optimistic archaeology. The question may well be asked whether anthropological models have any practical relevance for prehistorians: whereas anthropologists are able to observe their subjects directly, and even to cross-examine them, prehistoric archaeologists are confronted by a more or less vestigial record of circumstantial clues. This is the point at which archaeologists have to commit themselves. They can be pessimists and carry on with arranging their museum cases; or they can be optimists and seek to pursue their clues in quest of early man. I would not be writing this book if I were not an optimist.

In the final analysis a choice of this kind is an act of faith which does not need to be rationalised any more than an artist has to justify by argument the precise thickness of a line or a poet the choice of a particular word or, come to that, a scientist the choice of his area of commitment. One chooses because one is excited. Yet, the optimistic archaeologist, who aspires to find more than pretty patterns personal to his own vision or that of a small coterie (even if mediated to a complaisant public), can if pressed make a reasoned case for his choice.

At first sight the confrontation between conventional displays of archaeological data and the anthropologists' vision of a social organisation manipulating the resources of its environment to satisfy its physical needs is enough to confirm the pessimistic view: the disparity may appear so great that there is nothing more for the archaeologist to do than continue to play his games, speeded up perhaps by computers but in essence unproductive and essentially frivolous. Yet the disparity is more apparent than real, since it rests on the fallacy that archaeologists are condemned for the rest of time to play with pots and stones. In reality the data available for reconstructing prehistory are capable of almost indefinite amplification and extension, once one breaks out of the closed circle described by Oscar Montelius and his successors. So long as archaeological activity was held to be an end in itself, there was a positive inducement to restrict the pieces used in what had become a stereotyped game. But the converse is equally true. One of the most striking developments of recent decades has consisted precisely in this, that changes in the objectives of research have resulted not so much in the multiplication of conventional data as in a widening of the range of information. This has been brought about through purposive changes in the direction of research, including the selection of sites chosen for excavation and the manner in which their investigation is planned, in a radical widening in the scope of the data held to be relevant to archaeology, in the standard of the sampling techniques by which they were collected and in the quality of the briefing given to the experts invited to scrutinise them in the laboratory. Perhaps the most powerful argument in support of the optimistic view lies precisely in the elasticity of the data. The virtue of setting out to view the admittedly contemptible information available to many fields of archaeology in relation to hypothetical systems is surely that this is the best way not merely of appreciating but of remedying its deficiencies. The injunction 'ask and it shall be given' applies to archaeology as much as to any other field, just as it is no less true that if no questions are asked, none are likely to be answered. What archaeology needs and what it is now getting on an increasing scale is questions framed to elicit information about working systems. One may sum up so far by saying that it is only by viewing the materials available to conventional archaeology as vestigial relics of once living communities of men that we can appreciate fully how pitifully inadequate they are or visualise the means that have to be taken if they are to tell their story.

A second point to be made is distinct from, but closely linked with this, namely that it is not merely possible to extend very greatly the range of data available to archaeology; it is at the same time possible to extract much more information by considering archaeological data as clues to the functioning of systems. So long as archaeological evidence was regarded simply as a means of defining groups or periods, it follows that this was the limit of the information it was capable of giving. Conventional archaeology was limited by its conventions. It was a closed and hopeless circle and those trapped in it were and still are understandably pessimistic about what could or can be learned about the prehistoric past. So soon as archaeological evidence is viewed in relation to life and living systems, its potentialities are transformed. The contrast may be illustrated in a parallel field by considering the fossil bones of extinct animals. Of course these are vestigial, even if by exploiting opportunities like those offered by the frozen mammoths of Beresovka in Siberia or the salted rhinoceros of Starunia the soft parts can sometimes be recovered; but this does not mean that palaeontologists stop short at using them as zone fossils, still less of making typologies according to shape, size or colour. The converse is true that so soon as they are regarded as parts of animals that once lived, so soon as they are regarded in functional terms, then the mere fact that they are vestigial does not seemingly detract from their value as clues, any more than exponents of forensic medicine are deterred by the smallness or restricted range of their samples. The fossils, instead of being merely collected and sorted as small boys do, can be studied intelligently as components of organisms and, again, the geological deposits in which they are found, together with their contained clues to former climate, geography, plant and animal life, need no longer be regarded merely from a stratigraphical point of view, but also as sources of information of the highest ecological interest. The pessimistic palaeontologist is a contradiction in terms: if a man feels that way when confronted by fossils he had much better turn to classifying pots or sorting stamps, both blameless activities and the former even of potential value for defining cultural preferences and relations and establishing local sequences.

Once it is accepted that over and beyond the necessary task of building chronological frameworks and defining communities a reasonable prospect exists in theory of being able to discover how people lived and why and how development occurred in the course of time, the question next arises where to begin. If the fossils of former states of society acquire their meaning by being considered as components of systems that once functioned as living social organisms, it seems to follow that we ought to concentrate first on bioarchaeology, the archaeology of how men occupied territories and maintained life. In doing so, we do well to give weight to a point already touched upon, namely that men have psychic needs that arise from living in a type of society distinct from those prevailing at the animal level from which in the course of evolution they have emerged. Although therefore for practical reasons we may choose to begin by concentrating primarily on activities common to all animals – that is the occupation of territory and the extraction from it of food sufficient to ensure continuity – it will not be overlooked that the societies dealt with by archaeologists are human and need throughout to be considered at the social and ideological as well as at the merely biological level, even when attention is being concentrated on the most mundane levels of existence. Although as a semantic or even conceptual device we may choose to isolate some particular aspect of life for special study, the fact remains that every item of archaeological data, whether relating to subsistence, technology, shelter, transport, social emulation, redistribution or cult, forms part of a working system of which each component stands in some relationship, usually reciprocal, to every other.

Material culture. The very existence of the material equipment that comprises the basic data of archaeology is a sufficiently palpable indication of the uniqueness of the human phenomenon. The evolutionary hypothesis implies that material culture arose to supplement and improve the functioning of objects grasped and manipulated by primates in general, but its elaboration and above all its patterning reflects a type of social organisation and a means of articulate communication peculiar to the type of primate we designate as human. In any study of the human settlement of a region analysis of the way in which material equipment was employed in the quest for food and shelter and for assisting movement must necessarily play a leading part. On the other hand it is important not to fall into the error of imagining that artifacts

8

were merely extensions of men's limbs – they were also projections of his mind and embodiments of his history and owe much of their value for archaeology to this very fact.

Nevertheless, when considering the economic basis, tools and other gear can usefully be considered in the first instance in their role as aids to living, as in themselves incorporating raw materials and as designed to assist the communities employing them in the task of manipulating the environment to ensure survival. We can consider them on the one hand as embodying knowledge and skill in respect of the means employed in their own production and on the other as the actual means by which human communities exerted their will on their environment.

With regard to the first point it may be observed that disproportionate attention has in the past been paid to the typology of finished forms as compared with that given to the methods by which these were produced. This problem stems, like so many in archaeology, from a too narrow definition of aims. So long as analysis of form and style as a basis for building systems in the manner of Montelius and his followers was considered to constitute the essence of archaeology, the only relevant material comprised finished forms made in a restricted range of materials. From this it followed that generations of excavators let loose by an unkind fate on monuments in hitherto untouched condition and on settlement sites, as these were exposed in such large numbers during the great phase of land drainage and the construction of communications, were from a modern point of view scandalously selective in what they retained and studied. As a result the great archaeological museums have something of the character of mausolea, monuments to lost opportunities. The destruction of evidence by accredited archaeologists at a time when avenues for research opened up in all directions and excavation was still inexpensive is indeed terrible to contemplate. The existing work recently carried out on the techniques of production of artifacts in a wide range of materials including antler and bone, flint, stone and bronze, and the beginnings of similar studies on the shaping and ornamentation of pottery has only been made possible as a result of excavators retaining either total assemblages or at least adequate samples of the total range of archaeological data. The converse also follows that as excavators have become conscious of the value of what hitherto had cheerfully been discarded and of the kind of questions that could be answered by its study their standards of recovery and retention have improved beyond measure (Higgs 1972, Sect. II, nos. 1, 2).

On the question of the function of artifacts, advances are being made on three fronts: the recovery of implements or weapons in their hafts, analysis of the associations of artifacts, as for example of weapons or catching gear with bones of mammals or fish, and study of traces of wear and use on working edges (Semenov 1964). Success in the first two of these depends first and foremost in recovering artifacts under conditions that permit the survival of organic substances and this in turn involves making the most of chance finds and above all directing excavation to sites best calculated to yield these materials. Scandinavia as a whole is well provided with lakes left behind by the contracting ice sheets, the margins of which were particularly favoured by early man because they offered the possibility of exploiting the wide range of environmental resources; and in Denmark and south Sweden the chemistry of the waterlogged deposits forming the bogs that incorporate traces of former lake-side settlements favours the survival of a wide range of organic substances, including antler, bone, wood, bark and resin. For this reason there is an unusual wealth of evidence relating for example to the use of the bow and the methods of mounting the bone and flint armatures of arrows, to skis and sledges, to tread-traps and to the nets and traps used in fishing. Deposits of this kind are not less prolific in yielding animal bones in association with hunting and fishing gear, and in this respect silts deposited in the Baltic and its main gulfs when water-levels were much higher than today are especially rich in evidence for seal-hunting and the gear used in that activity. On the other hand Scandinavia offers no particular facilities for investigating traces of use on artifacts or conducting practical experiments with specimens. Important work has nevertheless been done and special mention may be made of Professor Moberg's experiments (C. A. Moberg 1955, 111 ff.) with Rovaniemi stone 'picks', checked by microscopic examination of working edges, or, again, of the experiments in tree-felling carried out by the National Museum of Copenhagen with polished flint axes.

Ecosystems. Since a principal, though not by any means the only, function of material equipment is to secure and utilise natural resources, it seems important next to say something of the relationship existing between human communities and the ecosystems in which they subsist. How do systems work that include human societies? This is where the findings of ecologically minded social anthropologists are so relevant. What they appear to have observed when studying recent primitive peoples is an exceedingly complex series of interrelationships. The economy prevailing at the time of observation appears as the outcome of a working relationship between social requirements, organisation, knowledge and technology on the one hand and the components of the habitat and biome on the other. The essence of an ecological model is that the relations between the several components are complex and reciprocal. There is no single determining factor. It is beside the point to discuss whether what we observe is the result of economic, social, ideological or environmental forces. What matters at any moment of time is that as a result of the interplay of these and other forces the system works in a particular way. The environment imposes certain constraints and offers certain opportunities: which options are taken up and how is determined by the interplay of a very large number of forces, which include psychic, social (and therefore historical) as well as economic or technological factors.

Now the environment can be considered at different levels of abstraction. In *Prehistoric Europe: the economic basis*, as earlier in *The Mesolithic Settlement of Northern Europe*, it was discussed only in extremely general terms. In the former a main concern was to show how the economy and general style of life prevailing during later prehistoric times related to the broad floristic zones recognised in Europe: thus the earliest European cities grew up in the Mediterranean zone; peasant societies developed comparatively early in temperate Europe and never spread in prehistoric times much beyond the mixed-forest zone of Scandinavia or the southern taiga of the Soviet Union; and throughout prehistoric times the circumpolar territories, comprising pine and birch forests and the open fjäll or tundra, continued to be occupied by communities whose subsistence was based primarily on catching and gathering. In the present work, dealing with a more restricted territory it has been possible to consider environment more closely as it related to the actual experience of individual communities. At this level the point can be made that, subject to the overall constraints, the most viable policy for human communities, the one that gave them the best chance of surviving local or temporary shortages or failures, was to exploit not one but two or three distinct ecological zones. The risk was spread by opening up the resources of two or more environments, whereas concentrating on a single one would risk total failure and possible extinction. Thus we may expect to find it commonly true that early settlements were so placed that the inhabitants were able to exploit coastal and inland or lowland and highland resources.

Territories. In practical terms physical environment is exploited in relation to territory. Before turning to this topic, it is perhaps worthwhile to emphasise two features of man's occupation of territory, neither of which applies to other forms of mammalian society, to anywhere approaching the same extent. First of all there is the question of the home base. The existence of some form of nest or shelter is common to all animals whose young are born in an immature and defenceless state. The need for a secure place in which the young can be kept warm, to which food can be brought and which the parents can most easily defend is especially necessary for the survival of human beings. There are two good reasons for this. First there is the length of the process of physical maturation and conversely of the period of weakness among human infants, but second, and much more important there is the need in human society to absorb the heritage of culture which in course of social evolution has shown a persistent increase in range and detail, but which even in the most primitive human societies known far exceeds anything existing among for example the surviving non-human primates. The acquisition of culture, which in human society provides not only the mechanism for coping with the environment, but is one of the basic sources of group identity and includes not merely articulate speech but particular kinds of articulate speech, as well as particular kinds of technology, subsistence patterns, social relations and ideology, involves a prolonged period of learning. The basis for this is laid in the home base that shelters mother, siblings and at least from time to time father.

The most elementary requirements of any home base are assured supplies of food and water. Since water is the most pressing need in the sense that it is the substance that can be dispensed with for the shortest period, the problem is best solved by locating the home base close to natural sources of supply, that is close to rivers, lakes, springs, rockpools or readily accessible underground sources. Food, though less immediately pressing, is nevertheless an insistent need, all the more so that over any period of time dietary requirements can only be satisfied from a wide variety of food stuffs. When settlements are permanently occupied or returned to at certain intervals dietary needs can be evened out by storage, but by and large food has continually to be replenished.

Whatever the means, whether animal or plant substances are obtained by gathering or catching or by farming or as frequently in Scandinavia by a combination of these, they all have to come from a territory or catchment area.

Among human societies it is useful to distinguish four main kinds of territory, the territory habitually used from the home-base, the annual territory, the social territory, and finally the techno-territory (Table 4). The extent of the home-base territory is limited by the amount of energy used up in concentrating food from the catchment area at the actual point at which it is consumed. In the case of people whose only means of travel is their own feet and who also have to carry food on their own persons the area is likely to be limited by what can be encompassed by a radius of one or two hours' walking (Higgs 1971, fig. 5). In a flat and entirely featureless landscape this might mean a circular area within a radius of five or ten kilometres, though in real terms, taking account of surface relief and other obstacles, the territory would be much more irregular in form. Again, even in prehistoric Scandinavia, walking was very far from being the only means of movement or transport. During the period of snow cover, which over much of Finland and northern Sweden extended over half the year, skis and sledges made it possible to move food and other commodities over greater distances for an equivalent expenditure of energy. Again over Scandinavia as a whole water transport, whether by sea, river or inland lake, would have provided an even more important way of moving goods and food: the capacity of boats to concentrate food from extensive catchment areas with a small expenditure, demonstrated most dramatically in the ancient world by the riverine or coastal location of cities, ought certainly not to be underestimated at a more modest level in prehistoric Scandinavia.

In the case of most societies that depend wholly or in any substantial measure on catching and gathering, it is necessary to move the home base in order to exploit seasonal opportunities. The home base may and generally does remain at one or more locations for periods measured in months during periods of cold or heavy rainfall as the case may be, but at other times of the year it may shift rather often and assume a peripatetic character. In this case it is useful to adopt the term annual territory to designate the total territory exploited by a group in the course of a whole year; whereas among permanently settled people home base territory and annual territory may be expected to coincide, among others the home base territory can be conceived of as moving around within the range of the annual territory.

By social territory I mean the total territory drawn upon for supplies, including raw materials and finished products as well as food-stuffs, by a given community by virtue of belonging to a larger social grouping. Here we touch upon another of the basic features which distinguish human societies from animal aggregations, the fact that men belong to structured hierarchies among which varying degrees of reciprocity obtain. More will be said about the importance of social structure and the nature of the evidence for this later in this introduction. Here I would only emphasise that it is basic to human societies that they are concerned with redistribution as well as acquisition; and redistribution not merely within biological breeding groups but ramifying in a structured way among extended groups based on common descent or in more sophisticated societies on allegiance to common political institutions. The topic of redistribution, for which there is a wealth of archaeological evidence, will be given separate discussion. Here it may only be noted that to judge by analogy with modern primitive peoples one has to reckon with the strong probability that foodstuffs entered into socially structured redistribution systems that might traverse many annual territories without necessarily involving the passage of individuals. Particularly striking instances could be quoted from New Zealand where the tropical food plants of the original Maori colonists and consequently the heaviest weight of population were concentrated in the North Island and the northerly parts of the South Island: detailed ethnohistorical studies have made it possible to reconstruct the routes along which products moved and it is known for example that mutton-birds, caught on Stewart Island in the extreme south, were favoured delicacies many hundred miles to the north (Clark 1965, 24).

Over and above territories marked by a relatively high degree of social interaction were those which shared substantial elements in technology, territories that may fitly be termed techno-territories. Thus in the final stages of the Late-glacial discussed in chapter 3 we find cultural assemblages grouped into three social territories by virtue of certain idiosyncratic traits, yet sharing basic characteristics common to the whole plain of northern Europe from the Netherlands to the Nieman with northward extensions into Scandinavia. Among these were a lithic tradition marked by blades, burins and steeply retouched flints, including tanged points, as well as a variety of objects made from reindeer, including antler clubs and barbed harpoon heads of a particular form with bases of pointed spade-like form.

Subsistence and seasonality. According to the stereotype embodied in the old literature the contrast between the 'Mesolithic' hunter–fisher–gatherer peoples of early Post-glacial times in temperate Europe and the later, 'Neolithic', farmers was so marked that it could only be accounted for in terms of revolutionary change; and this change was thought to have been brought about by the intrusion of new peoples from the south whose economy and material equipment stemmed from prototypes originally developed in the course of the 'Neolithic Revolution', which was supposed to have taken place in a comparatively restricted range of south-west Asia. On the other hand it had long been recognised that the old dichotomy could hardly apply so rigidly to the northern margins of the prehistoric farming territory in Scandinavia and in the taiga zone of the Soviet Union; and a distinct circumpolar zone was envisaged within which 'Sub-neolithic' communities were acquainted with such arts as pottery-making and the polishing of flint tools though practising a form of economy in which farming played at most a minimal role. The topic of the 'Neolithic Revolution' in general has been much discussed and I do not intend to add to this even by criticising some of the more extreme positions taken up in reaction to Childe's mythology. I shall concentrate instead on the situation in prehistoric Scandinavia.

The first point to be made is that the earliest inhabitants of Scandinavia of which we yet have adequate indications brought with them a knowledge of the ways of wild animals in particular, the product of a tradition of advanced hunting developed in central and southern Europe for at least a thousand generations and which itself represented a refinement of still earlier and more protracted experience. To say that man found himself as a hunter is only to admit, in view of the defectiveness of his equipment, more particularly during the longer, earlier phases, that he made his way essentially by understanding the habits of the animals on which he depended for an important part of his protein. During the Late-glacial period the early colonists of Denmark and south Sweden may be supposed to have possessed a highly sophisticated knowledge of how most economically to exploit the reindeer herds and other game of the region. If the sketchy knowledge we have at the moment is to be increased, some of the obvious key questions to be

15

answered concern the strategy employed, and the manner in which the annual territory was exploited season by season, as well as the size of the social groups at different times of the year. An overriding need is the recovery of more sites with an adequate supply of organic refuse and the analysis of such refuse in conjunction with site locations and artifactual material.

The way in which the successors of the reindeer hunters adjusted to Post-glacial conditions poses another set of problems. In particular it is of the highest interest to consider how the population exploited the increasing range of animals and plants that became available for food as temperatures increased and forests spread over most of the land. A topic of special interest, which also applies to the preceding period, concerns seasonality, since this brings out most clearly the way in which hunter-gatherers maximised their resources and in effect practised a kind of husbandry. The seasonal utilisation of resources, quite apart from its relevance to the patterns of subsistence and settlement also affected a wide range of material culture. Indeed, it seems plain that lack of appreciation of the relevance of this problem and consequently the lack of purposive research devoted to it, has resulted in serious errors of interpretation. Again, and incidentally, it has undermined the validity of much conventional classification including not least statistical essays of the type sponsored by F. Bordes (1950) and A. Bohmers and Wouters (1956), which appear to assume that assemblages of lithic artifacts reflect cultural or chronological differences and ignore the possibility that they may reflect no more than seasonal aspects of material equipment. As I have recently shown in respect of certain early Post-glacial lithic assemblages from England previously assigned to different cultural traditions (Clark 1973), it is highly probable that they reflect differences and variations in intensity in the activities carried on at different times of the year. Once accept that artifacts reflect activities and that activities are subject to seasonal variation, then correct interpretations can only be made when it is known at what times of the year the sites from which they came were occupied. Yet if one turns to the archaeological literature this topic is too often either ignored or accorded no more than a rather off-hand comment unsupported by adequate evidence: Haakon Olsen's work on the birds and fish from the Stone Age sites on the south shore of Varanger Fjord (Olsen 1967) is a brilliant exception which only serves to point the contrast. On *a priori* grounds it might be anticipated that the early Post-glacial inhabitants would have laid a greater emphasis on the exploitation of plant resources than their Late-glacial predecessors since the range of utilisable plants increased markedly under more genial climatic conditions then prevailing. Here the evidence at present available is even more exiguous. Plant remains, macroscopic as well as microscopic, have been collected from early sites almost entirely with the aim in view of gaining evidence for dating, hardly at all with the object of throwing light on the degree to which or the manner in which they were utilised. Systematic use of more effective apparatus for the recovery of plant materials may be expected to throw a flood of light on questions of seasonality and on the extent to which certain species were systematically collected.

The first domesticated animal species to appear in Scandinavia – and by domesticated species I mean operationally species introduced into the region by man and/or exhibiting genetic characteristics detectable in skeletal remains and which differentiate them from their prototypes – was the dog. This was certainly present as early as the middle of the eighth millennium B.C. It may have been introduced from south Russia, where it was already domesticated during the Late-glacial period, or conceivably have been bred from tame wolf-cubs in Scandinavia itself. Of the several animal species maintained by the earliest peasant societies in south Scandinavia the ox and the pig may also have been bred from indigenous prototypes, but sheep and/or goat and later horse must have been acquired from outside. Equally, since no wild prototypes are known from Scandinavia, it seems evident that the staple cereals of peasant Europe must have been introduced. Much has been learned about the methods used in land clearance, on the nature of the crops sown and of the way in which the ground was cultivated and crops harvested, but far too little direct evidence has been obtained about the arrangements for keeping livestock. Problems of peculiar interest are presented by the 'Sub-neolithic' economies mentioned previously; one would like to know much more about the gradient between communities in which farming played a major role and those in which even its practice is problematic; about the precise nature of the relationships established between men, elk and swine; and about the manner in which farming activities were slotted into the seasonal round, including the extent to which anything comparable to the *erämaanomistukset* practice obtained, in northern Scandinavia. Already it is abundantly clear that the pattern of subsistence in prehistoric

Scandinavia was immensely more complex and interesting than might be indicated by the mere juxtaposition of hunter–fisher–gatherer and farming economies.

The patterns by which territory was exploited in prehistoric Scandinavia were almost certainly more complex than so far suggested. As will become clearer still when discussing the basis of subsistence, the sharp dichotomy between settled farmers and nomadic hunter–fishers that features in so much of the archaeological literature was modified by several institutions. Certainly when historical records first begin to throw a steady light on the organisation of peasant societies in Scandinavia we find two important ways in which segments of households split off from permanent settlements temporarily during the course of the year in order to exploit favourable ecological niches at some distance from the home base. Thus in the systems known to the Norwegians as *seter* and to the Swedes as *fabod* parties of young girls would take cattle to clearings in the forest or out on to mountain pastures during the summer grazing period and return with the cheeses needed for winter use. Indeed the legal rights that go with the farmsteads even today are likely to include, together with the dwelling and its attendant buildings and a share in meadow and arable, rights in fishing and the use of woodlands perhaps as much as 20 kilometres distant. Less well-known is the *erämaanomistukset* custom by which peasant proprietors occupying farms in the agricultural zone were able to exercise recognised property rights over hunting and fishing grounds far away in the interior at distances of up to 260 kilometres. In this case it was presumably the mature able-bodied men who went off to tap the resources of wealth far beyond the settled home-base. While it is true enough that we cannot project these institutions recorded in history back into the prehistoric period as if they were verified facts, it is legitimate and rewarding to accept as a hypothesis that something like them prevailed in early times, more especially in territories like Norrland, the interior of Finland and the inland *fjäll* country of Norway.

Settlements. The high potential importance of settlement sites as sources of information about the economic and social organisation of prehistoric communities has been widely recognised since the pioneering activities of men like Gerhard Bersu and Gudmund Hatt and extensive stripping of Stone Age sites from the Middle Palaeolithic onwards has already brought substantial advances in knowledge. So far as the Stone Age is concerned Scandinavian archaeologists have in the main concentrated on the continuing task of sectioning sites and keying them into the general body of Quaternary research. This has brought important gains in establishing the territorial environment of settlements, but it is perhaps an indication of priorities that of the few sites extensively stripped none has yet for one reason or another been adequately published – and here one thinks in particular of sites like Barkær in north-east Jutland and Alvastra in Östergötland.

From a purely economic point of view much of course can be gained from traditional methods provided these are applied in a sophisticated way. The great advances recently made in Scandinavia in the critical interpretation of stratigraphic sequences are extremely welcome, but one result is to cast doubt on much apparently sound work carried out even during the last generation. The location of sites, provided that allowance is made for other factors, including the size of community, spacing in relation to other sites and in certain contexts defensive possibilities, can offer important insights into the way in which territorial resources were exploited; and, conversely, once the factors influencing the choice of prehistoric groups at any particular time have been understood, the key is there to recover the distribution of other sites in relation to the territory as a whole. So long as the factors that patterned, within certain limits, the location of sites remained unchanged, the same sites or ones closely contiguous were likely to be chosen again and again, something which applies pre-eminently to caves or rock-shelters that provide visible and localised advantages. This has important implications for the interpretation of archaeological data. It means above all that the value of the data stored in museums and in most cases published depends on the awareness of the excavator and his skill in isolating materials relating to particular phases of occupation. Again, the validity of interpretations is likely to be affected strongly by an appreciation of the seasonal context of occupations. And over and above this, apparent stratigraphic sequences are often complicated by natural processes of which earlier excavators were frequently unaware, affecting for example the accumulation of cave deposits, the formation and restoring of coastal deposits of special importance in areas like Bohuslän, where fluctuations of land and sea-levels have been especially complex (Mörner 1969), and the natural history of bogs with the complexities introduced for example by the occupation of temporary floating 'islands' (Troels-Smith 1953).

From the social standpoint the value of settlement sites can only be realised fully if they are stripped completely or sufficiently to yield, in conjunction with geophysical survey, a plan showing the number, nature, size and relations of structures. Such plans can yield vital clues under several heads, economic, demographic and social. Under the first heading, the nature of the structures can reveal not merely building techniques, but also the provision made for storage and for the stalling of livestock, as well as throwing light on the degree of permanency of occupation and in conjunction with small finds, provided these are adequately plotted, on the degree and nature of the subdivision of labour. Precise estimates of the number of households represented, in itself by no means a simple task to infer from building plans, can give reliable indications of the maximum number of inhabitants, but is only capable of yielding more precise information when it is possible to show how many of the structures were used at any one time, a consideration of particular relevance where, as in Finnmark, the more permanent sites were concentrated on particular strandlines. To establish the density of population in absolute terms on the basis of direct observation is hardly possible at present, since this would involve the location of every settlement and some degree of certainty about which were occupied at any particular period. On the other hand intensive ground survey and analysis of organic refuse from individual settlements of different periods, combined with even notional figures for the maximum numbers of their inhabitants, should be sufficient to point the course of demographic change. Cemeteries are also capable of contributing information on populations so long as individual burials can be aged and sexed. On the other hand they also offer many uncertainties, for example the proportion of dead accorded burial, the period over which burials continued and the number and geographical range of settlements served by each cemetery. Recovery of the complete plans of settlements and of individual buildings and complexes also offers insights into the structure of communities. Again, detailed plotting of stray finds and installations indicative of particular crafts may provide evidence for the sub-division of labour.

Social hierarchy. Although it is natural for archaeologists to concentrate on economic activities, which leave so many direct traces, it remains a fundamental objective to learn as much as possible about social organisation and structure. Social archaeology owes its crucial importance to the elementary but basic fact that all archaeological data are the product of the labours of men who not merely lived in society, but acquired their patterns of behaviour as members of social entities; moreover, as the anthropologists have shown us, the various branches of activity, which in modern thought and language are treated almost as though they had independent existence, can in fact only be correctly understood as aspects of the life of social communities. The terms in which Soviet prehistorians were once officially obliged (Thompson 1961, 29) to designate the main periods of social evolution and therefore of archaeology may have been crudely unilinear as well as politically motivated. This does not invalidate as a logical aim of archaeology the definition of styles of social life.

All human societies known to history are founded on the complementary institutions of the sub-division of labour and the redistribution of products and materials, including food. This applies even to primitive societies in which the sub-division of labour has only been carried to a limited extent. It follows that prehistorians should expect to find evidence for specialisation not only in the field of technology but also in that of social roles. Direct evidence for this may be provided by marked disparities in the provision of grave goods or merely by the presence in votive offerings of jewellery and parade weapons witnessing to conspicuous consumption. The converse is no less true that when grave goods recur at the same general standard one is entitled to assume the absence of any marked degree of social differentiation. This makes it fair to presume that both the hunter–fishers and farmers of the Scandinavian Stone Age were organised on a primitive egalitarian basis.

How far is it possible to detect social communities in prehistoric Scandinavia and how far can these be linked with our suggested hierarchy of territories? It is worth asking such questions even if as yet no certain answers can be given.

The smallest social unit recognisable in the archaeological material is the household, but the household only defines the basal level of the hierarchy of social networks in which the individual was enmeshed. Among most groups dependent on hunting, fishing and gathering observed by anthropologists the common working group is the microband comprising a cluster of up to three or four households, though at certain times of the year it may have happened under certain conditions that individual households fended for themselves. At a higher level of hierarchy bands comprising a number of micro-bands may be conceived of as occupying social territories, the most extensive territory of which the ordinary individual would probably at this time have been aware. The households united in social territories would have been knit together within the same network in two distinct ways, by sharing in the redistribution of materials and products and by displaying certain idiosyncratic styles. At a still higher level groups of bands lacking in all probability any formal association but sharing the same basic technology may be thought of as occupying techno-territories.

Redistribution networks. Redistribution is so deeply embedded in human society, as this is known from daily experience, from history and from ethnographic accounts of quite primitive communities, that it would be surprising not to find traces of it from prehistoric Scandinavia even allowing for the fact that relatively little evidence could be expected to survive. Frequently described under the anachronistic term 'trade', which represents a specialised form of redistribution proper to societies in which this function is discharged by full-time professionals, redistribution is witnessed by an abundance of evidence from Scandinavia. To cite only a few of the best known instances from the Stone Age, one may recall the occurrence of axe and adze blades of green Olonetz slate from the factories of Petrosavodek on Lake Onega, densely concentrated in Carelia, but widely distributed in Finland up to and beyond the Arctic Circle as well as in Esthonia and Latvia; thin-butted axes of Jutish flint in south Norway and daggers of the same material commonly as far north as the Trøndelag and sporadically beyond the Arctic Circle; hollow-edged thick-butted axes of south Scandinavian flint in the coastal tract of Norrland; greenstone axes from factories on Bømlo off the extreme west coast of Norway as far east as the frontier and as far north as Nord-Trøndelag some 600 km in a direct line; stone bracelets on either side of the Gulf of Bothnia; and amber objects from the East Baltic across the Caledonian mountains to the west coast of Norway. The need here is mainly for systematic petrological survey like that applied to stone axes in Britain. The probability is that similar patterns of extreme complexity will emerge, testifying to the wide ramifications of social reciprocity and interaction. One fact already evident is that the sea, so far from impeding redistribution, appears in fact to have facilitated it. Another is that, to judge from the presence of East Baltic amber on the west Norwegian coast, material moved along river courses even upstream. The evidence from imperishables reminds us further of what has been lost through the decay of organic materials. If we may rely upon early historical accounts furs were a particular product of northern territories to find their way into the redistribution network and this may be expected to have happened particularly at a time when settled life had begun in territories not too far remote. The same applies to foodstuffs, notably game birds, dried or smoked fish and possibly seal fat.

Idiosyncratic styles. The existence of social groups at a higher level in the hierarchy of organisation than those which habitually lived together in individual settlements is implicit in the material evidence for redistribution. Yet redistribution patterns can hardly serve of themselves to define precisely the boundaries of social groups occupying neighbouring social territories. It is only where such patterns appear to conform within the boundaries of stylistic provinces, as in the case of the axes of banded Galician flint that fall within the globular amphora province of the upper Elbe and the Oder and Vistula basins, that they can define precisely the dimensions of macro-groups.

The most reliable pointers to these are unquestionably the idiosyncratic features that in their day helped to denote group identity. In the flesh, no doubt, the most immediately noticeable features serving to proclaim group solidarity even at some distance would have been clothing and hair-styles, rather as birds proclaim their kind in the form of plumage. The only manifestations likely to survive in the archaeological record on the other hand are the styles and finish of relatively imperishable artifacts. Always provided that it is conducted with this specific aim in view, the time-honoured analysis of form and style offers the best promise of defining social groups.

Wolfgang Taute's painstaking analysis (1968) of the flint industries, characterised among other things by different forms of tanged point, has already provided evidence for the existence of a number of social territories on the north European plain during the final stage of the Late-glacial period (see Table 4, p. 69); and some of the boundaries, surprising though it may seem, have continued to operate down to recent times. The existence of a wealth of antler and bone from Mesolithic sites offers an even more sensitive medium for stylistic nuances, and even better opportunities exist in cases where a wider range of material survives. Already it seems possible to detect the existence of a number of social groups in the 'Sub-neolithic' world extending from Norway to north Russia, though the picture is blurred by the fact that artifacts of clearly defined form and style such as the slate daggers with elk head terminals themselves entered the redistribution system. A new situation emerged with the widespread adoption and intensification of a peasant way of life. Permanent settlement intensified regional loyalties. On the other hand the scale of social units increased and redistribution networks widened in range, so that during the second millenium B.C. first flint daggers based ultimately on exotic metal prototypes and then bronze artifacts incorporating imported copper and tin spread with a remarkable degree of uniformity, though of course differing in density over much of the richer farming territories of southern Scandinavia. Corresponding with this went a move towards a greater degree of social and political hierarchy culminating before the close of the prehistoric period in the emergence of chieftainship as an institution.

Stability and change. One of the main problems to emerge from the study of human settlement over a period of some ten thousand years is how to explain the process by which one form of society has given place to another. How is it that when archaeologists classify material traces from this period they find no great difficulty in making out temporal sequences in terms of variations in the objects found? And why, despite the apparent differences between material from successive periods, it is no less easy to detect elements of continuity extending sometimes over thousands of years? Paradoxically the nature of change can best be understood by considering how stability itself was maintained. Pioneers of social anthropology were impressed by the analogy of working systems, systems that comprehended everything from ecosystem to ideology and ensured by manifold sanctions the cohesion, coherence and continuity of social life. Evans-Pritchard (1940, 92) wrote of Nuer that: 'Oecological relations appear to be in a state of equilibrium. As long as present relations exist cattle husbandry, horticulture, and fishing can be pursued, but cannot be improved. Man holds his own in the struggle, but does not advance.' In the same way the system which regulated the social lives of the peoples studied by anthropologists had built-in mechanisms that up to a point ensured their survival in the face of factors making for disequilibrium. Just as according to the principle of homeostasis organisms 'regulate the internal environment of the body and adjust it to meet changing needs' without altering their

24

fundamental character and so ensure resistance to external factors, so human societies can only survive and in due course feature in the archaeological record thanks to built-in checks against innovation. Traditional societies were by their nature resistant to change since they could only survive by exacting a high degree of conformity. Cultural patterns survived so long because they were of high adaptive value. No society after all in which every member would be free to behave entirely in accord with personal whim would have much prospect of enduring for long. Thus cultural patterns would tend to survive because up to a point they were of high adaptive value, quite apart from the fact that men are by nature disposed to conform to the basic law of the conservation of energy. One may expect that the force of inertia institutionalised in custom was at least as powerful in prehistory as it is today.

Yet from another point of view the equilibrium in which societies may appear to exist is an illusion. In every society the existing form masks the interplay of underlying tensions. The pressure for conformity cannot hold these in check indefinitely. Once the threshold is passed at which the cost of maintaining conformity exceeds the benefit that this conformity confers, then normal evolutionary forces would favour a radical readjustment, the striking of a new balance, the appearance of new social norms. In Marxist terms revolutions occur when the contradictions inherent in society and normally contained by the forces of conservatism reach a point at which more or less violent change is the price of a new period of stability. After such a change a society would once again return to a state of apparent equilibrium, but its cultural face would be different: some traces of continuity might be expected, but other features would have vanished and new ones would have taken their place. In other words we should expect the archaeological material from any region to show threads of continuity, but also some quite radical changes of form.

Before considering the forces that made for change as they are being discussed by archaeologists at the present time something must be said of the attitude of a former generation more concerned with ordering than understanding phenomena in terms of process. When archaeologists examined excavated material from different periods, they were inclined to overlook continuity in their anxiety to use differences as chronological markers. The differences when not merely accepted as observed facts were liable to find explanations in mythological terms not unlike those offered by the ancients or by modern 'primitives' to account for the Creation. One of the commonest devices employed in British or for that matter Scandinavian archaeology has been to account for changes in material equipment in terms of the replacement of one population by another. As a hypothesis this is a possibility that ought always to be considered, but accepted as self-evident facts 'invasions' have a tendency to inhibit discussion and indeed research itself (Clark 1966), especially when as they so easily do they rapidly assume the guise of historical 'facts'. Movements of peoples there undoubtedly have been and these were potent forces making for change. What I am concerned to stress is first that these should not be assumed as self-evident and sufficient explanations for change and second that the capacity of people long settled on one piece of soil to absorb immigrants or cultural influences from outside is hardly to be exaggerated.

This is no place to discuss the causes of change in philosophical terms. Instead I will concentrate on some of those most relevant to this book. Before doing so a distinction needs to be drawn between the cumulative micro-changes which manifest themselves in every sphere of human activity given a sufficient range of time, whether in flint-knapping or calligraphy, and the kind of macro-changes on which archaeologists rely to define major periods or cultural stages. As I shall hope to illustrate later on, the former can be valuable for tracing continuity in cultural traditions, but it is with the latter, involving not single traits or even groups of traits but rather systems, that I am immediately concerned. It is best to admit that for the prehistoric period the proximate causes even of major transformations are likely to elude definition both on account of their small scale and because they might well be the outcome of contingencies, such as incidental brushes between neighbouring communities, rivalries between outstanding individuals, disease, shifts in the movements of fish or a spell of dry summers which of their very nature can hardly be detected in the archaeological record. What can usefully be done is to consider some of the underlying pressures that weaken systems to the point at which they could be overturned by trifles too small to be detected in the archaeological record.

Before attemping to analyse the impact of such pressures two qualifications need to be made. First, it should be made clear that what is under consideration is not the process of social change as such, but changes in the occupation and utilisation of a geographical region, namely Scandinavia, much of which was beginning to be opened up to settlement during the period covered by this book: two kinds of process are thus involved, one of economic dynamism, the other of environmental change, even if for obvious reasons these must have interacted one with another. Second, the various pressures vary very greatly in the degree to which they can be precisely measured or even identified by means of archaeological or Quaternary research. If greater attention is inevitably directed to what can be measured, no formulation that ignores more impalpable factors is likely to approximate at all closely to the truth. It is easy enough, as the literature shows, to construct 'models' using only a few easily measured variables; and these may even be useful provided that their limitations are fully appreciated.

Remembering these qualifications it may be useful to consider the underlying pressures making for change in the occupation and utilisation of Scandinavia during prehistoric times. Very broadly these may be distinguished as what for want of better terms we have called inherent dynamism and environmental change. By inherent dynamism is meant the kind of dynamism inborn in any system, comprising human populations and territories, more especially territories as marginal to the inhabited world as parts of Scandinavia were during prehistoric times. Under the heading of environment, I include not only the natural ecosystem but also the social environment as this was affected by contacts whether peaceful or warlike with communities occupying neighbouring or sometimes even quite remote territories.

Central to the notion of economic dynamism is that sometimes referred to as population pressure. When land is occupied it is likely to be taken up selectively in accordance with social preferences and technology up to the limits imposed by environmental constraints: some tracts will be ignored, others occupied and within these certain kinds of site will be preferred. During this pioneer stage the total population will increase until the point is reached at which its needs can no longer be met by customary means from the available preferred land. What happens next will depend on reaction to the closing of the frontiers. If social constraints are used to maintain population at its existing density, then economic and social life may continue without changes of a kind likely to be reflected in the archaeological record. The converse is true that if any one or more of a number of ways of increasing the food-supply are adopted – for instance through the more effective use of areas already settled, through the taking in of poorer secondary land areas or through increased exploitation of sea-foods – then more or less marked changes are likely to occur in economic and social structures allowing increased densities of population; and this in turn may precipitate significant changes in settlement and social hierarchy. It goes without saying that the story is likely to be greatly complicated in the context of marked changes in the environment.

If there is any truth in the ecological approach to archaeology, if social systems are so to speak locked into ecosystems by way of their economic and above all their subsistence bases, it follows that changes in the habitat or biosphere will set up pressures for change in total systems and in the archaeological residues of such systems. It is hardly sensible to categorise environmental changes as in themselves favourable or hostile, since they are inevitably both; by altering the conditions under which social systems operate they merely handicap some ways of doing things and facilitate others. The natural environment certainly exercised constraints, but it is important not to forget it also provided opportunities. It is true enough that so long as much of Scandinavia was covered by ice no human settlement was possible except in Denmark and southernmost Sweden, but what is of more positive interest is that in the long run its retreat laid open progressively larger areas for colonisation. The changes in land and sea levels that resulted from deglaciation were permissive in some areas, but imposed constraints in others. Isostatic recovery of the land in areas central to the old ice-sheet, when it came after some time-lag allowed major extensions in the area of settlement, for example in middle and north Sweden and in Finland. On the other hand the eustatic rise of sea-level in the North Sea area and later in the south and west Baltic by causing a reduction of hunting grounds may well have exerted pressure in the direction of new adaptations, notably through greater emphasis on sea-food and the adoption of farming. The northward and upland shifts of climatic and vegetational zones that accompanied the rise of temperature brought a rather abrupt end to regimes based on reindeer in south Scandinavia, but opened new possibilities for adaptation to a forested environment, an adaptation that for archaeologists marks the transition in this part of the world from 'Upper or Advanced Palaeolithic' to 'Mesolithic'. When, as temperatures reached their Post-glacial maxima and deciduous forests became dominant and even spread beyond their present northern limits, the conditions existed for the spread of mixed farming. Again, when the decline of temperature from the Post-glacial maximum took place towards the end of the prehistoric period this may have diminished the profitability of cultivating the older crops, but equally surely it favoured others and made possible a regime in which hay-making became of key importance.

Other pressures for change came from the socio-cultural environment. Notable among these were the effect of contacts with other systems informed by different values, having different social structures and technologies and adapted to extracting a living from different ecosystems. Contacts come about in a variety of ways and, since the only alternative would have been unregulated conflict, it can be assumed that these were to some degree at least formalised. If as we know to have happened actual objects could move across socio-cultural divides, it seems likely that ideas could also do so; and it should not be overlooked that by common consent and in the general interest it is usual for individuals or small parties to be granted freedom of passage. It is to be assumed that knowledge of technical devices and of usages of different kinds, as well as ideas of a more general nature, moved freely and rapidly over considerable distances, even if only able to penetrate the hard crust of established ways in alien societies when for some reason they happened to be timely. Another factor came into play when there was a marked difference in economic development between two societies in contact, namely social emulation, something all the more powerful where social stratification existed in the less developed of the two. One of the characteristic ways in which social elites have sought to establish their identity is by acquiring exotic possessions and adopting exotic ways; and innovations have always tended by a process of devolution to filter down the social scale and modify or even transform the prevailing pattern of behaviour. Contacts between neighbours were thus capable of generating new needs and as we can see so well in the transition from Neolithic to Bronze Age economies in Denmark, these had often to be satisfied by means of substitutes. There is no difficulty in visualising changes, even sweeping ones, proceeding without any substantial movement of people. On the other hand when invasions can be adequately documented it does not follow that they necessarily implied drastic changes. This was only likely to happen when warriors were accompanied by women and children. The overriding fact about most regions remains that of continuity over long periods of time.

Periodisation. An appreciation of Scandinavian, as of any other pre-history, depends on setting the data in their correct chronological context. Three ways of doing so will be used in this book, namely archaeological periodisation; the correlation of different kinds of archaeological data with stages in the evolution of the environment; and the application to each of radiocarbon dating.

By archaeological periodisation is meant the arrangement of arti-factual data in temporal order with reference either to a particular site or to a defined territory. Recourse will only be made to the time-honoured blanket terms of stadial connotation when rapid sign-posting is needed for diagrams or broad reference. When such terms are em-ployed they will be used in their conventional meaning.* Typological development, find associations and straightforward stratigraphy will be used in the context of social territory. By definition the sequence of stylistic or even functional lines of development can only apply to social territories, that is territories of relatively intense social interaction which achieve their identity in some measure by sharing idiosyncracies of behaviour and are knit together by the operation among other things of redistributive systems.

Since the basic theme of this book is the process of settlement and resource exploitation, it is logical to emphasise the context of archaeo-logical assemblages in the unfolding history of the habitat and biome (see chapter 2). If the underlying function of the cultural apparatus, of which archaeology studies the detritus, is to adapt to and manipulate the environment to subserve social and therefore to some extent ideo-logical ends, it follows that the accurate placing of archaeological assemblages in their geological and palaeo-biological contexts is a vital prerequisite to understanding. Conversely the fact that many different aspects of the environment underwent measurable changes in time offers another means of dating phases of human settlement. Here, again, chronology needs to be informed by spatial reference. Just as archaeological chronology is only valid in relation to specific

* Palaeolithic and Mesolithic are applied to communities that maintained themselves by hunting, fishing and foraging and lacked pottery respectively during the Late-glacial and early Post-glacial periods.

Neolithic denotes ones that depended to a substantial degree on farming, practised certain arts, including pottery making, and whose technology continued to be based primarily on flint and stone tools.

Sub-neolithic is applied to communities whose economy rested primarily on catching and gathering, but who practised certain of the Neolithic arts, including pottery making.

social territories, so correlations with environmental history only apply without qualification to particular locations. Thus coastal sites can only be dated in terms of the broad evolution of the Baltic and in particular to the progress of isostatic land recovery by measuring heights in relation to local strand-lines and taking account of tilt (e.g. Siiriäien 1969, 1971); and in the same way sites or individual finds can only be dated in terms of the evolution of climatic and forest history by fixing them stratigraphically in relation to locally determined pollen zones (e.g. Nilsson 1958; Tauber 1965).

The task of synchronising local sequences has been greatly aided by radiocarbon analysis and this has been valuable both for dating archaeological finds directly and even more relevantly for keying them into different aspects of environmental change. As might be expected of a region that pioneered so many basic techniques of Quaternary research, Scandinavia was among the first to welcome and apply this new method of dating. In drawing on the work done by the several radiocarbon centres operating in Scandinavia certain basic rules have been followed. With few exceptions the only dates used are those published in *Radiocarbon*. The object of doing this and of quoting laboratory numbers has been to facilitate checking the quality of determinations. Second, in accordance with the decision of the Cambridge Conference (Godwin 1962), dates are quoted on the basis of W. F. Libby's original half-life of 5568 ± 30 years. Thirdly, no attempt is made to calibrate radiocarbon dates with solar chronology by taking account of correlations with bristlecone pine growth rings. Radiocarbon dates will be quoted as radiocarbon dates, since, until a formula for calibration has been validated and internationally agreed, confusion would only be worse confounded by converting them prematurely into solar dates on the basis of incomplete experiments. Two considerations are nevertheless worth bearing in mind. Present indications are that solar and radiocarbon chronologies may have diverged to a maximum extent of 600 to 700 years between three and five thousand years B.C. (Libby 1970, 7). One implication of radiocarbon dates being too young in terms of solar time would be that Atlantic time lasted longer than at present appears. Again, the deviation curve, which appears to have returned to around zero at the transition from Late-glacial to Postglacial time, was far from being a smooth one: indeed its course was subject to steep oscillations, a fact that greatly increases the area of

31

uncertainty attaching to the dating of particular samples. This is only another reason for treating individual dates with scepticism and for relying only on consistent patterns of a substantial number. A final point to remember is that whatever their precise value in terms of solar years they have the priceless facility of bestowing simultaneity within a certain range of probability on the most distant and disparate phenomena.

2
Habitat and biome

Much of the interest of Scandinavia as a theatre of early settlement by man centres on the magnitude and rapidity of the environmental changes that have unfolded themselves during the last ten thousand years. Yet the basic geological structure of the region is also important both for the constraints and options it offered to the prehistoric inhabitants and for the insights it can give for the proper understanding of the diverse character of different parts of the territory. A marked contrast has always existed between the rocks of the Scandinavian shield comprising Norway, Finland and most of Sweden and those younger formations that comprise Denmark and the southernmost parts of Sweden. The Fennoscandian shield was itself the product of two main periods of orogenesis. The earlier, designated Archaean by Scandinavian geologists, included several cycles of mountain-building, but denudation and degradation has been so effective since, that almost the whole of Finland lies below 200 metres and much of Sweden consists of plains and undulating landscapes. The only prominent relief in Scandinavia, that provided by the Caledonian mountain system of Norway and adjacent parts of Sweden, was the outcome of the later phase of mountain-building dating from the early Palaeozoic era. The main types of rock found in both formations are hard crystalline rocks, granites, gneisses and schists, but each also includes Cambro-Silurian sediments deposited in geosynclines that preceded periods of folding and mountain-building. These sediments were to prove exceptionally important at a certain phase of settlement because they were those best suited to agriculture. In Sweden the most important outside the Cambro-Silurian regions of Scania and Blekinge were: the Falbygden area of Västergötland between the southern parts of Lakes Vänern and Vättern; the part of Östergötland between north-east Vättern and Roxen; a smaller area west of Hjälmaren; the islands of Öland

and Gotland; and a region on the north side of Siljän famous as a main focus of peasant culture during the historic period. Extensive tracts of lime-rich soils also extended over fan-shaped areas to the south of all but the first of these, the result of transport by ice-sheets. The same mechanism accounts for the even more extensive tract extending over Uppland, parts of Västmanland, Stockholm and Söder-manland which was enriched by lime derived from formations in the western part of the Gulf of Bothnia from Gästrikland to Medelpad. Although much of this was still submerged under the Litorina sea during the Stone Age, isostatic recovery made increasing areas available to farmers during the closing stages of the prehistoric period. Cambro-Silurian formations, where altitude and latitude permitted, were also important in Norway, as guides to agriculture, notably in respect of east Østlandet, Vestlandet and the Trøndelag.

In marked contrast to the Fennoscandian shield, the rock formations of Denmark and southernmost Sweden including most of Malmö-huslan were Mesozoic and Tertiary in age and sedimentary in origin. Landscapes were of low relief. The highest point in Denmark is no more than 173 m above present sea-level. The territory, and Denmark in particular, offered almost unbroken expanses of potential agricultural land, which made it relatively speaking far richer during late pre-historic times than other parts of Scandinavia. Within Denmark there were particularly important differences in this regard as between those parts of the country – east and north Jutland and the islands – covered by the Weichsel ice-sheet and those parts of Jutland which remained outside. Whereas the morainic soils of the former developed mould (Danish *mull*) and brownearths, more or less pronounced podsols and sand cover (cf. Dutch *deckzand*) formed on the glacial outwash deposits of the south-west.

There were also significant differences in the availability of raw materials for technology. The territory of the Fennoscandian shield was rich in a variety of rocks, including quartz and quartzite, slates that lent themselves to splitting and polishing, fine-grained greenstones capable of being flaked and gneisses and other rocks that could be pecked and ground into shape. The only flint in a primary situation in this territory was the dolomitic variety that originated as small concre-tions in limestone rock and was used during the Stone Age in Finnmark (Bøe 1936, 134). Chalk flint on the other hand was only locally available in the form of pebbles on the sea-shore (Gjessing 1942, 25) or of concentrations of nodules transported by ice like those on the west coast of Sweden deposited by retreating glaciers calving in the south Kattegat. Further supplies had to be obtained from the south Scandinavian territories where flint occurred in its parent chalk. Flint of high quality occurring in nodules large enough for making axes and daggers was one of Denmark's main sources of wealth and the material was certainly being mined from the time that thin-butted axes came into use to that during which flint daggers were current, that is, from around the mid-third to the mid-second millennia B.C. (Brøndsted 1957, 333 and 383, n. 189). Metal ores were confined to the Fennoscandian shield, but there is no evidence that either the copper or iron ores of Norrland were exploited during prehistoric times; and no tin is known. On the other hand, the formation of bog-iron, precipitated in the form of small lumps in still pools of water, and found today under peat, would have been favoured by the higher rainfall of sub-Atlantic times and there is abundant evidence that this was exploited by peasants in antiquity all over Scandinavia as it still was until recent times (Clark 1952, 202).

From an archaeological point of view the territories differ in that conditions for the survival of organic materials were generally more favourable in south Scandinavia. Thus antler and bone, so immensely revealing for the technology and subsistence of pre-historic communities, survive from Finland – the Åland Islands apart – only in the form of calcined fragments or exceptionally from marine silts; and a similar scarcity exists for much of Norway – not a single trace of animal fauna or bonework is yet known for instance from the coastal sites with Fosna or Komsa lithic industries – and Sweden north of Scania–Blekinge. The main exceptions relate to areas with lime-rich soils, to swamps and old lake-beds and to formerly submarine deposits. The wealth of organic materials from the southern territories on the other hand is exceptionally high, although locally these include poor zones like the glacial outwash sands of Jutland outside the limit of that last (Weichsel/Würm) glaciation.

The dichotomy in the basic geological structure of Scandinavia was modified profoundly and in ways peculiarly relevant to man by the effects of glaciation and its aftermath. On the other hand significant differences exist even here. The fact that the ice-sheet began to form and reached its greatest thickness on the Fennoscandian shield meant in the first place that the marginal territories in the south were the first to be uncovered and were therefore settled first; and indeed that the extreme south-west corner of our territory, the part of Jutland south of latitude 56° 30′ N and west of longitude 9° 20′ E, escaped the last glaciation completely. In the second place it meant that the Fenno-scandian shield, and more particularly the region centred on the Both-nian Gulf, was isostatically depressed under the weight of the growing ice-sheet and in consequence was subject to progressive uplift of land throughout the Post-glacial period, whereas much of the west and south Baltic area lying outside the area of isostatic displacement, was predominantly affected by the eustatic rise of sea-level that resulted from the melting of the ice.

Another difference between north and south Scandinavia arises from the fact that it extends over some 16° of latitude. It was not merely that the southern region was freed from ice before the Fennoscandian shield, so that vegetation and land fauna came in progressive waves from the south, but that even when the ice-sheet had been reduced to ice-caps and valley glaciers and temperatures had reached the Post-glacial maxima a substantial difference remained in the constraints and oppor-tunities of north and south. This is true even if climatic, vegetational and faunal differences between Temperate and Circumpolar zones have never since been sharply defined or coincided at all precisely with the geological divide. The point may be made in terms of the situation prevailing today. Between the north-European deciduous forest zone comprising basically Denmark and much of Late-glacial Sweden, but extending along the eastern and northern coasts of the Skagerrak and under the genial influence of the Gulf Stream as far as Møre in south-west Norway, and the Boreal Coniferous Region confined to the Fennoscandian shield, plant geographers recognise an intermediate north-European mixed-forest zone equivalent to the southern taiga of European Russia. The northern margin of this zone traverses the flank of the Fennoscandian shield: between Carelia and east Norway it follows an irregular course along latitude 61° N with a major loop in south and middle Sweden: and westwards it is deflected even further south by the mountains before responding to more temperate con-ditions on the west coast of Norway where it extends as far north as the Trøndelag. The influence of the Gulf Stream, which kept the coast free of ice as far as Finnmark in marked contrast to the Gulf of Bothnia and made it possible to practise a kind of farming, introduces another element and reminds us again of the danger of monolithic thinking in relation to Scandinavia.

GLACIATION AND DEGLACIATION

The scale of the last (Weichsel/Würm) glaciation of Scandinavia can be judged from the simple fact that it covered an area of 1,650,000 square miles as compared with the mere 2,416 square miles comprised by the ice-caps and valley glaciers of today. Basic conditions for the growth of the ice-sheet were a lowering of temperature and adequate precipitation. Even quite a modest fall in temperature would have been sufficient to cause existing areas of ice to coalesce, and, given an adequate supply of moisture, a substantial ice-sheet, once formed, would be capable of resisting minor fluctuations and continuing to thicken and expand. Conversely, when a sustained rise of temperature passed a critical threshold the melting and contraction might be expected to have been rapid, as indeed we know it was in this case.

The Scandinavian ice-sheet was nourished by cyclonic air masses from the south-west, one skirting the Norwegian coast and causing precipitation on its western flank, the other passing over territories lacking any continuous mountain barrier and depositing snow on the southern margin of the ice-sheet. Although at first ice developed more strongly on the western side of the Caledonian mountain system, the steepness of the slope and the proximity of deep water entailed a rapid loss due to the calving of glaciers. The eastern slopes on the other hand, being gentler, favoured the formation of piedmont glaciers which nourished by snow brought by the more southerly air flow expanded both laterally and vertically. This in time caused the ice divide to shift gradually east so that in the course of time the ice-sheet attained its greatest thickness on that side of the mountain crest. At its maximum the ice-sheet covered the whole of Scandinavia out to the edge of the Continental shelf of the coast of Norway, excepting only for Jutland south and west of the Main Stationary Line at approximately latitude 56° 30′ N and longitude 9° 20′ E.

Glaciation on this massive scale left direct traces of significance to early man, quite apart from the associated environmental changes dealt with in later sections of this chapter. The driving force of glaciers descending the steep western and northern slopes of the main mountain system carved out the fjords that played a leading part in early settlement and ground rock-surfaces smooth, thus providing scope for engraving and painting. From an economic standpoint glaciation exerted its most profound effect through the surface soils it left behind, boulder-clays deposited in great sheets and glacio-fluvial sands and gravels left by meltwater flowing under the ice-sheet. Among topographical features that affected the location of settlements and burial grounds and in some cases facilitated movement were the drumlins and moraines associated with boulder-clays and the eskers sometimes formed by glacio-fluvial deposits. Other products of deglaciation were the lakes and ponds that attracted early settlers to their shores and in silting up preserved records of organic materials of the highest importance for interpreting economy as well as for dating.

Much has been learned about the speed and nature of the contraction of the Scandinavian ice-sheet by a study of surface topography. The existence of systems of prominent terminal moraines in Denmark, north Germany and Poland, and not least in Sweden argues that the process was spasmodic rather than gradual, being interrupted by periods of standstill or even of minor readvance. Systematic studies of sequence of finely layered deposits or varves laid down in glacial meltwater have been used by de Geer and Sauramo and their followers to date the final stages of the process. Although subject to influential criticism (e.g. Flint 1947, 394–7), varve chronology has received some general support in respect of the last twelve millennia in Scandinavia from the finds of other branches of Quaternary research, notably from pollen stratigraphy and radiocarbon dating. Thus the Fennoscandian moraines, equivalent to the mid-Swedish, Norwegian ra and Finnish Salpausselkä, systems are well matched in the Younger Dryas period distinguished by pollen-analysts in Denmark and Scania; and the last stages of the rapid Gotiglacial retreat from the Scanian moraines finds a counterpart in the Allerød oscillation. Indeed, the fact that the radiocarbon age for the close of the Younger Dryas period agreed rather well with that of the varve data for the final departure of the ice from the Fennoscandian moraine was even used to validate radiocarbon dating on the assumption that both varve dates and radiocarbon dates were equivalent to solar dates. As we can now appreciate (p. 31) it was a coincidence that solar and radiocarbon dates happen to have agreed fairly closely at this time, though subsequently diverging by as much as some seven centuries. Even so until the bristlecone pine record has been finally validated and extended back to 10,000 or 11,000 years some uncertainty must remain about the absolute as distinct from the radiocarbon age of the final oscillations of Late-glacial climate. It is perhaps premature to discuss as critically as Mörner (1969, 175–83) has recently done the precise age of the end of the Late-glacial period as defined by the withdrawal from the Fennoscandian moraine: accepting the conventional varve date 8213 B.C. for the beginning of the departure of the ice from the Fennoscandian moraine and accepting also that radiocarbon ages were the equivalent at this time of solar years, Mörner arrives at the conclusion that the new half-life for radiocarbon allows a better approximation at 8350 than the old half-life which gives c. 8050/8000 B.C.

With these reservations it is still worth illustrating the speed at which the ice withdrew across eastern Sweden during different stages. Measuring along a line from Karlskrona to Linköping prolonged north the results are as follows.:

B.C.	Glacial stages	Annual rate of withdrawal (m)
8,300–6,800	Finiglacial retreat	315
9,000–8,300	Fennoscandian moraines	50
10,300–9,000	Gotiglacial retreat	215

The many problems (cf. Zeuner 1950, 30 f.) relating to the ice-margin in southern Scania and the correlation of the Scanian moraines with those of Denmark, and the south Baltic lands (Pomeranian moraines) need only to be touched upon in the next chapter, since by the time human settlement had effectively begun in Scandinavia the ice seems to have withdrawn already some distance north of the Scanian border.

LAND AND SEA

Of all the changes in the environment that accompanied the process of glaciation and its aftermath of deglaciation few can have made a greater impact on the conditions for human settlement or on the availability of primary archaeological data than those which affected the relative dispositions of land and sea. In Scandinavia these were the product of two main forces which operated with varying force at different stages in the process of glacial retreat and in different parts of the country.

Isostatic displacement of the earth's crust under the weight of ice-sheets was confined to the glaciated area and was most intense where the ice was thickest. As Map 15, giving the isobases or contours of displacement, clearly indicates, the Gulf of Bothnia showed the most marked effects; much of it was depressed by more than 200 m and the most elevated shore line measured on the Rosstjärnsterget in the vicinity

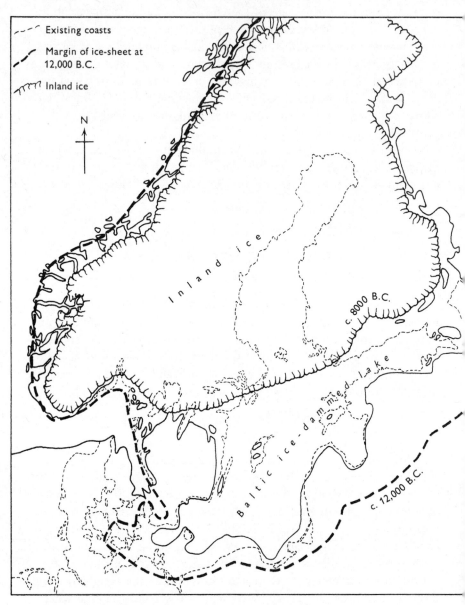

Existing coasts

Margin of ice-sheet at
12,000 B.C.

Inland ice

N

c. 8000 B.C.

Inland ice

Baltic ice-dammed lake

c. 12,000 B.C.

1. Northern Europe at the close of the Late-glacial period. The extent of the inland
ice is shown at the time of the Fennoscandian moraine.

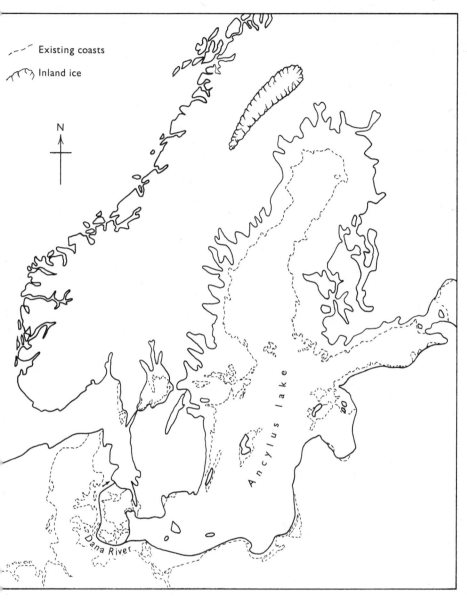

2. Northern Europe at the time of the Ancylus Lake.
Note the greatly reduced size of the ice-sheet.

of Skuleberget between Härnösand and Örnsköldsvik in Ångermanland is 295 m above sea-level, something like the height of an English
mountain. The map also brings out that isostatic depression hardly
extended beyond the ice-sheet as this existed during Late-glacial times.
This in turn meant that the contours of depression were steep and in
consequence that individual shore lines must have tilted perceptibly
from the centre. Another factor that needs stressing is that upwarping was
a slow process that got off to a slow start and is in fact still proceeding.

By contrast the eustatic rise of sea-level resulting from the release
of water formerly locked up in ice-sheets worked in the opposite
direction, affected all seas open to the oceans and followed immediately
on any reduction in ice-sheets. It also involved considerably less
vertical displacement than was the case in areas central to isostatic
warping. Since the two factors were opposed and one was local and
operated with some time-lag, the outcome in geographical terms
varied both locally and in time. And it must be remembered that both
responded to the process of deglaciation which itself was subject to
certain variations in intensity. It follows that precise results of the kind
needed for dating archaeological occupations depend on intensive
systematic local research.

The history of the Baltic as worked out by H. Munthe (1940) and
refined by his successors is too well known to require detailed exposition. In essentials it is part and parcel of the process of deglaciation, as we
are reminded by the elementary fact that when the ice margin stood
at the Pomeranian moraines the basin was wholly submerged by the
ice-sheet. Ten or twelve thousand years ago when the ice was retreating
across Väster and Östergötland the waters of the exposed basin were
ponded against it. In the northern parts of the basin, which were still
isostatically depressed, the waters of the ice-dammed lake (Map 1)
covered much of the ice-free territory of east Sweden, the Baltic islands,
Esthonia and Finland. Access to the open sea first came about when
the ice-sheet withdrew from the Fennoscandian moraines and entered
on its Finiglacial retreat, an event which allowed the waters of the
ice-dammed lake to drain westward to the Skagerrak. As the gap
between the Dano-Swedish land mass widened with the rapid retreat
of the ice-margin, salt water penetrated the basin and brought in
marine organisms. Prominent among these was the mollusc *Yoldia
arctica* adapted to the low temperatures still prevailing at the time and
commonly used to designate this phase. After the usual time-lag isostatic

recovery of the land began to outstrip the eustatic rise of sea level. One result of this upwarping in the north was that in the south the waters of the Ancylus Lake flooded the south and west shores causing a considerable loss of land between Mecklenburg and Latvia and the insulation at a certain stage of Bornholm. A more substantial result was that around 7500 B.C. the basin was once again cut off from the sea to become a lake (Map 2) appropriately named after the freshwater mollusc *Ancylus fluviatilis*. Yet the recovery was still very far from complete. The Gulf of Bothnia was two or three times broader than it is today, eastern Sweden was to a large extent submerged and Finland was only slowly beginning to take shape. To begin with the Ancylus Lake drained into the Skagerrak by way of the Svea river, Lake Vänern and the Göta river, but as isostatic recovery made further progress outlets had to be found further south first by way of the Dana river that flowed east and north through what are now the Fehman and Great Belts and also by a channel through the isthmus separating the Baltic from the Kattegat. Continuation of the same process, upwarping in the north and transgression in the south, coupled with a continuing eustatic rise of sea-level, finally breached the Danish land barrier and converted the Ancylus Lake into the Litorina Sea around 5000 B.C.

At this point it will be useful to take stock of what was going forward in the open sea. Here again, there was a marked contrast between north and south. Whereas along the Norwegian coasts isostatic recovery of the land so greatly exceeded the eustatic rise of sea-level that strandlines progressively receded, in the southern part of the North Sea basin the eustatic factor was dominant and the fen deposits which covered the low-lying territory that still joined Britain to the Continent at the beginning of the Post-glacial period were flooded over. During the period of the Ancylus Lake, Britain was insulated and much territory lost on the southern borders of the North Sea.

Continued upwarping in the isostatically depressed territories of Bothnia, east Sweden and Finland brought about notable enlargements of the land area during Litorina times, though even as late as 2000 B.C. broad coastal zones were still submerged. Indeed, the land at the head of the Gulf of Bothnia is still recovering at the rate of a metre, and even Stockholm is rising by about half a metre a century (Flint 1947, fig. 79).

The effect of these geographical changes on prehistoric man was in the main permissive. It is true that land loss by reason of transgression by lake or sea would have entailed some reduction of food resources, but the process was too gradual to have precipitated changes in any well-balanced system even though the possibility must remain that the culmination of marine transgression may have disturbed economic relations in a territory as confined as Denmark. Against this the extensive and rather rapid emergence of extensive land areas in the north of Scandinavia must have provided exceptional opportunities for the expansion both of human settlement and of the animal and plant species by which this was sustained.

Changes of this kind also exerted a profound influence on the primary evidence available for reconstructing prehistory. To take the negative aspect first, the flooding over of ancient shore-lines entails a serious loss of information bearing on the utilisation of coastal resources. In the west Baltic area, for example, we know hardly anything about the extent to which coastal resources were exploited by Palaeolithic and Mesolithic man and it is only in the northern part of this area that information is available even for the Litorina phase and then only spasmodically for periods of marine transgression. On the other hand, in regions where upwarping has been predominant the evidence confirms the evident attraction of coastal settlement to early man, offering as it did complementary sources of food. As an added bonus to archaeologists, strand-lines, where these are available for study, offer interesting possibilities for establishing systems of relative chronology. In the case of a country like Finland, where organic residues are rare, such sources of information are particularly welcome.

VEGETATION AND CLIMATE

The spread of plants into territories made available by the contraction of the ice-sheet and by the subsequent recovery of land within the zone of isostatic displacement is a very paradigm as well as a necessary antecedent for the colonisation of Scandinavia by man. From an ecological point of view the history of vegetation is of basic importance from several distinct but closely interconnected reasons. It provides an important clue to climatic change and reflects, though to a lesser degree, topographical and soil changes. It exerts powerful constraints on herbivorous animals which, along with the plants themselves, are the basic source of human food. Further, as botanists have recently recognised under the lead of Johs. Iversen (1949), human activities – the 'anthropogenic factor' of science-jargon – have themselves been a fac-

44

tor and sometimes a major factor in shaping vegetation. By recovering the history of vegetational change in sufficient detail and linking this directly with human settlement there is some prospect therefore of being able to throw light on the way the landscape has been utilised and shaped. Again, vegetational history is capable of providing a chronological system by means of which changes in many other spheres may be calibrated and synchronised, a basic requirement for an ecological approach to the history of human settlement before written records.

Information about vegetational change depends on the systematic study of plant remains from stratified deposits. The recent vogue for pollen analysis, stemming from Lennart von Post's elegant demonstration of a simple graphical means of presenting fluctuations in the proportions of pollens from different species of tree from samples taken from successive levels of vertical sections (von Post 1916) should not obscure the crucial value of macroscopic traces. It was in the guise of leaves and fruits that an arctic flora was first recovered from Late-glacial clays in Scania more than a hundred years ago (Nathorst 1871) and Axel Blytt (1876) formulated his hypothesis of wet and dry phases on the basis of alternating layers of peat and tree-stumps. Again, Gunnar Andersson (1902) first demonstrated that temperatures rose during the Post-glacial period to a peak from which they have since declined, by systematically collecting remains of hazel from deposits north of the recent distribution of this shrub. Macroscopic remains in the form of leaves, fruits, seeds, roots, bark, branches and trunks retain their crucial importance as keys to the use made of vegetation for artifacts and food. Collections of the kind available from a site like Alvastra merely illustrate what could be learned from systematic deployment of an effective froth flotation method. Again, macroscopic traces of vegetation that can be assumed to have grown at or close to a particular locality form necessary complements to the fossil pollen blown in sometimes from quite distant areas.

On the other hand, critically used (Tauber 1965) and systematically applied, pollen analysis is able to yield a most valuable insight into broad changes in the history of vegetation. Further, by providing a convenient means of zoning pollen-bearing deposits with some precision, it affords a useful framework for synchronising cultural and environmental situations. As the method matured and came to be systematically applied to territories outside those centring on south Sweden and the west Baltic area where it was first developed, its

Table 1. *Scheme showing the evolution of the physical environment of man in northern Europe during the last 12,000 years*

Conventional periods	Baltic phases: Munthe 1940	Pollen zonation W. Norway: Fægri 1940	Denmark: Jessen 1935/8	Scania: Nilsson 1948	Nilsson 1961	Radiocarbon dating Nilsson 1964a	Berglund 1966	Mörner 1969
Post-glacial (Blytt–Sernander)								
Sub-atlantic		XI	IX { b	I	SA 2	A.D. 650	A.D. 700	A.D. 700
			a	II	SA 1	300 B.C.	200/250 B.C.	200/250 B.C.
Sub-boreal	Litorina Sea	X	VIII	{ III	SB 2	17/1800	1700	1650
				IV	SB 1	3300	3150/3100	3100
Atlantic		IX	VII { b	V	AT 2	4600 (?)	4300	4400
			a	VI	AT 1	6200	6000	5800
Boreal { late	Ancylus Lake	VIII	{ VI	VII	BO 2	6800	6750	6550
Boreal { early			V a, b	VIII	BO 1	7900	7400	7750/7330
Pre-boreal	Yoldia Sea	VII	IV	IX	PB	8300	8000	8050/8000
Late-glacial (Hartz)						Tauber 1971		
Younger Dryas	Ice-dammed Lake	VI	III	.	DR 3	8200	.	.
Allerød	Lake	V	II	.	AL	8900	8600	9000/8950
Older Dryas		IV	I c	.	DR 2	9700	9750	9800
Bølling		III	I b	.	BO	9900	.	9950
Oldest Dryas		I, II	I a	.	DR 1	10200	.	10300/10350

46

practitioners have rightly been assiduous in developing independent zoning systems of local reference. One by-product of regional research has been a tendency to use different systems of notation in various parts of Scandinavia (Table 1). Another has been a concerted effort to synchronise regional zonations by seeking to obtain radio-carbon dates for crucial points in local sequences. In Table 5 an attempt has been made to present in diagrammatic form the results of applying radiocarbon analysis to the Danish and Scanian sequences, the two most complete ones at present available from Scandinavia.

Late-glacial. When referring to different phases of Late-glacial and Post-glacial time it is for some purposes convenient to employ terms of general application rather than numerical notations devised for zoning regional vegetational histories. Those in common use are of varying origin. The Late-glacial terminology rests on an application of strati-graphic observations made at Allerød in Zealand at the beginning of this century (Hartz and Milthers 1901). At this locality a layer contain-ing temperate fossils was found sandwiched between ones containing *Dryas octopetala* and associated arctic species whose presence in south Scandinavia had been recognised in a previous generation (Nathorst 1871). Pollen-analytical and other stratigraphic studies have since con-firmed the existence of a comparable temperate oscillation over an extensive area of Europe as far west as Ireland and as far south as the Pyrenees, to which the designation Allerød has commonly been given. The geographical status of an earlier minor oscillation, first noted near the former Bølling Lake in Jutland, is rather less clear, but its existence locally in the west Baltic has been judged to be sufficiently distinct to form a stratigraphic sub-division. Recognition of the Allerød and Bølling oscillations equivalent to Jessen's Zones II and Ib has involved sub-dividing the Dryas deposits into Younger, Older and Oldest, corresponding with Jessen III, Ic and Ia respectively. Since the Allerød oscillation was so exceptionally clearly defined both stratigraphically and pollen-analytically at the name site, it was made the first target of the C14 dating apparatus established at Copenhagen in the fall of 1951 (Anderson, Levi and Tauber 1953). The mean of five determinations (at Ruds, Vedby, Zealand) set the transition from Allerød to Younger Dryas at 8880±200 B.C. The fact that dates from comparable deposits in Britain and the Netherlands agree within the standard deviation with those from Allerød suggests that at least within comparable latitudes in north-west Europe the Allerød oscillation was broadly synchronous. The dates adopted in our table for marking the transitions between Zones I, II and III are based on the comparative study made by Godwin and Willis (1959). The fact that by general agreement the Allerød phase lasted around a thousand years means that it is something of which serious account will have to be taken when considering early settlement of the ice-free parts of Scandinavia by man.

We are particularly fortunate that the Late-glacial flora of Denmark should have received exceptionally detailed treatment. Although the flora of the Dryas deposits is commonly designated in shorthand as 'Arctic' it is widely agreed that ecologically speaking this would be misleading and inadequate as a description. As Krog has emphasised (Degerbøl and Krog 1959, 76), conditions prevailing in the periglacial area of south Scandinavia were not really comparable with those prevailing in the Arctic, since the angle of the sun was higher, the summer longer and the winter shorter. Iversen was impressed by the unique character of the Dryas flora and wrote of 'the curious open country that spread over immense regions at the close of the glacial age, and with its mixture of grassland and tree-islands provided ideal living conditions for the rich late-glacial flora'. This included a number of arctic plants of alpine habit, including *Dryas octopetala* itself, *Betula nana* (dwarf birch), *Salix polaris* (arctic willow), *Rumex*, *Oxyria* and *Thalictrum*. The grasses which also featured in the landscape were more luxuriant than those of the present Arctic regions and ericaceous plants were less frequent (Degerbøl and Iversen 1945, 56–7; Godwin 1956, 18). In addition, it included plants such as *Ephedra distachya*, *Artemisia* and *Hippophäe*, unknown in the Arctic, but at home in the steppes. In its totality the Late-glacial flora of Denmark, Scania and for that matter of Britain finds no living counterpart. It was the product of unique conditions and combines elements of alpine and steppe, as well as of Arctic character. As Iversen (1954, 104–5) and Godwin (1956, 290–1) have pointed out, the presence of a steppe component in the vegetation, as well as in the contemporary fauna, argues that the Dryas climate was continental in character with strongly contrasted seasons including rather dry summers (Iversen 1954, 104–5). As Iversen has further shown, the precise character of the vegetation existing even in an area as relatively small as Late-glacial Denmark and Schleswig-Holstein varied in different localities. For instance, where birch trees expanded into Holstein and Zealand in sufficient strength during the Allerød oscillation to create a true forest enrivonment, in mid-Jutland the landscape took on more of the nature of a park tundra with only a few trees in sheltered places. Again during the Younger Dryas when colder conditions returned there was a perceptible gradient in the degree of severity from Holstein to north Jutland.

Although Iversen was careful to emphasise the difficulty of trying to infer temperatures from fossils, he has nevertheless offered estimates which at least give an idea of their course during different phases of the Late-glacial phase in Denmark. Thus whereas he considered that Older Dryas July temperatures were under 10° C, his estimate for the Late Allerød is between 13–14° C, and for the Younger Dryas approximately 10° C. The high temperatures estimated for the Allerød argues that the dominance of birch in the forest was probably due to its having established itself before the slower moving pine. The presence of aspen in the Allerød *gyttja* (Iversen 1954, 96) is worthy of note because it was a favourite food of elk which was also represented in deposits of this age. Another aspect of climate particularly relevant to early man and the herbivorous animals on which he so largely depended, was precipitation. Here Iversen (1954, 103) was able to observe the presence of a number of plants, including *Dryas octopetala* itself as well as *Hippophäe rhamnoides*, *Arctostaphylos uva-ursi* and *A. alpina* 'which do not tolerate more than a thin and transient snow cover'. The presence of such chianophobous species is of special relevance to the seasonal movements of reindeer discussed in chapter 3.

Post-glacial. The terms by which phases in the history of Post-glacial environment are commonly designated in our area are now used in a conventional sense as labels and nothing more. They no longer imply endorsement of Blytt and Sernander's hypothesis for explaining what they assumed to be wet and dry phases in the stratigraphy of peat bogs. The notion that, when eustatic sea-levels were low and Denmark lay at the centre of an extensive land area, climate would tend to be continental or Boreal in type with relatively low rainfall and a strong contrast between summer and winter temperature, and that conversely, the transgression of the sea over much of the old land area joining Denmark to England on one side and Sweden on the other would have favoured a more Atlantic type of climate, moister and having a more equable temperature, may have had and may still retain a certain plausibility for the west Baltic area. Yet it was at best parochial and offered no convincing explanation for a repetition (Sub-boreal and Sub-atlantic) even there.

The most widely held hypothesis to emerge from intensive and long sustained research is that summer temperatures rose to a peak during the Post-glacial period well above the levels obtaining at the present time in the Scandinavian region. The period of maximum temperature has commonly been termed the Post-glacial Climatic Optimum (Zeuner 1950, 67; Godwin 1956, 28 and 330) as though the transition from Late-glacial climate to one in which maximum summer temperatures were even higher than those now prevailing was a self-evident improvement. But this would be to evaluate changes of temperature in terms of our own contemporary norm, the norm to which our own economy happens to be adjusted. Perhaps it would be best to drop such an emotive term and remember that the environment as such is neutral. In human terms the best adjustment to ecological circumstances whatever these may be is that which is most appropriate. In effective terms the change from Late-glacial to the Post-glacial warmth maximum was 'good' for farmers but 'bad' for reindeer hunters. In more objective language one can say that Arctic to sub-Arctic conditions called for one adjustment and Temperate conditions for another.

Comparisons between the present and fossil distributions of a sufficiently large number of organisms, including hazel (Andersson, H. 1902) (Map 3), prickly sedge (*Cladium mariscus*)(von Post 1925), water-nut (*Trapa natans*) (Nordhagen 1933, fig. 57), *Najas flexilis* (Sandegren 1920) and tortoise (*Emys orbicularis*) (Degerbøl and Krog 1951, 43–9), suggests that mean July temperatures have fallen by 2° or 2½° C since their maximum expansion. The danger of trying to infer details of climatic changes from fossils is such that it is still too early to estimate at all precisely the profile of the Post-glacial temperature curve. The indications are that mean July temperatures may have risen rather more steeply than has sometimes been assumed. One is the rate at which the ice-sheet contracted as soon as it left the Fennoscandian moraine (see p. 39). Another is the evidence of pollen analysis. The rise of the birch (*Betula pubescens*) and the decline of pollen of open vegetation was so rapid as to suggest the early formation of closed birch forest. The comparative suddenness of the transition from open landscape to closed forest has been noted by palynologists, as far west as Ireland (Mitchell 1951, 192). In respect of Denmark Iversen expressed the view (1954, 98) that 'At the end of the Younger Dryas period the temperature seems

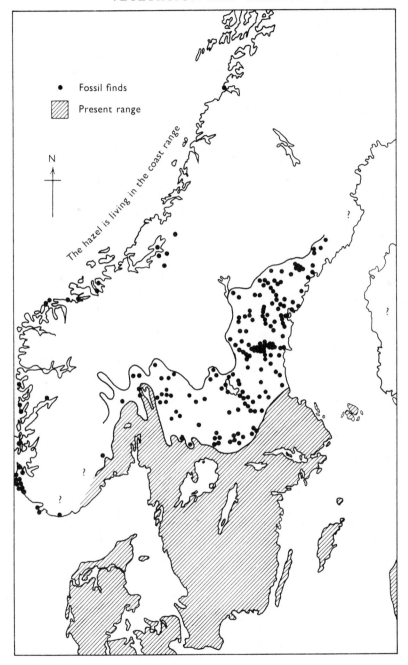

Fossil finds

Present range

N

The hazel is living in the coast range

3. Map illustrating the extent of the contraction of hazel (*Corylus avellana*) in Sweden since the Post-glacial temperature maximum. (*After Andersson*)

to have risen so quickly that the forest development could not keep step with the climatic improvement' and in another place (1960, 8), he spoke of 'the sudden and radical climatic improvement'. Whatever room for research there may still be in relation to the rate of vegetational response, there can hardly be any doubt that the main outcome of the rise of temperature in this field was the replacement of a predominantly open landscape by one largely dominated by forest trees. It was not for nothing that in Britain for example the Post-glacial was designated the Forest Period long before details of the composition of forests at different stages had been worked out by means of pollen-analysis (e.g. Tansley 1911, 65–6). The combined study of macroscopic plant remains and pollen by competent plant ecologists has resulted in a broad consensus that forest trees extended up to the tree-line in a solid cover broken only by lakes, water-courses, swamps and the sea-shore. Writing of the situation in Denmark, Iversen (1941, 31) put the matter in a nutshell: 'A continuous forest, with dangerous swamps as the only openings, covered the entire country.'

Several factors determined the composition of forests at particular times and places, but everywhere a pervasive control was exercised by climate. It was, above all, a rise of temperature that allowed trees to spread from their refuge areas in the south and east. To a significant extent it was increasing warmth that determined the succession of forest trees. Different species were able to colonise more rapidly than others and forests, once established, might be difficult to penetrate and replace. Nevertheless, it was broadly true that the earliest forests were made up of species best able to tolerate relatively low temperatures and that species demanding higher temperatures tended to appear later and rise to dominance later. Thus, Pre-boreal forests were composed of trees already present in the region during the Allerød period, and which contrived to survive the colder Younger Dryas, notably birch (*Betula pubescens*), aspen (*Populus tremula*), willow (*Salix* sp.) and Juniper (*Juniperus communis*). The comparatively low values for pine (*Pinus sylvestris*) need not in itself imply a low temperature. The pine had to spread from a more distant refuge area, travelled more slowly than the birch and on arrival may well have found it difficult to gain a good hold in the birch forests (Fries 1965a, 273). That the transition from Pre-boreal to Boreal forest in Denmark and Scania was marked by some increase of temperature is suggested by the rise to predominance of hazel (*Corylus avellana*), which began to form extensive scrub on the better soils, leaving very dry ones to pine. During the later Boreal period (Zone VI), the thermophilous broad-leaved trees, notably alder (*Alnus*) and the components of the mixed oak forest – oak (*Quercus*), elm (*Ulmus*) and lime (*Tilia*) – commonly attained high values in the forests of south Scandinavia. Both these developments reflect the Post-glacial rise of temperature. On the other hand, the increase in hazel permitted by climate may locally have been occasioned or at least assisted by the use of fire for hunting, a practice which though it might affect only limited areas at any particular moment would, if continued over any length of time, come to exert a profound and widespread influence on the vegetation of extensive territories (Rawitschur 1945). The ability of hazel to survive burning and so to be in a position initially to take over areas cleared by fire is due to its ability to send out side-shoots from low down on the root stock (Iversen 1941, 46). It has been observed to colonise areas cleared by recurrent prairie fires in parts of Wisconsin (Chavannes 1941). The presumption is a fair one that hazel would have responded to fire whether caused by natural forces, by hunting or by slash and burn farming. The coincidence of a fall in tree pollen with rises in that of grasses and weeds including *Artemisia* and *Plantago* at a level marked by charcoal at Hoxne, Suffolk, reminds us that man may have been making an impact, however local and temporary, on vegetation as far back as the Lower Palaeolithic (West and McBurney 1954, 135).

In Denmark and south Sweden the moment at which the rise of warmth-demanding trees crossed the declining curves for the older forest components marks the effective boundary in pollen diagrams between the Late Boreal and Atlantic phases (VI/VII). Further north the deciduous trees of the mixed oak forest made their presence felt well beyond their present northern limits in middle Sweden and south-west Finland. Again, as we learn from the occurrence of pine stumps dated to the Atlantic phase by radiocarbon analysis (Map 4), the coniferous forest extended at this time well above the modern tree line on the Caledonian mountains of Norrland (Lundqvist 1962). As more has been learned about the vegetational history of middle and northern Sweden it has become evident that thermophilous trees continued to flourish there, as they did in south-west Norway (Fægri 1943), during the Sub-boreal phase (Fries 1965b, Pl. I, 3). The fact that temperatures still remained high at this time is indeed amply supported by the detailed study of the stratigraphic occurrences of tortoise shells in south Scandi-

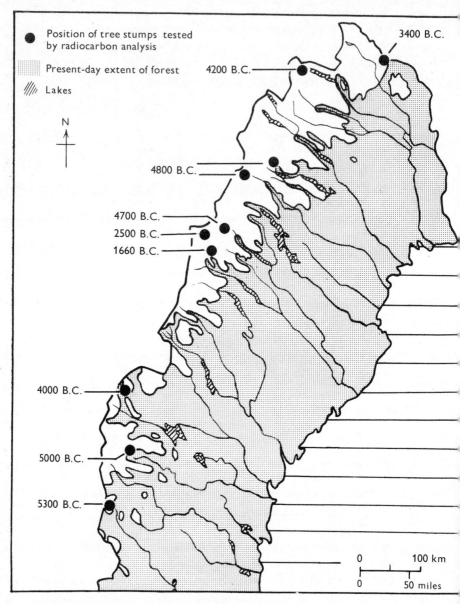

Position of tree stumps tested by radiocarbon analysis

Present-day extent of forest

Lakes

N

3400 B.C.

4200 B.C.

4800 B.C.

4700 B.C.

2500 B.C.

1660 B.C.

4000 B.C.

5000 B.C.

5300 B.C.

0   100 km

0   50 miles

4. Map showing that forest trees were growing high up on the *fjäll* of northern Sweden at a time when Post-glacial temperatures and tree-line were higher than today. (*After Lundqvist*)

54

navia beyond the present northern range of the breeding population (Degerbøl and Krog 1951). If allowance is made for the longer duration of the Atlantic phase, it will be seen from the following table taken from Degerbøl and Krog that there was no diminution in the presence of this warmth-demanding animal until Sub-atlantic times:

Forest history zones	Numbers of occurrences of tortoise (*Emys orbicularis*)
IX	0
VIII	32
VII	49
VI	12
V	18
IV	0

This suggests that from the point of view of temperature there was little to choose between the Atlantic and much at least of the Sub-boreal (cf. Magnusson 1964) and it is an interesting fact that Norwegian palynologists are inclined to place the Post-glacial temperature maximum in the latter period. This has an obvious bearing on the expansion of farming economy witnessed by archaeology for the Sub-boreal in northern territories from west Norway to the coastal tracts of the Gulf of Bothnia and south-west Finland.

In south Scandinavia the Sub-boreal phase of climate was marked by a series of closely interlocked changes in vegetation which in the light of the previous paragraph can hardly be explained adequately in terms of climate. The most outstanding were locally pronounced if temporary reductions in the mixed oak forest and corresponding recoveries in open vegetation of the kind driven into restricted habitats by the Post-glacial spread of forest trees. Prominent among the Late-glacial species to stage a recovery during the warm Sub-boreal were narrow and broad-leaved plantain (*Plantago lanceolata* and *P. major*), *Artemisia* and *Chenopodiaceae*, plants traditionally associated in north-western Europe with cultivated fields or meadows. The notion that botanical changes of this kind might indeed have been due to the activities of prehistoric farmers, that the virgin forest was 'being changed into cultural forest' was first expressed and worked out in detail by Iversen in his classic paper of 1941 (53). Although not unchallenged (Nilsson 1948 but cf. Iversen 1949), Iversen's hypothesis has received wide acceptance and similar land occupation (*Landam*) phases have been recognised in Sub-boreal deposits far and wide over the territories farmed by prehistoric man in different parts of Scandinavia and frequently in close association with Neolithic sites. Yet the impact of farming on vegetation might be expected to have varied in some respects according both to local ecological circumstances and to the precise nature of the farming system. The *landam* system envisaged by Iversen involved the temporary clearance of successive patches of forest by axe and fire to provide grazing for livestock and seed beds for cereals. Archaeologically this *landam* phase related to the final or C phase of the early Neolithic of Denmark and stratigraphically it occurred well up in Zone VIII of the Danish pollen sequence.

An earlier form of farming economy contrasting in several respects with Iversen's *landam* has been claimed by Troels-Smith (1953) to equate with the marked decline of elm that served to define the beginning of the Sub-boreal. Whereas under the regime inferred by Iversen livestock were free to graze at will and cereals must therefore have been surrounded by some kind of enclosure, under Troels-Smith's the cattle were envisaged as being kept in stalls. The presence of ramson (*Allium* cfr. *ursinum*), a prime favourite of cattle, meant that cattle can hardly have been given a free range. Instead, Troels-Smith argued with some local ethnographic and historical support that they were fed on branches of elm which was for this reason inhibited from flowering and releasing pollen. The fact that he was able to point to the presence of weeds that commonly accompanied farming, as well as his discovery of an analogous conjunction in connection with Neolithic settlement in Switzerland, helped to attract some support for his hypothesis. On the other hand, Iversen (1941, 34–6) firmly placed the zone border VII/VIII at the elm decline on the basis that this was climatically conditioned. Again, the very pervasiveness of the elm decline has led many to doubt (e.g. Fries 1965*a*, 279) whether it is best explained in terms of a change in land utilisation that was to begin with local and sporadic, especially in view of the recurrence surface, premonitory of the major change of climate reflected in the transition from Zones VII to VIII, which has been so widely recognised at the beginning of the Sub-boreal. What is sure is that territories subject to even a minor fluctuation of climate would have been that degree more sensitive to economic change; and the opposite would, of course, apply.

Another question which probably does not repay further discussion at the moment is the extent to which the many plants that appeared in forest clearings and meadows were introduced by man, or represented an ecological response to greater light on the part of plants which had been restricted to small refuge areas so long as forest trees exercised an almost total dominance. In the case of cultivated wheat or barley, where no prototype existed in the Late-glacial or early Post-glacial flora of north-western Europe, we can be sure that the plants concerned were humanly introduced. In other cases, where for example weeds of cultivation are not to be distinguished from Late-glacial relicts, no definite answer can be offered. From an ecological point of view indeed the question is irrelevant. What is significant is that a change in the way in which men utilised their landscape was reflected by a series of interrelated changes in the composition of vegetation. Another possibility to be entertained is that the Scandinavian flora was enriched accidentally from time to time as a direct result of extensions in the range of the social territories or spheres of social interaction of the human population. A particular instance of this has recently been touched upon by Magnus Fries (1969, 32), who has pointed out that plant materials must frequently have traversed great distances in the form of packaging materials: the example of the bronze and glass vessels known to have reached even quite remote parts of Scandinavia from the south during the Iron Age finds many counterparts in the re-distribution of fragile objects like flint axes or daggers or slate orna-ments which during earlier periods of pre-history had travelled great distances and traversed many floristic zones.

The Sub-atlantic phase is widely accepted as a time of increased precipitation and reduced temperature. Stratigraphically its beginning has often been defined by a boundary horizon (*Grenzhorizont*) separat-ing an old *Sphagnum* peat, highly humidified, denser and dark-coloured from a younger one, paler and generally unhumidified; and it was supposed by its discoverer, C. A. Weber, that the change in the condi-tions of peat formation was a simple product of climatic changes from Sub-boreal to Sub-atlantic.

Although this hypothesis has undergone some modification, it is widely accepted that the younger *Sphagnum* peat was formed under conditions like those under which raised bogs are at present being formed in the cool Atlantic climate of central Ireland (Godwin 1956, 34). The recognition of earlier boundaries or recurrence surfaces, in-cluding one at the Atlantic/Sub-boreal transition, has suggested brief episodes of heavier rainfall and flooding before the major change to Sub-atlantic climate. The formation of extensive areas of raised bogs, for instance, in south and central Sweden (Fries 1965*a*, 279) in itself affected the landscape as a scene of human settlement. The Sub-atlantic phase is often described as one of climatic 'deterioration'. Certainly it was less favourable for cultivating wheat in northern latitudes. On the other hand the new conditions suited oats and rye and offered special opportunities for the growth of grass, the basis of the hay-making on which so much northern husbandry is still based. So far as natural vegetation is concerned the Sub-atlantic was marked in south Scandinavia by the expansion of beech (*Fagus*) and hornbeam (*Carpinus*). In the north three main developments occurred: the spruce (*Picea*) extended its range over the rest of middle Sweden, the tree line on the Caledonian mountains receded and the treeless *fjäll* underwent a significant expansion.

ANIMAL LIFE

The herbivorous mammals which were of greatest importance to man as sources of food were precisely those most directly linked with vegetation. They thus provided a main link between the human populations of Scandinavia and the history of environmental change, more particularly during the early phase of settlement before effective farming had been undertaken in the region. They also affected very directly the sources of materials available for artifacts and hence to some degree the types produced.

Late-glacial. For the Late-glacial period our knowledge of the animals occupying the ice-free territories of Denmark and south Sweden depends upon the recovery of antlers, bones and teeth from natural deposits. Moreover, it is only in a few rare cases that finds have been made under controlled conditions, notably at the Allerød settlement site of Bromme in central Zealand (Mathiassen 1946*a*, 228). Most of the finds have been made in the course of ordinary economic activities. This is liable to introduce some distortion of the sample, since younger deposits are liable to be disturbed or even opened up more frequently than older ones. Thus, of the 49 finds of reindeer known from Denmark other than Bornholm, it is interesting that 32 have been ascribed (Degerbøl and Krog 1959, 138) to the Younger Dryas (Zone III), 9 to the Allerød (Zone II) and only 8 to the Older Dryas (Zone I), which to judge from the flora was at least as favourable, if not more favourable to reindeer than Zone III. Since only scrappy finds are available from

Table 2. *Faunal occurrences during the Allerød (II) and Younger Dryas (III) periods in Denmark*

Animal species	Zone II Allerød	Zone II Younger Dryas
Herbivores		
Reindeer (*Rangifer tarandus*)	×	×
Wild horse (*Equus caballus ferus*)	×	×
Elk (*Alces alces*)	×	×
Bison (*Bison priscus*)	.	×
Giant deer (*Cervus giganteus*)	.	×
Fur-bearers		
Wolf (*Canis lupus*)	.	×
Alpine hare (*Lepus timidus*)	.	×
Mouse hare (*Ochotona*)	.	×
Ground squirrel (*Spermophilus rufescens*)	.	×
Wolverine (*Gulo gulo*)	×	×
Beaver (*Castor fiber*)	×	.
Birds		
Ptarmigan (*Lagopus* sp.)	.	×
Swan (*Cygnus cygnus*)	×	.
Fish		
Perch (*Perca fluviatilis*)	.	×
Pike (*Esox lucius*)	.	×

Zone I, the Late-Glacial fauna of Denmark may be listed from Zones II and III (Degerbøl and Iversen 1945, 25) respectively. In addition to the herbivorous mammals whose importance to man has been stressed, the lists include a number of fur-bearing animals of particular import- ance during a cold climate, and a few birds and fish.

Some of these animals, including the most abundant, reindeer, are at home today in tundra-like environments, but certain species, notably wild horse, bison, giant deer and *Spermophilus rufescens* are adapted to steppe environments and so complement the steppe component in the Younger Dryas vegetation. Another point to note is the presence in both phases of the elk and in the Allerød of the beaver, both species adapted to forest. The relative mildness of the Allerød phase is also reflected in the occurrence of the freshwater mollusc *Bithynia Leachi* in the culture layer at Bromme (Mathiassen 1946a, 227).

In Denmark itself remains of reindeer dating from the Late-glacial period (Map 5) have been found as far north as Nørre Lyngby on the north coast of Jutland and as far east as Bornholm which during the Late-glacial was still attached to the mainland of Germany. The only part of Denmark in which finds are sparse is that which lay outside the Weichsel ice-sheet and in which bogs were too acid for animal bones to survive under most circumstances (Degerbøl and Krog 1959, 103). Information about the occurrence of reindeer in Sweden has been less precisely recorded and not all the identifications are to be relied upon.

The concentration in southern and west Scania shown by Isberg's map (Isberg 1930a, fig. 1) is no doubt connected with the acidity of peat bogs north of the calcareous zone. Stray finds published since (Nybelin 1943) have shown that in fact reindeer expanded to the limits of south Sweden during the Late-glacial period. The dating of the south Swedish finds has been the subject of some discussion. Whereas in Denmark 159 finds can be assigned to the Late-glacial (14 to Zone I; 9 to Zone II; 32 to Zone III) and none to the Post-glacial, the Swedish investigator Isberg (1930a and b) assigned slightly more than half to the Post-glacial (15 Late-glacial; 14 Boreal; 4 Boreal/Atlantic). Isberg's results have since been put in question as the result of the investigation of the find from Nebbe Mosse (Althin, Brorson-Christensen and Berlin 1949) dated to the Younger Dryas phase. On the other hand, the criticism that analyses taken from old specimens of the kind relied upon by Isberg are inherently unreliable could also be applied to the great majority of the Danish specimens. The possibility, though not a strong one, cannot be entirely eliminated that a pocket of reindeer may have been as it were trapped in the northern marches of their old territory and managed to maintain themselves by adapting to Post-glacial vegetation.

The expansion of reindeer into the rest of Scandinavia most probably took place from the south and the east. The direct route from the south to Norrland would hardly have been practicable. By the time isostatic recovery had set in sufficiently to open up a route, closed forests established themselves and, as we have noted, pine trees expanded high up on the Caledonian mountains. On the other hand, even before a continuous land connection was established between the Göteborg and Oslo regions, the possibility existed, while temperatures were still low, to cross at any rate in winter the frozen sounds between islands (Degerbøl and Krog 1959, 103). In this way reindeer herds could have

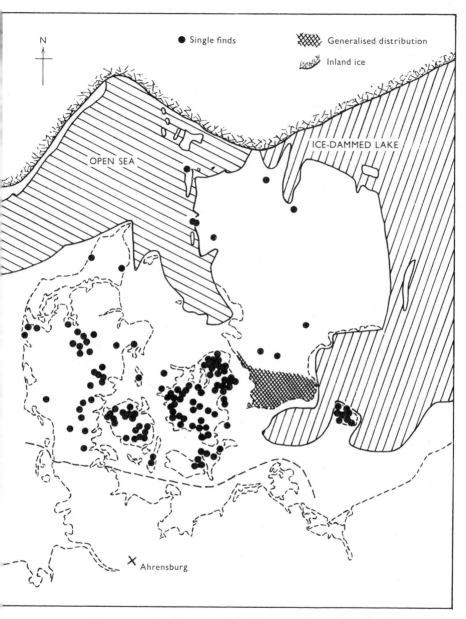

5. Map showing the distribution of skeletal remains of reindeer in south
Scandinavia. (*Based on Degerbøl, Isberg, Nybelin et al.*)

entered southern Norway (where on the high *fjäll*, of which the Hardangervidda is a conspicuous example, they still exist today) at an early stage of the Post-glacial, if not indeed slightly earlier. The eastern route from Russia, certainly followed during more recent periods might also have been used about the same time. It is even possible that reindeer herds passing between the Scandinavian ice-sheet and the White Sea may have reached Finnmark by Late-glacial times. Expansion southward into Norrland is unlikely to have occurred on any scale until the open *fjäll* country expanded with the contraction of forest during Sub-atlantic times.

Post-glacial. The transformation of vegetation which accompanied the onset of a warmer climate, while it made southern Scandinavia untenable for reindeer, created an environment favourable to a number of other animals of value to man. These included several species of particular importance as sources of meat, notably elk (*Alces alces*), aurochs (*Bos primigenius*), red deer (*Cervus elephas*), roe deer (*C. capreolus*) and wild pig (*Sus scrofa ferus*). The implications of these changes for the economy of prehistoric man will be touched upon in the appropriate contexts. Here the obvious point can be made that instead of being able to rely primarily on a single herbivore habituated to moving over extensive areas of more or less open landscape, the inhabitants of southern Scandinavia had to adapt to exploiting a broader range of animals accustomed to living in smaller groups and collectively suited to a broader range of local environments. Since as we have already seen the vegetation on which browsing and grazing animals depended underwent a continuous series of changes in the course of Post-glacial times, it is necessary to consider the sub-fossil remains of mammalian fauna from this period as precisely as possible in their correct chronological context. As we have already seen in the case of the Late-glacial, the critical application of pollen-analysis has at least given us a tool by which to do this and thanks to a number of valuable studies it is already possible to establish some of the broad outlines.

The habits of the elk, which as noted above (p. 59) had already made its appearance in Denmark during the Allerød oscillation, are comparatively well-known because it inhabits (in the case of the New World under the designation moose) vast tracts of circumpolar forest extending south into territories with a deciduous component and penetrating on occasion beyond the forest zone and into the open tundra. At the present day the elk is marked above all by the catholicity of its tastes: in the U.S.S.R. as a whole it is known to eat some 175 species of plant, including 110 grasses and herbs, 39 trees and shrubs and a variety of algae, ferns and lichens; and a single young tame elk in the Mordwin nature reserve has been seen to graze 133 varieties during the summer and autumn, including 61 of some importance (Heptner and Naumov 1956, 335). It follows that these animals avoid thick closed forest. They prefer tracts with open patches where they are able to browse off a mosaic of vegetation. Again, they tend to avoid steep ground and seek lakes, marshy areas and river valleys. Here they can indulge during the summer in bathing – they are excellent swimmers – and obtain a wide variety of foods including water plants, herbs, grasses and the leaves and shoots of aspen, birch, oak, or willow. During the winter diet is more restricted: the branches of the already mentioned trees are favoured, but the twigs, needles and even bark of coniferous trees form an almost limitless reserve for times of dearth. With these tastes it is easy to see why in Denmark feeding conditions for elk should have been 'excellent in the Pre-boreal, and very good in the greater part of the Boreal period' whereas when the mixed oak forest reached its maximum and darkened the forest 'environmental conditions became increasingly poor' (Degerbøl and Fredskild 1970, 131-2). One of the attractions of Scandinavia for the elk is the abundance of lakes and in some parts of the country of rivers, not to mention the numerous lakes of Late-glacial origin. In the early stages of forest development vegetation in Denmark and south Sweden must to some extent have resembled those prevailing today in the southern part of the circum-polar forest and it is hardly a surprise that elk remains should have been so relatively common on the settlements from this time. Conversely the rarity of elk from the Atlantic period, although basically due to worsening conditions for feeding, may well have been emphasised by more intensive hunting at a time when extensive tracts of land were being lost in Denmark.

It is much more hazardous to speculate on the ecological requirements of the aurochs because as Degerbøl has recently conceded (Degerbøl and Fredskild 1970, 132) this animal can no longer be observed in its natural habitat. What is certainly known is that in Denmark it appeared at the end of the Late-glacial sequence (one find each from Zones III and III/IV), was common in the Pre-boreal (fourteen finds), and more abundant still in the early Boreal (twenty finds), declining in the late Boreal (eleven finds) and in Zealand, though not in Jutland, disappearing completely in the Atlantic phase, a pattern closely comparable with that observed for Scania (Isberg 1962). The conclusion drawn from this by Degerbøl is that the aurochs, like the elk, flourished best during the earlier phases of forest development when grasses and herbs were still available locally in sufficient quantity to make, when supplemented by leaves and twigs, an attractive and adequate diet.

At the present time red deer flourish best in deciduous forest, though they are able to exist in a very small form in the largely disforested territories of the Scottish highlands. On the other hand their abundance, together with roe deer, at Star Carr shows very well that birch and willow forests with pine stands were sufficiently congenial to result in well developed animals, inferior indeed to those of the central European forests but outstandingly superior in size to those surviving in northern Britain today (Fraser and King in Clark *et al.* 1954, 79). Unlike elk, red deer and roe deer survived the dominance of the mixed oak forest in south Scandinavia. Although regarded as sylvan species, red deer and roe deer prefer to graze and to browse shoots and foliage on the forest edge. Roe deer for instance favour the foliage of birch, oak, ash, beech, elder and hazel and in winter go for blackberry fronds, wild rose leaves, juniper, crab apples, beech-mast, holly, fungi, broom and if necessary bark (Tegner 1951, 23–4). It is a characteristic of deer that they tend to follow a more or less regular cycle of movement in response to changes of temperature. In territories where there is any marked relief they normally feed on high ground in the summer and shelter during the winter on low ground (Fraser Darling 1969, 31–2). In the case of west Norway sheltered fjords provide the most congenial winter refuge, whereas in summer the herds seek upland pastures (Ingebrigsten 1924, 55).

As a rule wild pigs tend to occupy fixed territories, though ones subject to seasonal extension. Their diet, while including an animal component, notably earthworms, eggs and small rodents, consists mainly of vegetable foods, above all roots, fruits and the concentrated nourishment afforded by acorns and beech-mast. This means that in northern Europe they fit ecologically into a context of mixed oak forest and explains why they were so sparsely represented at a site of the age of Star Carr and so strongly at a Late-boreal site like Sværdborg I.

Other land mammals to enter Scandinavia during Post-glacial times included beaver (already present during the Allerød), brown bear (*Ursus arctos*), fox (*Canis vulpes*), wild cat (*Felis catus fera*), badger (*Meles taxus*), otter (*Lutra vulgaris*), wood marten (*Martes sylvatica*) and squirrel (*Sciurus vulgaris*). Apart from their value for food these animals provided in their furs a resource of major economic value.

Anthropogenic factors played a part in Post-glacial fauna as well as in vegetation. The dog (*Canis familiaris*) appeared during the Boreal, possibly as a local domesticate of the wolf (Degerbøl 1961). Genetically modified forms of ox (*Bos taurus domesticus*) and swine (*Sus scrofa domesticus*) appeared at the beginning of the Sub-boreal and horse (*Equus caballus*), present in the Younger Dryas but extremely rare during the early Post-glacial, reappeared later in the period in close association with man. Sheep (*Ovis aries*) and goat (*Capra hirca*), neither of which had predecessors in the region, appeared in the context of farming economy in south Scandinavia.

The geographical evolution of the Baltic was another factor under-lying changes in animal food resources. It is likely for example that the ringed seal (*Phoca hispida*) and the Greenland seal (*P. groenlandica*), both habituated to arctic conditions and the former even able to make holes through fast ice for breathing, were already present during the Late-glacial period. If they entered from the east by way of the White Sea – something which can hardly be tested until more is known about the early geography of northern Carelia – they could have existed in the Baltic ice-dammed lake. Alternatively if they came from the west they may not have arrived until the time of the Yoldia Sea. Seals with a more southerly range, the grey seal (*Halichoerus grypus*) and the common or spotted seal (*P. vitulina*), presumably did not arrive until Post-glacial times. This applied also to andromous fish, notably salmon (*Salmo salmo*) and white fish (*Corregonus* sp.). These Atlantic fish, which today regularly ascend the great rivers of Norrland to spawn, can hardly have obtained access in any numbers until the breaching of the Dano-Scanian barrier and the formation of the Litorina Sea.

3
The Late-glacial settlement of Denmark/Scania

Before turning to the record of more or less continuous human settlement in south Scandinavia during the final stages of the Late-glacial period, the possibility, indeed the probability, that it was temporarily occupied as early as the Eemian or last Inter-glacial period needs to be considered. If it is correct as our authorities confidently state (Nordmann 1936, 37; Flint 1947, 328; Oakley 1969, 28 and fig. 12) that temperatures at this time were as high, if not indeed higher, than those prevailing today, it might after all be expected that warmth-demanding organisms including ungulates and their human predators would have extended their range into our area. On the other hand no fully convincing archaeological evidence has yet been advanced to substantiate this. There has been no lack of flint artifacts of typologically archaic form, collected either from the surface of cultivated ground or from the foreshore. On the other hand, when it is recalled that flint implements frequently pass through an archaic-looking phase in the course of manufacture and were not for various reasons always finished, the recovery of such objects out of any secure geological context ceases to convince (cf. Becker 1971b). In the case of roe deer bones recovered from Eemian deposits at Hollerup, near Randers, the only question is whether the holes noted by Møhl (1954) were in fact made by man.

CHRONOLOGICAL FRAMEWORK

As indicated in the last chapter the Late-glacial period in northern Europe has been conveniently zoned in terms of vegetational and climatic change so as to provide a framework, controlled and validated by radiocarbon dating, for the beginnings of continuous human settlement in south Scandinavia. As a background to our study it may be convenient to review the sequence established for the Hamburg region

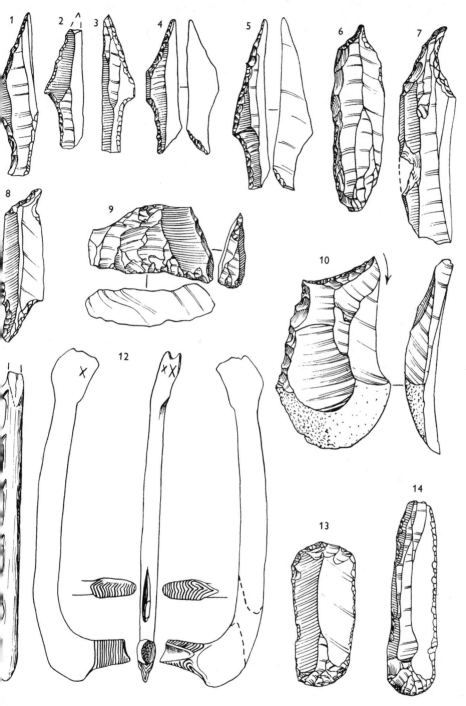

Fig. 1. Hamburg flint and reindeer artifacts
(3/4, except (9) and (12) at 1/2).

Table 3. *Schematic sequence in the Ahrensburg tunnel valley, with archaeo-logical levels in their Late-glacial contexts*

Section	Archaeological levels	Pollen Zones (Jessen)	Climatic periods
Brushwood peat	.	VII	Atlantic
Reed peat	.	IV–VI	Boreal
Mud (*Faulschlamm*)	Ahrensburgian	IV	Younger Dryas
Sedge peat	.	II	Allerød
Calcareous mud (*Kalkmudde*)	.	Ic	Older Dryas
.	.	Ib	Bølling
.	Hamburgian	Ia	Oldest Dryas

by Gustav Schwantes and his pupil Alfred Rust. Working in conjunc-tion with a team of natural scientists, the geologist Karl Gripp, the palynologist Rudolf Schutrumpf and the zoologists Walter Krause and Walter Kollau, these prehistorians succeeded in establishing well docu-mented phases of human settlement in their correct contexts.

Indications that man had penetrated the Hamburg region during the Late-glacial period were first given by flint assemblages collected from the surface of localities near Lavenstedt and Neumünster during the opening decade of the twentieth century, but it was not until some years later that their significance was appreciated (Schwantes 1928). Realising that their inventory of blades, tanged points, end of blade scrapers and burins compared with that of Advanced Palaeolithic assem-blages, Schwantes saw the necessity of establishing their true strati-graphical position in the sequence of the region. He therefore turned to the Ahrensburg tunnel valley near Neumünster. By choosing flint sites adjacent to depressions in the bed of the tunnel valley formed through the melting of buried ice he hoped to recover scatters of archaeological material in position at successive levels of the infill. Again, since these deposits were likely to be water-logged the possi-bility was evident that organic remains including animal material and a record of vegetational change would be preserved.

The first main excavation was carried out in 1933–4 at Meiendorf. This established the context of a flint industry first noted on German soil in 1932 at Wellingsbüttel only a few kilometres distant, an industry

Table 4. *The hierarchy of human territories on the north European plain during the final stages of the Late-glacial period*

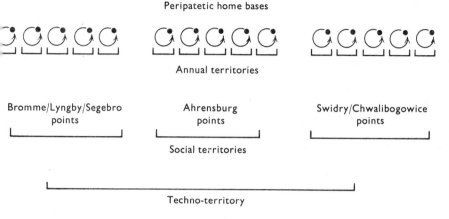

Peripatetic home bases

Annual territories

Bromme/Lyngby/Segebro points

Ahrensburg points

Swidry/Chwalibogowice points

Social territories

Techno-territory

(Blades, burins, end scrapers and tanged points of flint; reindeer antler clubs or mattocks; barbed harpoon-heads)

first published from this part of Europe by Popping (1931). The wealth of organic data recovered from Meiendorf (Rust 1937) led Schwantes to accord separate status to the cultural assemblage which in time-honoured fashion was termed Hamburgian (Fig. 1). Excavations at Stellmoor nearby confirmed the context of the Hamburgian but were above all notable for fixing the stratigraphic position of the assemblage which first attracted interest to the region and received the name Ahrensburgian (Rust 1943). The stratigraphic results obtained by these two key excavations can be set out in tabular form (Table 3).

It will be seen that the two archaeological levels in the tunnel valley are separated by a wide gap extending from Zone Ia to II, represented by *c.* 3 metres of deposit. Since reindeer are known to have penetrated Denmark during Zone I there is no *a priori* reason why their human predators should not also have done so; and in fact we know (p. 87) that man was present at least by Ic. On the other hand by the time we are able to point to a definite settlement, that is by the Allerød phase (Zone II), south Scandinavia apparently formed a distinct social territory.

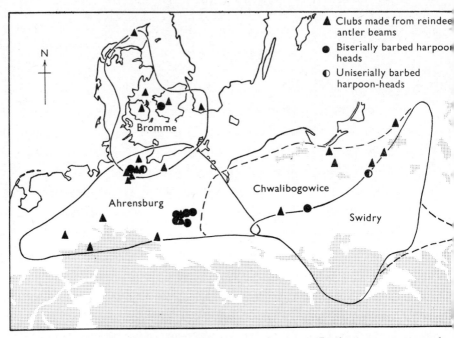

6. Map of the north European plain showing the main tanged point territories and the distribution of individual finds of leading reindeer antler artifacts.

SOCIAL TERRITORIES

Several factors contributed to a marked degree of uniformity in the technology of the inhabitants of south Scandinavia and adjacent parts of the north European plain during the closing stages of the Late-glacial. The region presented an ecological setting that despite some local variation was broadly similar as regards terrain, climate, vegetation and fauna, with reindeer as the dominant source of protein. Equally, all the inhabitants of the plain were heirs of an Advanced Palaeolithic heritage. In each case flint-work was based on the techniques of blade production, steep retouch and the burin blow and each made extensive use of antler and specifically of reindeer antler as material for artifacts. In respect of these latter it is significant that the two main classes are each distributed widely over the whole techno-territory (Map 6). Thus mattocks or clubs of reindeer antler extend from Westphalia to Poland and as far north as northern Jutland and Scania. Again, a particular form of harpoon-head having a base of pointed spade form (Figs. 2 and 3)

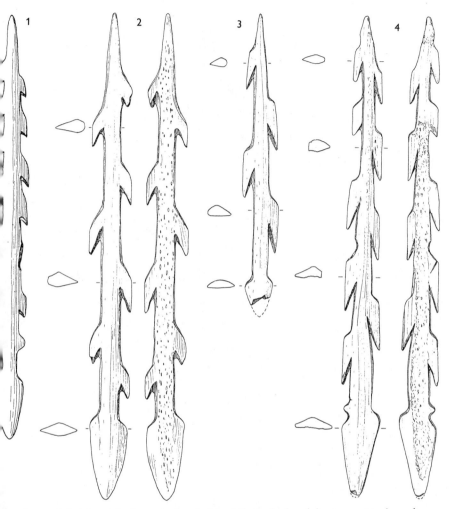

Fig. 2. Reindeer antler harpoon-heads, biserially barbed and having pointed spade shaped bases of Younger Dryas age from northern Europe. (1) Lachmirowice, Poland; (2) Gorz, Havelland; (3) Stellmoor, Schleswig-Holstein; and (4) Skaftelev, Zealand. (*After Taute*) (1/2)

and having either two series of barbs disposed alternately either side of the stem or more rarely only one row of barbs is distributed over Denmark, north Germany and Poland.

The feature which allows one to distinguish distinct social territories within this extended province of basically uniform technology is

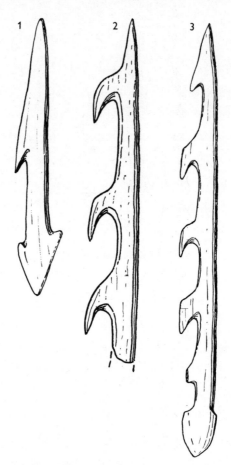

Fig. 3. Uniserially barbed harpoon-heads of reindeer antler of Younger Dryas age from Stellmoor, Schleswig-Holstein (1)–(2), and from Eckertsdorf, Kr. Sensburg, former East Prussia (3) (1/2).

characteristically idiosyncratic. As Taute (1968) has so admirably brought out in his masterly survey of the lithic industries of the north European plain dating from the Late glacial-period, three more or less complementary geographical zones can be distinguished, each marked by a predeliction for a particular method of making tanged flint points:

(a) An eastern (Swidry–Chwalibogowician) zone extending from the Warta to the Nieman, and comprising an area of c. 100,000 sq. km, in which tangs were shaped in part by an inverse retouch and by flat flaking on the bulbar surface.

(b) A western (Ahrensburgian) zone reaching from Belgian Limbourg to Schleswig-Holstein, Mecklenburg and Brandenburg and covering an area of c. 120,000 sq. km, in which the tang was shaped exclusively by flaking from the under flake surface.

(c) A northern (Lyngby–Bromme–Segebro) zone extending over Denmark, south Sweden and Schleswig-Holstein, an area of c. 70,000 sq. km, in which the tanged points were characteristically made on heavy pointed blades.

There are indeed signs that these three territories had already become distinct during the preceding Allerød phase. At this time the cortical area of Poland was occupied by the Swiderian and north Germany by the Rissen and allied groups marked by knife blades with backs blunted for the finger (Schwabedissen 1954). As the site of Bromme itself shows, the northern group was already established at this time.

Swidry–Chwalibogowice. It is unfortunate that the great bulk of evidence relating to the Late-glacial settlement of Poland recovered by archaeologists (Krukowski 1922; Kozłowski 1926) derives from eroded sanddunes. This means that it consists almost entirely of flint assemblages. Hardly any direct information is available about the basis of subsistence, and knowledge of other aspects of technology is almost lacking (Šturms 1970, 8). On the other hand, even though antler and bone objects have yet to be found associated with these flint assemblages, there is a strong presumption that the reindeer antler mattocks found within this territory relate to the same settlement. The same applies to the well-known biserially barbed harpoon-head from Lachmirowice (Fig. 2, 1) which closely matches specimens from Stellmoor and from the intermediate Havel lakes; and also to the uniserial point recovered from a Younger Dryas deposit at Eckertsdorf, Kr. Sensburg (Gross 1940, no. 17), which matches another piece from Stellmoor (Fig. 3, 2).

Investigation of dunes at the name site Swidry Wielkie in the fork of the Swidry and Vistula south of Warsaw showed long ago that the industry occurred in sand under a humus layer marking a phase of stability and containing flint industries ranging from 'Tardenoisian' to Neolithic; and this general sequence was found to be valid for other dune formations in the Vistula basin (Sawicki 1936). More refined

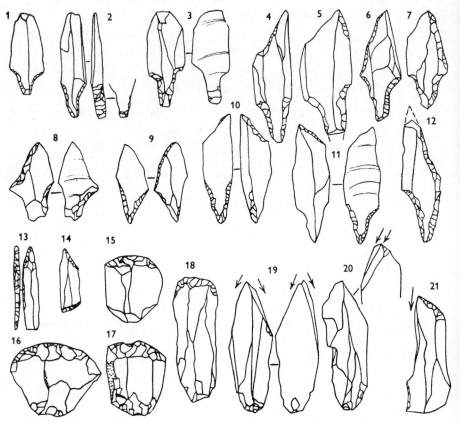

Fig. 4. Swidry–Chwalibogowice flint assemblage from Staňkowice, Poland (1/1). (*After Szmit*)

stratigraphical studies, like those carried out by the Chmielewskis on the dune of Witow *c.* 100 km west of Warsaw (Chmielewska and Chmielewski 1960; Taute 1968, 133–5) and some limited applications of pollen analysis and radiocarbon dating have made it possible both to arrive at a more detailed sequence and to synchronise this with the sequence of Late-glacial climatic history. In this book Taute (1968, 233–8) has committed himself to a five-fold division of these assemblages, the first three of which he assigns to the Allerød and the last two to an early and late phase of the Younger Dryas respectively. There are two reasons for questioning the validity of this five-fold sequence: the samples are in most cases too small to be of much statistical value; and the assumption that variations in the composition of artifact assemblages in the same tradition necessarily reflect chronological differences ignores the possibility, indeed the strong possibility, that variations in tool-kits may on the other hand be due to changes in seasonal activities. A broad typological distinction nevertheless exists between assemblages of Late-glacial II (Allerød) and Late-glacial III (Younger Dryas) age. The earlier group, of which that from Swidry Wielkie I may serve as exemplar, is marked by Swiderian points with pointed bases (Fig. 4, 9–11) and long and short end-scrapers. In the later group, represented by Chwalibogowice and Witow C, end-scrapers, among which shorter ones become commoner, continue but are now supplemented by round scrapers; a few backed bladelets appear; and Swiderian points decline in favour of Chwalibogowician ones with pronounced tangs (Fig. 4, 2–8). The presence of a few Ahrensburg points in the Younger Polish assemblages helps to confirm their Younger Dryas age.

Ahrensburg. The Ahrensburg and the Hamburg industrial assemblages shared a tradition common to the Advanced Palaeolithic settlement of Europe, north Africa and south-west Asia. They comprised in common a variety of artifacts from well struck blades shaped by a steep retouch to form weapon armatures, end of blade scrapers and burins or graving tools made by punching flakes into the main axes of blades so as to form the required chisel edge. Their makers also shared with other Advanced Palaeolithic groups an ability to work antler and bone by the groove and splinter technique for making a variety of artifacts, a task in which burins almost certainly played a leading part. The industries also agree in that neither were equipped with flint axe or adze blades, which first seem to have appeared on the north European plain in the context of the Post-glacial forest. There were also some important differences. The Ahrensburgian occupants of Stellmoor got along without two tool forms of which the Hamburgians made significant use, namely notched blades (resembling in many cases the 'strangled blades' of French pre-historians) and pronged tools (*Zinken*) made on blades and having oblique points. More significant are differences in a functional component common to both groups, namely the points.

There is circumstantial evidence that both Ahrensburgian tanged and Hamburgian shouldered points served not merely to arm weapons but to act as the heads of projectiles. There can be no doubt that tanged points were at least in certain instances used to tip arrows (Fig. 5) since

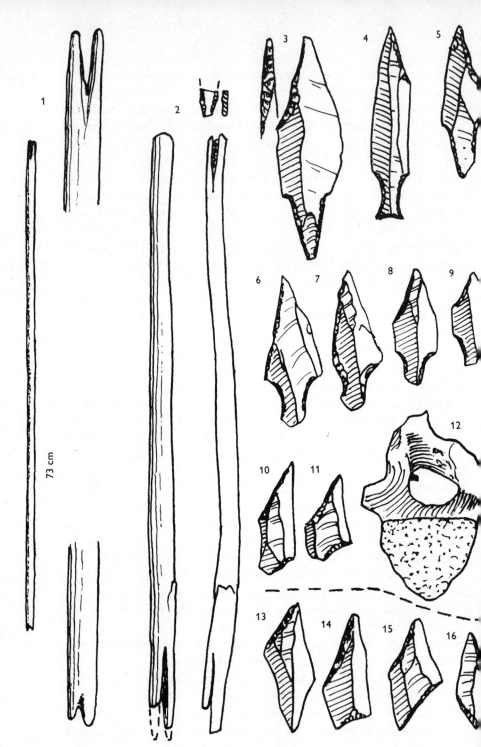

Fig. 5. Ahrensburg arrowshafts and armatures: Stellmoor (1/1, except (1a): 73 cm long).
[Note: Tanged points (nos. 3, 9) and rhombic points (nos. 10, 11, 15, 16).]

in two instances at Stellmoor their tangs were found in position in the foreparts of arrowshafts (Fig. 5, 2) and in a third a complete specimen was recovered along with parts of a wooden shaft (Rust 1943, Taf. 93 and 94). The arrows themselves, of which over a hundred fragments were recovered ranging in length from 5 to 75 cm, were made of pine wood, as were the pointed pieces interpreted by Rust (1943, 192–3 and Taf. 97–8) as bow ends. The use of this material is consistent with Schutrumpf's conclusion (in Rust 1943, 18) that in southern Schleswig-Holstein the temperature never declined enough during the Younger Dryas to drive out forest trees completely. The arrows themselves display some sophistication since they were made at least in some cases in two parts with the forepart (15 to 25 cm) dovetailed into the main shaft. Again it is worthy of note that grooved sandstone shaft rubbers of the type used in northern Europe down to the early Bronze Age had already come into use in the Ahrensburg territory (Rust 1943, Taf. 88). That they were used with effect is shown by the flint embedded in a reindeer vertebra (Fig. 5, 12) from the Ahrensburg level at Stellmoor (ibid. Taf. 87, 1). Whether the shouldered points of the Hamburgian were used to tip arrows or spears cannot yet be certainly determined but the thickness of bone through which they passed – 2 cm in the case of a reindeer shoulder blade and an appreciable amount in that of a rein-deer vertebra (Rust 1943, Taf. 34–5) – means that if spears were used they must have been propelled with exceptional force. If size is any criterion for distinguishing between arrowheads and spearheads, it may first be noted that Hamburgian shouldered points stand much closer to Ahrensburgian tanged points than either does to the heavier Lyngby points. As between the former two there is no distinction in size sufficient of itself to call for a difference in use. If as the diagram shows (Fig. 6) there is a higher proportion of Ahrensburg points under 35 mm in length and correspondingly an increase in that of Hamburg ones between 45 and 55 mm, this is counter-balanced by the fact that the only two specimens over 65 mm were both of the former group. The same applies if the length–breadth ratio is taken into account: it is the Lyngby group that stands apart. In the absence of hafted specimens from Hamburgian levels there must nevertheless remain some question whether these people used the bow as the Ahrensburgians undoubtedly did. What is not in doubt is that both armed their projectiles with flints and, again, that reindeer bones from each have been found with flint heads deeply embedded in them. Short of adopting the perverse

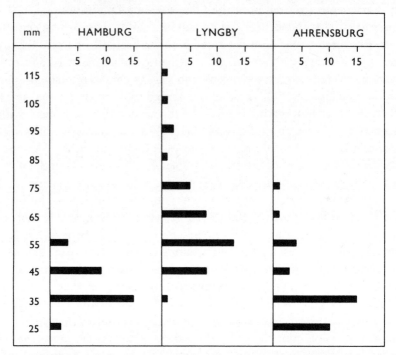

Fig. 6. Histograms illustrating lengths respectively of Hamburg, Lyngby and Ahrens-burg tanged flint points. The samples comprise all specimens illustrated by Rust 1937 (Taf. 17) and 1943 (Taf. 22); Mathiassen 1946 (figs. 6, 14, 16); and Rust 1943 (Taf. 46).

notion that these embedded flints were in every instance the result of misses between human combatants, we may conclude that reindeer were in fact hunted and shot during the Late-glacial period in northern Europe.

Certain differences have been noted in antler and bone work. Rust even held that the Ahrensburgians had given up the groove and splinter technique used by their predecessors for obtaining the blanks required for harpoon heads, but in fact he illustrates the stump of an antler subjected to this treatment (Rust 1943, Taf. 66). An innovation in the Ahrensburgian level at Stellmoor was evidence for the manufacture of mattock heads and clubs made from reindeer antler: in fact, this one excavation yielded substantially more than the total number of stray finds from the north European plain and south Scandinavia as a whole. Yet we cannot be quite sure from its absence from Hamburgian levels at Meiendorf and Stellmoor that this kind of tool was unknown to

78

this earlier group; after all it was known to the Gravettians of central Europe at Pavlov (Klima 1956, Taf. x) many thousands of years earlier. Differences in the form of harpoon head from each period would be more diagnostic if the sample were only big enough. For what it is worth the single specimen from Meiendorf (Fig. 1, 11) was unilaterally barbed, whereas the Ahrensburgian level at Stellmoor yielded two biserially barbed specimens of a type widely distributed on the north European plain (Fig. 2) as well as one with a single barb and another with a single row of prominent barbs of rounded profile (Fig. 3).

Lyngby–Bromme–Segebro (Map 7). The first indication that Denmark was occupied as early as Late-glacial times came in 1889 when an artificially shaped beam of reindeer antler was found at the foot of the cliffs at Nørre Lyngby on the north coast of Jutland. The number of reindeer bones and antlers recovered subsequently from the bed of a lacustrine basin exposed in the cliff-section and subject to rapid erosion argues that the original find comes from the same context, especially since the later recoveries include an antler beam, in this case broken out of the skull and presumably from a slain animal, of which the crown has been detached and the brow tine reduced to a stump (Hjørring Mus. 14382). In the case of the original find from Nørre Lyngby the beam has been neatly detached and the brow tine much reduced in length, the stump hollowed out to form a shallow socket.

This antler object from Nørre Lyngby first attracted interest mainly by reason of the material from which it was made, pointing as it did to a period of settlement when reindeer were still present. As a result many more specimens were recognised and in some few instances could be related to geological deposits of Late-glacial age. Sophus Müller (1896) published additional ones from Denmark and R. Stimming (1917) from the Havellund, Brandenburg. In 1923 Gustav Schwantes filled the geographical gap by publishing examples from Schleswig-Holstein and extended the distribution eastwards to Poland. It only needed records from Westphalia in the west (Brandt 1933), Scania in the north (Althin, *et al.* 1949) and East Prussia (Gross 1940) in the east to establish that, as seen on our map (Map 6), these artifacts of reindeer antler were to be found distributed over the whole of the north European plain including south Scandinavia. Schwantes also drew a useful distinction between three ways of treating the brow tine (Fig. 7): one represented by the

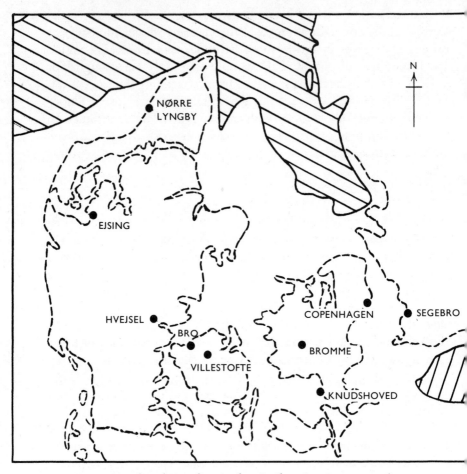

7. Map of south Scandinavia, showing key sites. Present coastline
shown by a broken line.

Nørre Lyngby specimen in which the stump was hollowed to form
a socket; and two others in which the tine was truncated obliquely to
form a working-edge parallel to or at right-angles with the beam. By
analogy with handled wood-working tools he designated these last
respectively as axes and adzes. Having done so, he proceeded to use
them as indicators of adaptation to a forested environment and thus
a convenient dividing line between the Palaeolithic and Mesolithic in
northern Europe. This trail, followed by many, myself included
(Clark 1936, ch. 3; Rust 1937), proved to be a false one. In practical

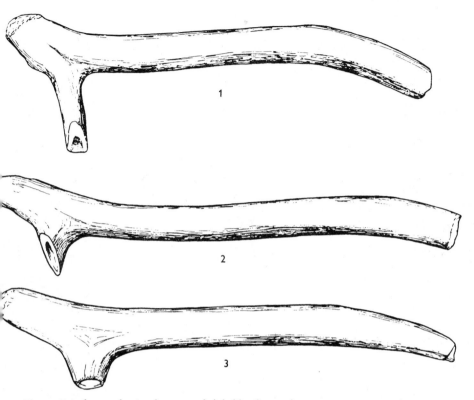

Fig. 7. Reindeer antler implements of club-like form of Younger Dryas Age (Zone III) from north Germany (Langenfelde, (1)), Fünen (Odense, (2)) and Jutland (Nørre Lyngby, (3)). The brow tines have been shaped to form axe-like or adze-like blades (1)–(2) or alternatively to provide a socket (3). (2/7)

terms the objects would have been quite inadequate for felling or shaping forest trees; where dated they belonged to a predominantly Dryas vegetation on the north European plain; and they were later found by Czech archaeologists at Pavlov in a Gravettian context of much greater antiquity.

The Nørre Lyngby cliff again came into the news in 1915 when a heavy tanged flint blade was recovered in position together with remains of a Late-glacial flora, including dwarf birch (*Betula nana*) and arctic willow (*Salix polaris*). Pollen analyses of samples (Iversen 1942) collected at the time of discovery later confirmed that the find dated from the Younger Dryas (Zone III). The flint itself had been accurately struck from a core so effectively prepared that the tip of the flake was

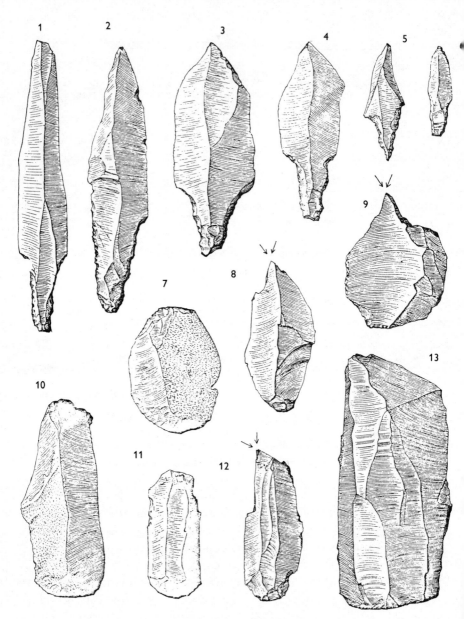

Fig. 8. Flint assemblage of Allerød (Zone II) age from Bromme, Søro, Zealand (1/1). (*After Mathiassen*)

sufficiently symmetrical not to require secondary retouch. The lower end had been reduced in width by steep flakes struck from the under surface on either side of the bulb of percussion of the primary flake, the middle part of the striking platform of which remained intact. This was the first indication of the existence of a distinctive group of Late-glacial flint assemblages corresponding to the northern social territory.

The first site at which tanged points of the type first recognised at Nørre Lyngby came to light as components of an industry was discovered by Erik Westerby in 1944 in the parish of Bromme near Søro on Zealand. Excavation by the National Museum showed that the flints were concentrated in a dark layer sealed under peaty soil and sand and resting in part directly on a moraine and in part on an old surface in the sand overlying this moraine. Although disturbed by glacial action during the Younger Dryas the archaeological layer proved to yield an uncontaminated flint assemblage (Fig. 8). Of the 427 finished artifacts burins represented c. 61%, end of blade scrapers 17%, tanged points 15% and core scrapers or block planes 5%. The high proportion of burins, more than four-fifths of which were of medial type, argues for great industrial activity and makes more regrettable the complete absence of antler or bone artifacts. Of the tanged points approximately half had been struck from cores so carefully prepared that, like the example from Nørre Lyngby itself, the points required no secondary retouch; rather more than another quarter had slight secondary flaking at the tip; and rather less had been retouched obliquely. The function of these points has been much discussed. Rust's (1943, 215) ingenious suggestion, supported by the analogy of the caribou antler clubs inset with bifacially flaked stone points from northern Canada (V. Nordmann 1936, fig. 34a) that the Lyngby point was mounted like a halberd blade in the socket of the antler from the same site is not supported by the practical facts of the case: the socket does not match the tang. The alternative, which finds support in the care taken to make the points symmetrical, is that they were mounted as the heads of projectiles. Comparison with Ahrensburgian or even with Hamburgian points shows that Bromme–Lyngby points were as a group substantially larger. This is no doubt why Mathiassen (1946a, 178) and Becker (1971a, 135) interpret them as spear rather than arrow-heads. Yet Bromme–Lyngby points are no larger than the flake arrows of the middle Neolithic in Scandinavia and, until specimens have been found in their hafts, it is best to leave their function open; conversely the need to find an answer only adds urgency to the quest for sites where the conditions of conservation offer promise of finding these points mounted.

In publishing the Bromme find, Mathiassen was able to map many other finds of Lyngby-type points from different parts of Denmark (Mathiassen 1946a, fig. 20). Stray specimens need to be treated with reserve because typologically they may closely resemble preliminary stages in the manufacture of middle Neolithic flake arrows. More impressive are flaking sites with a range of associated forms. Mathiassen was able to point to one such, Velhøj in Ejsing parish, north-west Jutland, and others have since been added from the Knudshoved peninsula in Southern Zealand (Becker 1971a), from Bro in north-west Fünen (Søren Andersen 1970), from Segebro near Malmö in the south Swedish province of Scania (Salomonsson 1962) and from mixed sites in Schleswig-Holstein (Taute 1968, nos. 65, 72, 77, 89, 119). There seems no reason to doubt that Denmark and Scania formed parts of a single social territory which at times overlapped with Schleswig-Holstein and may have extended up the west coast of Sweden.

Although conditions did not favour the survival of organic components of the artifact assemblage, sufficient organic traces were recovered to indicate that the Bromme site was occupied during the time of the relatively temperate Allerød oscillation; whereas non-tree pollen predominated in the overlying sand, the occupation layer yielded indications of the birch (*Betula alba*) and pine (*Pinus*); the mollusca included such forest species as *Bithynia tentaculata* and *B. leachi*; and the mammalian fauna was marked by beaver and a predominance of elk, as well as by (scarce) reindeer, horse and wolverine. Since the original point from Nørre Lyngby has been securely dated to the Younger Dryas, this gives a longish time span to the Bromme–Lyngby industry. It is unfortunate that the sand deposit containing a similar flint assemblage from Segebro near Malmö in Scania cannot be dated more precisely than to Allerød–Younger Dryas (Salomonsson 1962, 2). On the other hand, preliminary work on the geology of the Bro site suggests a Younger Dryas date (Søren Andersen 1970, 97) and it is significant that Lyngby points occur alongside Ahrensburg (Taute 1968, 80). The evidence suggests that Denmark and south Sweden formed a single social territory during the Allerød and Younger Dryas. In this case Becker (1971a, 137) may be sanguine in expressing the notion that 'it is only a question of time before we find the Ahrensburg culture in Denmark' and some other explanation must be found for the occurrence of stray specimens of points typologically of Ahrensburg type.

SETTLEMENT AND SUBSISTENCE

In discussing the evidence for social territories on the north European Plain during the closing stages of the Late-glacial period it was established that south Scandinavia formed a unitary northern territory, though one in contact with a western territory in Schleswig-Holstein. This is extremely important because it defines our problem. By Allerød times, south Scandinavia was an autonomous self-contained territory.

This only emphasises the need to improve the quality of the local evidence. Extrapolation from the sites in the Ahrensburg tunnel valley is only permissible with major reservations. What is needed above all is the recovery of settlement sites in different parts of Denmark and south Sweden furnished with adequately preserved food-refuse and a tool-kit having components made from organic materials as well as of flint and stone. What we have at the present time are flint assemblages of well-defined Bromme–Segebro character, stray points of Lyngby type and isolated finds of worked reindeer antler. If this material can tell a story this is largely due to the exceptional care taken, especially since the Meiendorf–Stellmoor excavations, to record and where possible to date even stray finds by means of pollen-analysis. In this respect the study of occurrences of reindeer in Denmark, by Degerbøl and Krog (1959), is outstanding.

Since, as Iversen has emphasised (in Mathiassen 1946a, 199), the Late-glacial deposits of Denmark are likely to be buried under thick layers of muds and peats of Post-glacial age, the recovery of traces of occupation from this time in their parent deposits is likely to be a rare occurrence. The same reasoning argues that younger Late-glacial finds are more likely to come to light than those of earlier phases which for this reason are likely to be more thickly covered by overlying deposits (Degerbøl and Krog 1959, 139). This probably explains why, compared with 32 finds from Zone III, Degerbøl and Krog record only 8 from the much longer lived Zone I. The only finds referable to a particular sub-phase of Zone I were the skeleton of a well-built male reindeer from Villestofte (Pl. I, *upper*) and an artifact made from the outer part of a brow tine from the bed of the Sound off Copenhagen,

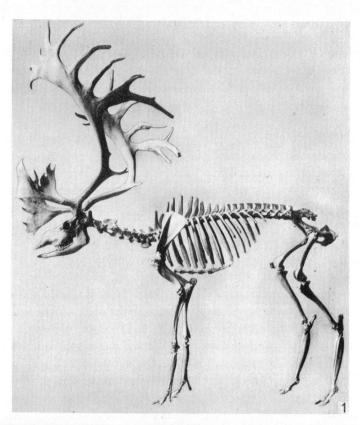

both from Zone Ic. The latter rates at present as the oldest surely dated artifact of Late-glacial age from Denmark, an indication that man was already present during the Older Dryas. A shouldered point of flint from Hvejsel in the county of Vejle, Jutland (Becker 1971a) is typologically even older, relating to the Oldest Dryas, the period of Meiendorf and the basal level at Stellmoor. On the other hand, as Becker (1971a, 133) has pointed out, the Hvejsel projectile head cannot certainly be used to indicate the presence of man in Jutland at this time. It is at least possible that the point was carried north in the body of a wounded reindeer. As many finds from prehistoric Europe, not to mention the evidence from modern primitive societies, have shown, wounded animals often escaped their pursuers, sometimes as in the case of the *Bos primigenius* from Vig for a second time – and the nearest Hamburgian site was only 150 km south.

Schleswig-Holstein. This raises the question what kind of economy was practised by the Hamburgians? For this we have to turn in the first place to the sites of Meiendorf and Stellmoor in the tunnel valley between Hamburg and Ahrensburg. The samples of animal skeletal material recovered from these sites was sufficiently large and well preserved to prove that both Hamburgians and Ahrensburgians depended for animal protein almost exclusively on reindeer at least at the time of the year they represented in their occupation of these sites. As the histograms show (Fig. 9), other animals were represented in such insignificant quantities as to suggest casual hunting rather than systematic exploitation of the kind suggested by the overwhelming predominance of reindeer. There are several reasons why reindeer lend themselves to concentrated exploitation of this kind. The first point to emphasise is that the reindeer is capable of satisfying not merely the subsistence but also the technical needs of peoples living in the same ecosystem. As Burch has recently specified (1972, 362) 'people who consume all of the meat, viscera, stomach contents, and fat of caribou are able to satisfy all of their nutritional requirements'. The importance of stomach contents is that they provided a particularly important means of acquiring the rich supplies of vitamins and iodine from the lichens grazed by reindeer, and fats (Nordenskiöld 1881, 1, 435). Their skins

PLATE I. Reindeer and environment. (*upper*) Skeleton of Late-glacial (Zone I) age from Villestofte, Fünen. (*lower*) Reindeer herd swimming Norwegian river with birch parkland background.

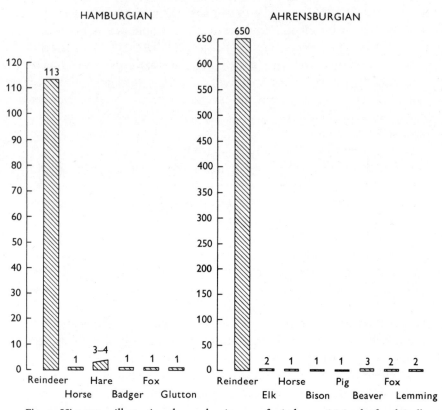

Fig. 9. Histogram illustrating the predominance of reindeer at Meiendorf and Stell-moor. The Hamburg figures combine the samples from both stations. The Ahrensburg ones refer to the upper level at Stellmoor.

could have provided material for tents, skin clothing and possibly for boats. Sinews would have served for sewing these as well as for binding weapons and providing lines for harpoons. Owing to its toughness, antler could provide a raw material of particular value for weapon-heads, though for this purpose the beams had first to be cut into strips; and beams were also capable of being used to make mattocks or clubs after removal of their crowns and surplus tines. In this respect, it was a bonus that in reindeer both sexes bear antlers, whereas in elk and red deer only the males do so. The importance of reindeer for subsistence in Late-glacial times on the north European plain is amply reflected by the wealth of discarded meat bones from sites like Meiendorf and

Stellmoor. On the technical side it is possible to offer a convincing hypothesis for each of the main categories of Hamburgian flint artifact in terms of killing and exploiting reindeer, from the shouldered points embedded in reindeer bones to the scrapers needed for preparing the skins and the burins and *Zinken* designed to cut through the hard outer wall of the antler and detach the splinters used as blanks for making weapon-heads. The survival of antler has even made it possible to study in some detail the groove and splinter process (Clark 1953; Clark and Thompson 1953) as well as end products in the form of harpoon heads.

A second point of importance is the gregarious nature of reindeer which makes them easy to kill when contact is established, an important qualification which needs further discussion. Since they move in bands it is hardly possible to miss even with defective weapons, especially since when moving in large numbers reindeer 'are practically oblivious to all dangers from an inanimate source' (Burch 1972, 361). Individually also reindeer are handicapped by curiosity which offsets their sharpest warning sense, their keen eyesight. Another reason why they are among the easiest game animals to take is that they tend when migrating to move in definite directions. The fact that reindeer commonly occur in such large groups means that they have continually to shift their grazing grounds.

This has obvious implications for their human predators. It does not mean that people could ever have followed herds at all closely. As Burch has shown so vividly, no hunting band including women and children could possibly keep pace with a reindeer herd in course of migration. Even when the animals are walking they can maintain speeds of over 7 km per hour and when trotting, which they can keep up for some time even over rough country, their speed rises to *c.* 40 km p.h. A variety of strategies was possible for men exploiting reindeer or caribou as these are termed in North America. Those practised by Eskimo groups in Alaska and the western Hudson Bay region summarised by Burch (1971, table 1) illustrate some of the main possibilities and offer useful models when considering the vestigial data from the Late-glacial period in northern Europe. Groups like the Asiaquiut of the Kazan river west of Hudson Bay or the 'Mountain People' of the interior of north-west Alaska, who depended primarily on caribou, moved around over extensive annual territories, not in close pursuit of an individual herd, but moving camp as supplies ran out, a routine which involved risks and meant that groups had to be small. Groups who only depended on caribou seasonally had to exploit some alternative source of food: an inland group like the Kuuvakmiut Eskimo of Alaska might exploit fish, often engaging in more than one seasonal fishery and smoking or drying a proportion of the catch; whereas groups whose annual territories extended to the coast, like the Kivalinaquiut of Alaska or the Patliquiut of west Hudson Bay might move to summer camps and engage in sea-mammal hunting.

Examination of the reindeer bones from Meiendorf and in particular analysis of the dimensions of the tibia, femora, metatarsals, vertebrae and sacra convinced Krause (in Rust 1937, 48–9) that the assemblage was not as complete as one might expect if the animals had been killed throughout the year, but was consistent with seasonal slaughter; and Kollau concurred in this view (in Rust 1943, 83–4, fig. 1) in respect of the larger assemblage from the Ahrensburgian level at Stellmoor. Since reindeer accounted for more than 99% of the mammals represented in both assemblages, this can only mean that the sites were occupied seasonally. The further assumption made with special emphasis by Rust himself (1937, 115–16; 1943, 135 and fig. 35) that the sites were occupied during the summer, is much more questionable. Indeed there are powerful reasons for accepting that on the contrary they represent the residues of winter occupation. Rust made great play with the idea that the Hamburgians were camping at Meiendorf close to the ice-margin and that they can only have done so in the winter, yet (*pace* Schwabedissen 1944, Taf. 125) the indications are that the ice-margin was in fact far away at this time. Owing to difficulties in effecting precise correlations between Danish and south Swedish moraines (Zeuner 1950, 31) dogmatism is out of place, but it is more likely that during the Oldest Dryas the ice-margin coincided with Munthe's E 1 which traversed the east and south coast of Zealand, passed west of Langeland, east of Fehmarn and joined the north German coast near Rostock (cf. Brøndsted 1, 1957, map 33). We are on much firmer ground in respect of the position of the ice at the time of the Ahrensburgian occupation during the Younger Dryas: by common consent this was marked by the Fennoscandian moraine which at its nearest point was some 570 km distant from the Ahrensburg tunnel valley. Since the Hamburgian and Ahrensburgian reindeer assemblages were so closely similar, what goes for one may be presumed to go for the other. The argument about proximity of the ice must therefore be discarded. The decisive factor governing the whereabouts of reindeer during the winter is the depth of snow, a factor of special importance in view of the fact that this animal is exceptionally choosy in respect of grazing. This is particularly relevant in relation to our problem because there are good reasons for thinking that in general the snow did not lie thickly on the northern lowlands. Thus, Iversen was able to demonstrate (1954, 103–4) in the Late-glacial flora of Denmark 'a number of plants...which do not tolerate more than a thin and transient snow cover ('chianophobous' species), e.g. *Arcostaphylos uva-ursi, A. alpina* and *Dryas octopetala'*. And strong confirmation that conditions were favourable to reindeer during the winter was provided by Degerbøl and Krog's survey (1959) of reindeer remains recovered from Late-glacial deposits in Denmark. The fact that, as shown in our Map 8, over four-fifths of the antlers from Denmark were shed is particularly significant since stags, to which most of the finds belong, shed their antlers during November–December; moreover, as Degerbøl points out (1959, 98) some of these finds that retain them, notably the complete skeleton of Older Dryas age from Villestofte, must have succumbed about the month of October to judge from the degree of polish on the antlers. In other words, so far from the reindeer herds that fed the Hamburgians and Ahrensburgians in their tunnel valley wintering in the south and only coming north during the summer, it was already evident that the real situation was the precise opposite. The case has since been clinched by Sturdy's application of hardness tests to the total assemblage of antlers from the Ahrensburgian level at Stellmoor. This has shown (1972, ch. 6, 22; ch. 8, 26) that the vast majority of the reindeer had been killed in the autumn on the way north to their wintering grounds with a smaller number in the spring on their move south. This makes extremely good sense. The strategy of intercepting reindeer on their seasonal migrations tallies admirably with the circumstance that the animals are most easily taken while on the move in herds (Pl. I, lower, p. 87). And it is particularly significant that far more were taken on the northward than the southward trek. By making the main kill in the late autumn enough meat could be stored frozen for use during the winter, whereas camp was presumably broken soon after the spring movement south. Another point worth making is that at this time of the year the reindeer were carrying their antlers, something that agrees not only with the well-known rarity of shed antlers from this tunnel-valley site (Rust 1937, 62; 1943, 106–7) but also with

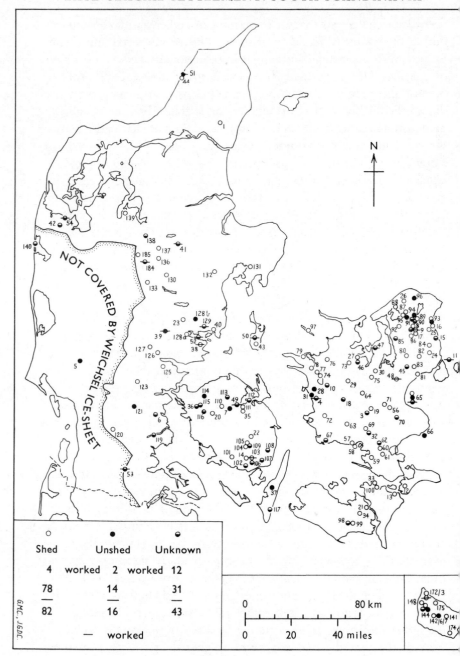

8. Map showing distribution of Late-glacial reindeer antlers from Denmark.
(*Based on Degerbøl and Krog*)

evidence that antlers were worked on a massive scale. The one drawback might have been that skins were rather past their prime though presumably still useful for purposes like tent-making, an extremely necessary task before settling in for the winter and one for which there is plenty of evidence in the area (Rust 1958*b*).

If, like the Asiaquiut, the Hamburgian and Ahrensburgian bands depended primarily on reindeer the year round, they no doubt moved their camps south. This does not mean that they followed closely on the heels of the reindeer herds but rather that they set up bases along their lines of movement, possibly even as far as the highlands of central and southern Germany as suggested by Sturdy (1972, map 7–18). Whichever hypothesis is followed it is common ground that the Ahrensburg tunnel valley was situated near the northern frontier of the Hamburgian and Ahrensburgian distributions or, as I would prefer to say, social territories. All this is consistent with and indeed supports Becker's explanation for the presence of the stray Hamburgian flint point at Hvejsel. The territory of Denmark and south Sweden lay outside the range of the Hamburgians and for that matter of the Ahrensburgians.

Denmark/Scania. What kind of strategy was adopted in this northern province, the social territory of the Lyngby–Bromme–Segebro group? Very little can be said except in general terms until several accurately dated sites are available in different locations with an adequate complement of organic materials and in particular of animal skeletal material. The antler implement dredged from the Sound off Copenhagen dating from Zone Ic and the crown artificially detached from its beam found at Copenhagen and dating from the very beginning of Zone II (Degerbøl and Krog 1959, nos. 11 and 15) merely indicate that reindeer were being hunted in this area before the more temperate conditions associated with the Allerød oscillation were fully established. Although very few animal materials are available from the Bromme settlement dating from the full Allerød they are sufficient to indicate at least that at the time of the year represented elk were being hunted as well as and in greater quantity than reindeer. Other finds from Fünen as well as Zealand indicate that reindeer were still available during the full Allerød and the fact that these finds included shed antlers (Degerbøl and Krog 1959, nos. 17, 20) argues that the reindeer were certainly present during the winter. While it is likely that the inhabitants of the northern province hunted reindeer during the Allerød they can hardly have depended primarily on this animal.

With the return of arctic conditions during the Younger Dryas the situation was quite different. From this period there is an impressive number of finds of reindeer antlers scattered widely from north and south Jutland to Scania and Bornholm, including several mattocks and clubs, a harpoon head and what may be a knife handle, as well as discarded antlers from which individual tines have been removed (Degerbøl and Krog 1959, nos. 38, 39, 41, 45, 47–55). The inference is that at this time reindeer was the only land mammal of much importance. It was one on which one might therefore expect to find some primary dependence. A hint of this is given by the number of antler fragments and bones recovered from the bed of a small lake as this has been eroded on the Nørre Lyngby cliff, among them the original Lyngby club and the artificially shaped beam now in Hjørring Museum (14382). Of the various alternatives outlined for Alaska and Canada (pp. 89 f.) it seems unlikely that the Kuuvakmiut system was followed. The low-lying territories of Denmark and Scania have no substantial rivers. In his study of the sub-fossil fish remains of Denmark, Degerbøl noted only one find of salmon, namely two vertebrae from Meilgaard (Degerbøl 1945, 126) on the coast of east Jutland facing on the Kattegat, at a time when these fish were entering the Baltic to run up the great rivers of Norrland. The only fish known to have been present in Late-glacial Denmark were pike (*Esox lucius*), *Coregonus lavaretus* and perch (*Perca fluviatilis*). It is of interest to note that the first two occur, though in different species, on the Barren Grounds of Canada west of Hudson Bay.

The possibility exists that the alternative followed by the Kivalina-quiut and the Patliquiut was adopted, that of alternating reindeer-hunting with the capture of sea-mammals during the summer. The fact that the Younger Dryas coastline of our region is now under the sea makes it difficult to check this directly. On the other hand something can be learned from an objective analysis of Late-glacial animal materials dating from a period of relative land depression in north Jutland (Møhl 1907). Two points emerge, neither of them very suggestive of intensive summer hunting. The eight whale finds comprise six baleen (four Greenland; one Blue; and one Finwhale) and two toothed whales (one white, one killer). The complete absence of common porpoise and the comparative scarcity of other toothed whales, the only kinds hunted in south Scandinavia during the Stone Age, shows that these particular finds at any rate, can hardly reflect intensive summer hunting of marine mammals. On the other hand the relative abundance of baleen whales of a kind that could hardly have been hunted in the Stone Age argues that these large animals were being stranded at this time. In the case of seals the most noteworthy fact is that all eight finds were of ringed seal (*Phoca hispida*), a species commonly hunted through holes in the ice (*maupoq* method) and whose young are born on the ice during the period February/April. There seems no reason to doubt the possibility that ringed seals could have been taken in this way during the Younger Dryas – the stout single-barbed harpoon head from Stellmoor (Fig. 3, 1) would have been admirably adapted for this purpose, as a comparison with those associated with seal bones from much later sites reminds us (cf. Clark 1946, fig. 10) – and in this connection one may recall the seals engraved on objects from Upper Palaeolithic deposits in the Dordogne (cf. op. cit. fig. 2). The point to note is that this was a winter, and not a summer activity. The stranding of large baleen whales on the other hand, while it must have provided an occasional bonus that could hardly have been overlooked, would have been too unpredictable to have occasioned seasonal movements. Either way the hypothesis that the Late-glacial reindeer hunters in our region practised sea-mammal hunting in the summer finds scant encouragement from the existing evidence. On the other hand the hunting of ringed seal and the scavenging of baleen whales may well have been fitted into their cycle of movement.

The remaining possibility is that they followed the practice of the Asiaquiut of the west Hudson Bay area or the 'Mountain People' of north-west Alaska and moved camp from time to time to obtain reindeer, while supplementing their intake by fishing, shore-scavenging and perhaps fowling. As we have already noted in the case of the inhabitants of the Ahrensburg tunnel valley, it was quite possible, when the reindeer were in the habit of making long treks, to make a big killing in the late autumn as the herds moved north, live through the winter on frozen meat, and make a second though smaller killing in the spring before breaking camp and following the herds further south. In the northern area on the other hand there is no reason for thinking that such conditions prevailed. It may be that the reindeer shifted to-wards the coast during summer, but there is no evident geographical reason for distant treks. On the other hand, for reasons already discussed, it would not have been practicable to follow the reindeer closely or continuously. Again, it is not very realistic to imagine that hunting was carried on as a rule by single adults. The most likely hypothesis is that people normally lived in micro-bands of three to four primary families and that camp was moved from time to time in order to take reindeer under the most favourable circumstances. Under these conditions one might expect to find a number of sites reflecting a relatively short stay, which as Becker (1971a, 135) has remarked, is precisely what does occur.

The reindeer hunters seem to have lived in skin tents supported on light poles and secured by stone weights and guy-ropes, comparable with those in use among Eskimo groups. Structures of this kind could easily be dismantled and rolled up for transport to the next camping place. No investigation of settlement plans seems to have been made at Meiendorf or Stellmoor, attention being concentrated on recovering the rich waste discarded in the adjacent lakes or ponds. The site chosen by Rust to investigate living structures at Borneck near Ahrensburg was defined in the first instance by flint assemblages. Plans were recovered by stripping areas down to undisturbed subsoil taking care to define fire places and to isolate glacial stones. Rust interpreted concentric settings with outliers as evidence for double tents held up by weighted guy-ropes. Since the inner area was normally only about two paces in diameter such structures must have been designed to house single family units. There are two reasons why there is no firm evidence how many tents went with each settlement. Excavation has never been extensive enough to be sure that the whole plan had been recovered. And when traces of several structures occurred on the same site it was difficult to be sure which, if any, were occupied simul-taneously. Thus at Borneck the plans of four structures were recovered, one with Hamburgian, one with 'Magdalenian' and two with Ahrens-burgian flint industries. Clearly structures were erected on the site at three periods. What one would like to be sure of is whether the two Ahrensburgian ones were in fact inhabited at the same time and how many others would have been found if a larger area had been stripped. At other sites the areas stripped have been even more tantalisingly small – 187 sq. m at Deimern 45, an Ahrensburgian site in N. Soltau on the Lüneburg heath, and c. 266 sq. m at Segebro near Malmö, Scania, the only Late-glacial settlement site in south Scandinavia of which a plan is available. In each case the scatter of flint artifacts has

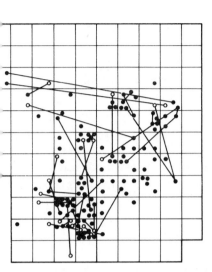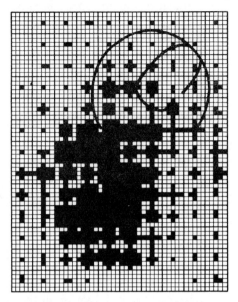

Fig. 10. Diagrams illustrating scatters of Late-glacial flints, (*left*) at Deimern 45 and (*right*) at Borneck-Mitte, Schleswig-Holstein. In the latter the outline of the tent structure waso bserved. In the former fitting flakes are joined by lines. Overall grid scale in metres. (*After Taute and Rust respectively*)

been carefully recorded and concentrations cover areas of *c.* 7 × 7 m and *c.* 7 × 8 m respectively. Do these imply single units or clusters of units? If the site of Borneck is any guide the answer must be that flint concentrations at Segebro and Deimern represent working areas relating to single dwellings (Fig. 10). The plan (Rust 1958*b*, Abb. 37) of Borneck-Mitte in particular shows a concentration, contiguous to a tent plan, of approximately the same size as that of Deimern 45. By linking joins between burins and spalls (Taute 1968, Abb. 16) one finds two discrete areas of activity in the Deimern plan, but these could well have arisen from a change of position by the same worker. On purely archaeological grounds there is insufficient evidence to determine the size of the average social unit. On *a priori* grounds already discussed (p. 96) one could on the other hand expect that the hunting micro-band would be likely to comprise three or four family units with the probability that these might under certain conditions split into its components or alternatively amalgamate into bands for short periods.

It may in conclusion be worth speculating on the likely size of the population of our social territory during the Younger Dryas period when reindeer may be assumed to have been the prime source of food. While no exact comparisons can be made because the environmental conditions of the Younger Dryas were to some extent unique, some idea can be obtained by considering the position in territories of which the carrying capacity is known. If, for instance, we apply the figures quoted by Helle (1966) for the reindeer territories of Finland, where *c.* 32,000 sq. km carried *c.* 150,000 reindeer in 1959–64, to the approximately 70,000 sq. km of the Lyngby–Bromme–Segebro territory, we arrive at a total reindeer population of *c.* 330,000. Accepting for working purposes Sturdy's estimate (Sturdy 1972, 8.3), of 500 reindeer as an annual requirement to maintain an average family unit, this would allow a human population of *c.* 660 units or 3,300 individuals. If these units were normally aggregated in groups of three or four this would mean that the social territory defined by lithic assemblages of Lyngby–Bromme–Segebro type would have been shared by anything from 165 to 220 micro-bands. To the extent that coastal or inland water resources were drawn upon this estimate would need to be enlarged, to a certain, but probably not very substantial extent.

4

Early Post-glacial settlement in south Scandinavia

The prospects for human life and settlement in northern Europe underwent far reaching changes as the environment responded to the onset of Post-glacial conditions. The effect of the rather steep rise of temperature signalised by the rapid retreat of the ice-sheet from the Fennoscandian moraines was the more dramatic that the Late-glacial inhabitants of south Scandinavia had relied so closely on reindeer, an animal adjusted to a rather narrow range of vegetation and capable of rapid movement. The very closeness of the symbiosis between predators and prey meant that the response to ecological change was correspondingly marked. The rapid replacement of the Dryas flora by forests, in which at first birch and later pine predominated, meant that for reindeer herds migration was the only alternative to extinction. When this happened their human predators had the choice of adapting to the new environment created by the immigration of new animals and vegetation or of following the reindeer herds northward. That some at least adopted the second alternative is suggested by the northward spread of a lithic technology closely associated with reindeer hunters in south Scandinavia during the Late-glacial, a theme discussed more fully in chapter 6. Another indication is that of cultural discontinuity at this time in south Scandinavia itself. The absence of tanged flint points or of antler barbed points of Late-glacial type, on the other hand, is not in itself conclusive one way or the other since cultural change can often be explained as well in terms of adaptation to altered circumstances as in those of population movement. Paradoxically the survival of the biserially barbed point with spade-shaped base on Bornholm, where it occurred in the bog of Vallensgaard (*DOI*, no. 160), is as suggestive as its otherwise complete absence from Post-glacial deposits in Denmark, since the island was in Pre-boreal times the tip of a marked promontory, a natural cul-de-sac: reindeer herds trapped there might have died out or been exterminated, whereas their predators could have survived by adaptation through the medium of their culture.

What is certain is that the rise of temperature was marked in south Scandinavia by the intrusion of plants and animals from the south and it is a reasonable hypothesis that the northward expansion of biological zones was accompanied by a comparable movement of ideas and even of people. The problem of deciding how far the inhabitants of this region stayed there and survived by adaptation and to what extent the area was resettled by newcomers at the time of the Late-glacial/Post-glacial transition is a difficult one. It is complicated by the fact that any newcomers would necessarily have stemmed from the same kind of background as that from which the Late-glacial inhabitants of south Scandinavia themselves derived. In certain instances potential sources of traits which appeared in this region at the beginning of Post-glacial times can plausibly be traced to proximate regions. The obliquely blunted microlith, the commonest component of this class in such assemblages as those from Klosterlund, Duvensee, Henninge Boställe and for that matter Star Carr in England is one example, since it had already appeared in north-west Germany during the Younger Dryas period at Hohle Stein, Callenhardt (Taute 1968, 300), a site with a transitional fauna with not only reindeer but also such forest and forest-margin species as red deer, roe deer and wild pig. The source of others is more difficult to define since they were common to a vast area of Europe during the late Pleistocene. A notable instance of this is the technique of obtaining blanks for antler and bone artifacts by removing splinters defined by cutting deep, more or less parallel, grooves through the thickness of the material. This technique well known in south Scandinavia during early Post-glacial times may well have been practised there already during Late-glacial times. Equally on the other hand it was practised during the late Pleistocene over a territory extending from Iberia to Siberia.

A promising field for tracing affinities is that provided by the symbolic art applied to artifacts of antler and bone during Boreal times in south Scandinavia and the south Baltic area. Since detailed attention is given to this later in this book (pp. 147 ff.), it will be sufficient to state there that the main elements of the repertoire were employed during the late Pleistocene not only in western but also in eastern Europe. As fuller information becomes available from the U.S.S.R. it is becoming ever more apparent that this territory was a main source from which the early Post-glacial inhabitants of south Scandinavia drew their inspiration. This is particularly plain in another sphere. The slotted bone equipment, both knives and projectile points, which first appeared in the north during Boreal times, finds no parallel in the late Pleistocene assemblages from the French caves, but occurred in contexts of similar age over a wide zone of Russia (see pp. 171–5). The fact that the inhabitants of northern Europe derived elements of their culture from this extensive area makes it easier to understand the features common to the widely separated Maglemose and Kunda assemblages, including for example slotted equipment and pit ornament.

CHRONOLOGICAL FRAMEWORK

Although the discovery at Nørre Lyngby had already suggested as early as 1889 that Denmark had probably been occupied as early as the Late-glacial period, it was not until 1900 when excavations were undertaken in the great bog (*Maglemose*) at Mullerup in Zealand that settlement during the period between the reindeer age and the kitchen middens began to be documented on a solid basis. Progress has since taken two main forms. Many more settlements have been excavated in Denmark and in adjacent parts of Germany and Sweden (Map 9). At the same time the various techniques of Quaternary research have been deployed in order to establish a secure framework into which settlement finds and stray discoveries alike may be fitted. The simplest way of summarising the most important sources now available is to set them out in tabular form (Table 5). The main finds have been grouped in each of three main phases in the climatic and biological history of each of five areas. The references quoted at the foot of the table should allow the reader to pursue more detailed information in the museums and in the literature.

SETTLEMENTS

None of the sites yet investigated from the Pre-boreal period, notably Klosterlund and Stallerup in Jutland and Henninge Boställe in Scania, have yielded information about the actual dwellings or about either the character of the technology other than its lithic component or the animals and plants taken for food. The water-logged deposit at Star Carr in north-east England gives some measure of what may yet be found when suitable sites are located in south Scandinavia.

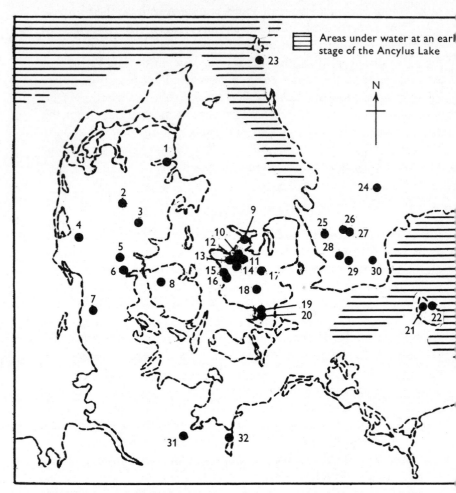

9. Map showing key sites dating from the Pre-boreal and Boreal settlement of south Scandinavia and proximate zone of north Germany.

1, Sønder Hadsund; 2, Klosterlund; 3, Vissinggaard; 4, Bøllund; 5, Springbjerg-lund; 6, Stallerupholm; 7, Kongens mose, Draved; 8, Koelbjerg; 9, Vig; 10, Ulkestrup; 11, Øgaarde, 12, Skellingsted; 13, Hesselbjerggaard; 14, Verup; 15, Vinde-Helsinge; 16, Mullerup; 17, Ryemarksgaard; 18, Holmegaard; 19, Lundby; 20, Sværdborg; 21, Vallensgaards mose; 22, Melsted; 23, Sandarna; 24, Loshult; 25, Baremose; 26, Agerød; 27, Henninge Boställe; 28, Linnebjär; 29, Harlösa; 30, Äsperöds mosse; 31, Duvensee; 32, Hohen Viecheln.

Table 5. *Some key sites of south Scandinavia and north Germany, grouped under main phases of early Post-glacial climatic history*

utland	Zealand	Bornholm	Scania	North Germany
		LATE BOREAL (B.C. 5600–)		
	Holmegaard[7]			
	Hesselbjerggaard[8]			
	Ryemarksgaard[9]			
	Skellingsted[10]			
pringbjerglund[1]	Sværdborg[11]		Agerød I: HC[23]	Hohen Viecheln
	Ulkestrup[12]			(upper)[29]
	Verup[13]			
	Øgaarde[14]			
		Melsted[20]		
		EARLY BOREAL (B.C. 6300–)		
ollund[2]	Koelbjerg[15]		Baremose IV[24]	Hohen Viecheln
tallerupholm[3]	Lundby[16]		Henninge Boställe[25]	(lower)
issinggaard[4]	Mullerup[17]		Loshult[26]	Duvensee[30]
	Vinde-Helsinge II[18]		Äsperöds mosse[27]	
ongens mose,			Harlösa[28]	
Draved[5]				
		PRE-BOREAL (B.C. 7000–)		
losterlund[6]	Vig[19]	Torupgaard mose[21]		
		Vallensgaards mose[22]		

1	Berthelsen 1944, 42–54, 75–8.	16	Brøndsted 1957, 73–5.
2	Vebæk 1940; Petersen 1966.	17	Sarauw 1903.
3	Blankholm and Andersen 1967.	18	Mathiassen 1943, 17–21.
4	Mathiassen 1937; Iversen, ibid, fig. 31.	19	Hartz and Winge 1906.
5	Kapel 1963; Blankholm and Andersen 1967.	20	Becker 1951, 97–102; 115–32.
		21	Ibid. 168–70.
6	Mathiassen 1937, 132–51.	22	Ibid. 167–9.
7	Broholm 1931, 1–73; Becker 1945.	23	Althin 1954, 74–5, pl. 10–19; Nilsson, T. 1967 b, 17–20.
8	Mathiassen 1943, 22–6.		
9	Mathiassen 1941 b; Troels-Smith 1941.	24	Welinder 1971, 71–8, fig. 20.
0	Mathiassen 1943, 107–11.	25	Althin 1954, 86–8, 157; Welinder 1971, 48–9; Nilsson, T. 1967 b, 55–61.
1	Friis Johansen 1919; Broholm 1931, 73–117.	26	Petersson 1951; Nilsson, T. 1968.
2	Andersen, K. 1951.	27	Ymer 1907, 453; Welinder 1971, 36–7.
3	Andersen, K. 1960; Jørgensen 1954, 160–72.	28	Salomonsson 1961, 12–14; Tilander 1961.
4	Mathiassen 1943, 148–53.	29	Schuldt 1961.
5	Troels-Smith 1943.	30	Schwantes 1939, 87–104.

If the situation is much better for the early and later Boreal phases this is due to the choice of lake or bog margins for settlement at certain times of the year. The investigation of such sites, frequently brought to light by peat-diggers, has provided us with a certain amount of information about dwelling structures as well as rather more complete evidence for the utilisation of such substances as wood, bark, antler and bone, and in addition food refuse of great value for reconstructing the basis of subsistence. Yet it is important to note that such information is not evenly spread geographically and relates only to the seasons during which the particular sites were occupied. Although many sites are located in present-day bogs, it can nevertheless be recognised that the driest places in these, low islands or peninsulas, were chosen for occupation. Even so excavators of sites like Sværdborg and Holmegaard were in no doubt that to judge from winter flooding at the present day they could only have been occupied during the summer (Friis Johansen 1919, 355). The first site where actual hut emplacements were observed was in fact outside our immediate territory at Duvensee near Lübeck. The debris of occupation were seen to overlie mat-like settings of birch and pine bark, appearing in one instance to form a 5 m square with rounded corners, the main function of which was to prevent rising damp. Fires were evidently set on spreads of sand, which appear in at least one instance to have been renewed on some five occasions, suggesting repeated seasonal occupations (Schwantes 1928, 201–11; 1939, 87–99). Similar bark flooring and sand fire emplacements have since been observed at sites on Zealand, notably at Holmegaard IV (Becker 1945) where a hut c. 6½ by 3 metres was uncovered and at Ulkestrup also in Aamosen (Andersen, K. 1951, 70), where traces of two were found. The better preserved of these had a floor formed of sheets of pine bark up to 2 m long and ½ m broad laid down to form a rectangular area c. 6·7 m by 4·5 m in extent, the interior of which was paved with smaller pieces of elm, birch and pine bark. Huts of this kind were probably walled and roofed by birch branches rammed in round the floors and pulled together at the top to make a roof. The fact that they were only provided with single fire-places argues that each sheltered a single family. How many such families lived together in the same settlements can hardly be determined. The extent of a site like Sværdborg I is large enough to have held a settlement of up to ten huts of the kind which occurred apparently singly at Sværdborg II and IV on the same peninsula jutting out into the marsh. On the other hand the total archaeological debris at Sværdborg could represent a number – at least twelve, but probably much more – of summer encampments of a single family unit. The same applies to the interpretation of a site like Nørre Strandegaard on Bornholm (Becker 1951a, fig. 4) with a number of discrete spreads of flint-work, each apparently indicating settlement. On balance it looks as though at the time of the year when the marsh sites of Zealand were occupied, the people were living in dispersed family groups and returning year after year to the same dry spot. It needs to be emphasised that as yet we know nothing of the winter settlements of the Zealand population and that we lack information from any season from other parts of Denmark or for that matter from south Sweden.

TECHNOLOGY

Since under primitive conditions the artifacts on which societies depended for manipulating natural resources were themselves abstracted almost entirely from their more or less immediate environments, it is consistent with an ecological approach to consider them under the heads of the main materials from which they were manufactured. Like other communities living at a comparatively elementary level of technology, those which inhabited north temperate Europe during the early Post-glacial period depended very largely on organic materials for their daily equipment. Yet it is precisely these which are most imperfectly represented in the archaeological inventory from which we seek to reconstruct their way of life. In south Scandinavia they are only likely to survive, and then incompletely, on sites in or immediately adjacent to waterlogged deposits, sites which occur in some localities more than in others and which in Denmark seem only to have been occupied during the summer months. Failure to appreciate the implications of this helped to support the old dichotomy of a Zealand 'Mere Culture' and a Jutland 'Gudenaa Culture' (see pp. 166 ff.). The technology represented on such classic sites as Mullerup, Holmegaard and Sværdborg owes its special character not to having been adapted to the exploitation of meres and adjacent territories so much as to having been found under circumstances which permit the survival of a much broader range of equipment, or at any rate the equipment used during the summer months. The technology of the same people found on sites relating to other seasons would often be represented almost if not completely by its lithic component. This apparently applied to winter sites on Zealand and to those from any time of the year in Jutland, where artifacts of organic materials normally occur in isolation from the lithic component in locations where conditions happen to have been favourable to their survival. The only components that can be relied upon to survive are those made from flint and stone.

Flint. The flint-work from this phase of settlement is important not merely because of its high capacity for survival and its consequent ubiquity. As the hardest and sharpest material available it controlled the way in which the inhabitants of South Scandinavia were able to exploit their environment, including the manner in which they were able to shape and process a wide variety of animal and plant substances. The composition of lithic assemblages from the early Post-glacial period is also important for another reason. It reflects on the one hand continuity with earlier traditions as these prevailed in contiguous regions to the south, and on the other innovation stemming from adaptation to a forest environment.

Ever since the paper by Gustav Schwantes (1923) the diagnostic value of the flint axe or adze has been recognised as an explicit index of adaptation to the new forested environment. The blades were shaped from nodules or thick flakes by bifacial flaking and sharpened by striking off single flakes transversely or obliquely to the main axis of the tool, a process that could be repeated when resharpening was required. Their more or less pronounced asymmetry in section (Fig. 48, 2) suggests that in most cases they served as the blades of adzes, a hypothesis that is fully confirmed by the evidence of specimens recovered still set in their mounts (Fig. 16, 1–2). That such adzes were in fact used for felling trees is supported by evidence from Star Carr, where the stumps of felled birch trees (Pl. II, *left*) are pointed like sharpened pencils suggesting downward strokes at an oblique angle. In the case of blades pointed at the working end (Fig. 48, 1) these are commonly described as 'picks'. The bifacially flaked axe having its edge more or less parallel with the handle did not become common until Atlantic times. A word needs to be said about the objects described in the litera-ture as 'flake axes', a form which appeared already during the Pre-boreal, continued through the Boreal and became extremely abundant during the later phases of Atlantic time (Fig. 48, 4–5). These objects were struck by a single blow from the sides of carefully prepared cores. No examples have been found certainly in their hafts and no systematic

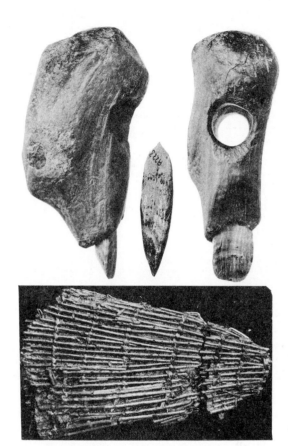

PLATE II. Early Post-glacial technology in northern Europe. (*left*) Felled birch trees of late Pre-boreal (Zone IV) age at Star Carr, England. (*right, upper*) Stag antler haft set with boar's tusk blade from Skellingsted Bro, Skamstrup par., Holbæk, Zealand. (*right, lower*) Part of plaited fish-trap of early Atlantic (Zone VII) age from Nidløse, Zealand.

work seems to have been done on micro-wear on their edges. Their use is still unknown. The description 'side-blow flake axe' is to be understood in purely conventional terms. By far the larger proportion of flint artifacts used at this time in south Scandinavia were made from flakes and for certain purposes from narrow and more or less regular micro-bladelets. Block cores from which blades had been struck were conspicuously absent. On the other hand the requirement for bladelets led to the production of more or less pyramidal cores. In later Boreal

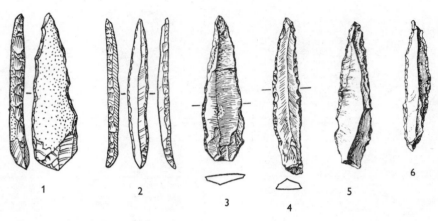

Fig. 11. Flint drills (*mèches de forêt*) from late Pre-boreal/early Boreal contexts in northern Europe. (1), (2) Star Carr, Yorkshire; (3), (4) Henninge Boställe, Scania; (5), (6) Klosterlund, Jutland. (2/3)

and early Atlantic times, exceptionally fine and regular bladelets were needed for insetting into slotted equipment; elongated handle cores shaped for gripping (Fig. 44) in the human hand were made so that bladelets could be removed from one end under strong control. Among the tool forms made from the larger flakes were ones with oblique or transverse retouch, end scrapers and burins. Narrow drills (*mèches de forêt*), formed by steeply retouching flakes or bladelets on either edge (Fig. 11), were a feature of Pre-boreal/early Boreal assemblages in Denmark, as well as in eastern England, but were no longer present as a leading form during later Boreal times. This suggests among other things that Althin (1954, 157) was correct in assigning Henninge Boställe, Munkarp, Scania, in which the type is well represented, to the same period as the Klosterlund industry, Welinder's recent opinion notwithstanding (1971, 49). Why it was that the narrow drill should have been prevalent from Yorkshire to Scania early in the Post-glacial and then have passed out of general use is one of those changes which requires an explanation. Useful indicators of continuity and change are provided by persistent traits. Flint microliths are a case in point (Fig. 12). As arrow armatures they played a vital role in economic life (Pl. III) and owing to their range of possible form they were especially sensitive to changes in fashion.

Examination of samples from successive phases of the early Post-glacial

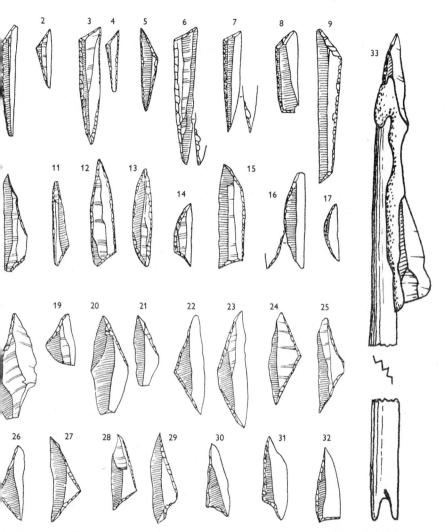

Fig. 12. Microlithic arrow armatures. (*lower rows*) Duvensee, Schleswig-Holstein (early Boreal). (*upper rows*) Sværdborg, Zealand (late Boreal). (*right*) Forepart with microliths inset in resin and nock end of pine wood arrow from Loshult, Scania (early Boreal). (1/1)

Table 6. *Changes in the proportions of the main classes of microlith* repre-sented in assemblages of Pre-boreal/early Boreal and late Boreal Age respectively from successive phases of human occupation in Jutland between c. 8000 and 5600* B.C.

			Classes of microlith (Fig. 13) (%)				
Period	Sites	Samples	A	B	C	D	Misc.
BO 2	Springbjerglund (mid.)	354	15·9	8·0	4·8	65·0	6·2
	Bøllund	280	28·9	26·1	19·3	19·7	6·1
BO 1	Stallerupland	80	35·0	32·5	6·25	15·0	11·25
	Sønder Hadsund	207	43·4	21·7	2·4	28·5	3·9
PB	Klosterlund	109	55·3	28·2	—	4·3	12·2

NOTE. The data have been taken from the following sources (reclassified): Kloster-lund (Mathiassen 1937, 144–6), Sønder Hadsund (E. B. Petersen 1966, 182), Stalle-rupland (Blankholm and S. Andersen 1967, 91), Bøllund (E. B. Petersen 1966, 183), and Springbjerglund (mid.) (Berthelsen 1944, 48).

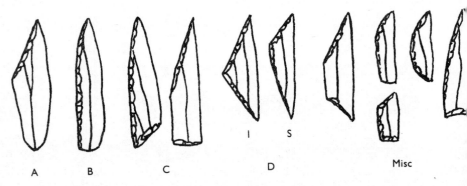

Fig. 13. The main classes of microlith used during Pre-boreal and Boreal times in south Scandinavia.

* Assemblages originally classified according to the systems of Mathiassen (1937, 94–5) and Becker (1951a, 118–21) have been reclassified for the present book in accordance with my own prior scheme (Clark 1934).

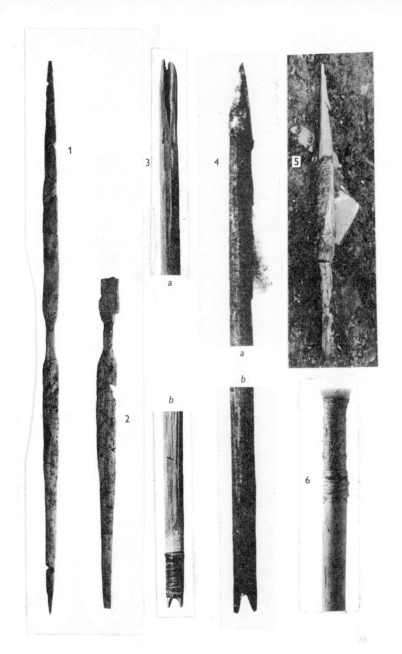

PLATE III. Weapons of Boreal and Atlantic age from south Scandinavia. (1), (2) Self-bows with constricted grip, from Holmegaard, Zealand. (3) Forepart (a) and nock end (b) of arrowshaft with groove for flint inset, from Vinkelmose (Zone V). The binding for securing the fletching is visible above the nock. (4) Forepart (a) and nock end (b) of arrow, from Loshult, Scania, dating from the early Boreal, with flint microliths inset in resin. (5) Barbed bone point mounted on part of original shaft from Ulkestrup, Denmark. (6) Forepart of arrowshaft mounted with transverse flint head from Tværmose, Ejsing, Jutland.

(see Table 6) reveals a number of changes. A noticeable feature is the sharply progressive decline of obliquely blunted points (category A) and in this respect it is interesting that the percentage for Star Carr is identical and that for Duvensee comparable, to that for Klosterlund. Both Star Carr and Duvensee diverge from Klosterlund in lacking categories B and C and including elongated trapeze forms in the miscellaneous category.

The Boreal sites in Jutland are marked by the presence, sometimes in quite high values, of points retouched at the base (category C), and by the relatively high values for triangles, which in the late Boreal form close on two-thirds of the Mesolithic assemblage. Again, among the triangles there is very pronounced change as between early and late Boreal in the relative proportions if isosceles and scalene forms.

Stone. Stone artifacts (Fig. 14) played only a very restricted role in the flint-rich territories of the north European plain. Hammerstones or unfinished spearheads with opposed hollows appeared first at Mullerup (Sarauw 1903, fig. 15) and later at Sværdborg (Broholm 1931, fig. 38). Maceheads perforated by hour-glass holes pecked from both faces occurred in two main forms during the late Boreal. Round to oval forms are known from Hesselbjerggaard, Aamosen, Zealand (Mathiassen 1943, fig. 6), from Agerød I, Scania (Althin 1954, p. 12 no. 2, 3) and from the upper level at Hohen Viecheln, Schwerin (Schuldt 1961, pl. 99d). Hohen Viecheln also yielded an elongated pick-like form (ibid. pl. 39) and Kungsladugard near Göteborg yielded a specimen with long tapered projections. There is also some slight evidence for directly perforated stone artifacts. The adze-blade of fine-grained gneiss with working edge bevelled by grinding from Holmegaard (Broholm 1931, 41–2) was admittedly recovered during preliminaries to the main excavation, but since the site was apparently uncontaminated by younger material there seems no sound reason for doubting this association. Of more dubious status is the star-shaped object from Orust Island, Bohuslän, a stray find, but one which bears engraved designs, including the net-like pattern, found on bone and antler objects of Boreal age. There is evidence from Agerød I (HC) that pecked stone axes and adzes of round or oval section and having ground working edges may already have begun to come into use in Scania before the end of the later Boreal, as well as polished stone chisels (Althin 1954,

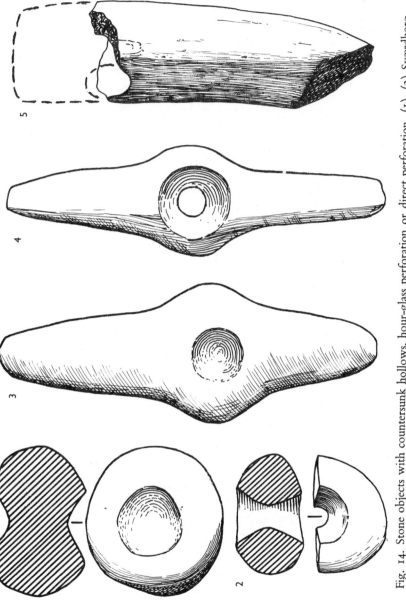

Fig. 14. Stone objects with countersunk hollows, hour-glass perforation or direct perforation. (1), (2) Sværdborg, Zealand (1/2). (3) Sandarna, Göteborg (4/9). (4) Kungsladugard, Göteborg (1/2). (5) Holmegaard, Zealand (2/3).

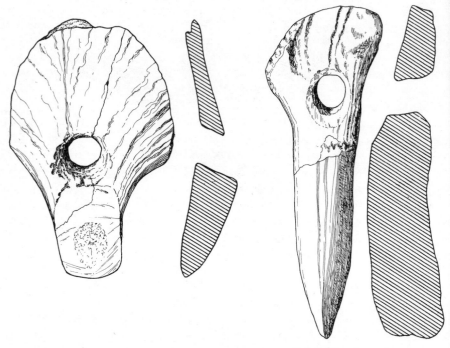

Fig. 15. Elk antler mattock-heads made from (*left*) shed antler and (*right*) one taken from slain animal: Star Carr, England. (1/3)

pl. 11, nos. 2, 3; pl. 14, no. 1). In parts of the east Baltic area where flint was absent, on the other hand, polished stone axes and adzes were already playing a leading role at this time.

Animal skeletal materials. One of the striking features of artifacts made from antler, bone and teeth is the discrimination exercised by the early Post-glacial inhabitants of Scandinavia in exploiting the characteristics of particular materials. Antler was highly appreciated. Although to judge from Star Carr red deer antler was keenly sought already during the Pre-boreal as a material for spear-heads, this period was also particularly favourable to elk. The antlers of this animal were not tough enough for spearheads but served admirably for mattock-heads. To judge from Star Carr (Fig. 15) and from stray finds from Scandinavia and the east Baltic, both shed antlers and ones broken out of the skull of slain animals were used. In each the palmated area had first to be

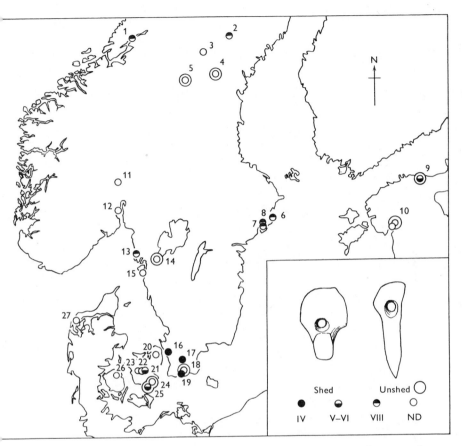

10. Map showing distribution of elk antler mattock-heads in Scandinavia and Esthonia ranging in age from Pre-boreal to Sub-boreal. See Appendix A.

removed and a perforation for the wooden handle made obliquely through the base of the actual antler. Where shed antlers were used the working edge had to be shaped from the base, but when antlers had been broken out it was possible to shape the working edge from the much tougher adhering bone. Since this represents an optimal exploitation in terms of the prevailing technology it is hardly surprising that these two basic forms should recur throughout the techno-territory wherever elk antler was available. Both were present at the English site, Star Carr (Clark *et al.* 1954, pls. xiv, xv), and alongside other variants at the Esthonian sites of Kunda and Pernau (Indreko 1948,

162 ff.). The numerous finds from Scandinavia are mapped (Map 10) and listed in Appendix A. Of the four from Scania three, all made from shed antlers, have been dated in terms of pollen-analysis, one from Harlösa sn. to Zone IV and two others (each from samples obtained from the specimens themselves) to Zone IV/V. From a chronological point of view the most conspicuous feature of the Danish finds is that with the sole exception of a single example in a preliminary stage of manufacture from Sværdborg (Friis Johanson 1919, fig. 111) none have been observed in the rich assemblages of Boreal age from Zealand. This and the early datings in England and Scania suggest that many of the Danish specimens belong to Zones IV or IV/V; and in this connection it is worth noting the elk antler haft from Torupgaard, in the parish of Klemensker on Bornholm, recovered from calcareous mud probably of Pre-boreal age. On the other hand in middle and north Sweden and in Norway the few dated specimens indicate that this form was a long-lived one, another indication of that continuity in utilisation of natural resources which I shall hope to indicate again and again in discussing in another volume the later prehistory of Scandinavia. The situation can be summed up by saying that whereas all the dated specimens of this type of mattock-head from south Scandinavia belong to Zones IV–VI in the pollen sequence, all those from the Scandinavian shield whose age has been established belong to Zone VIII.

When elk declined rather sharply during the Boreal period their antlers were no longer available in adequate numbers for mattock-heads, which as a result came to be made of red deer antler. The same material was also adapted because of its capacity for absorbing shock to form hafts for adze or pick blades (Fig. 16). These might be of flint or occasionally of boar's tusk (Pl. II, *right upper*, p. 107) or polished antler. The use of red deer antler for mattock-heads and haftings for flint adzes and picks during Boreal times meant that there was seldom enough of this material for making barbed spearheads like those found at Star Carr. Occasional finds of red deer antler beam bearing traces

---

Fig. 16. Adze (1, 2) and mattock heads made from a variety of materials from south Scandinavia (Boreal). (1) Flint blade in wooden haft from the Elbe–Trave canal (2/3). (2), (3) Flint and red deer antler blades in red deer antler hafts from Sværdborg, Zealand (2/3). (4) Red deer antler haft evidently cracked in use and repaired by binding secured by transversely incised lines: Sværdborg (2/3). (5) Red deer antler blade from Hohen Viecheln, Mecklenburg (1/1). (6) Single-piece mattock head of red deer antler from Sværdborg, showing parallel lines of pit ornament (2/3).

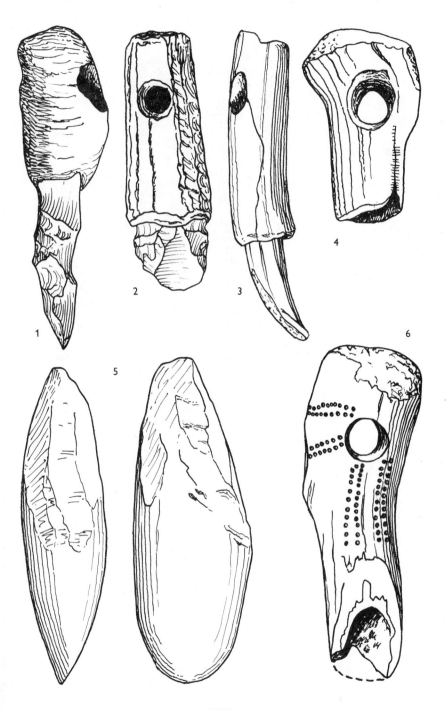

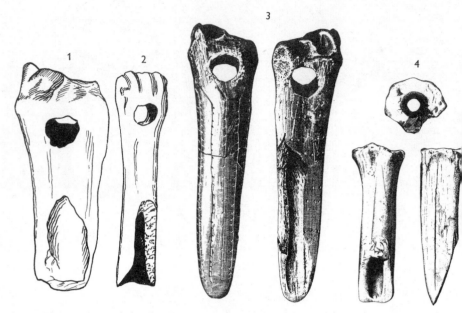

Fig. 17. Mattock-heads of aurochs bone of Boreal age from Denmark and north Germany. (1) Humerus, Skellingsted Bro, Aamosen. (2) Metatarsus, Sandlyng Skov, Stenlille sn. (3) Ulna, Hohen Viecheln, Schwerin. (4) Metatarsus, Hohen Viecheln, Schwerin. (1/2)

of the groove and splinter technique* and of the odd stag antler point like that from Sværdborg (DOI, 173) are exceptions which help to prove the rule. Having once opted for using stag antler for mattocks and hafts the early inhabitants of this small territory had to turn to bone.

The most useful bones for making artifacts were those from the limbs of the main food animals on account of their strength and straightness. The metacarpal and metatarsal bones of the largest species, aurochs and elk, were even used for mattock-heads by cutting through the bone at an oblique angle to form the working-edge and providing a hole for the insertion of a handle, either by breaking through the distaff end to the medullary cavity or by perforating the bone close to the proximal end (Fig. 17). Those of red deer and roe deer could, when cut into

* E.g. beams with parallel grooving in the National Museum of Copenhagen from Slagslunde, Zealand (Nat. Mus. A. 2583) from Harritslevgaard, Skorby sn., Odense (Nat. Mus. A. 20854) and from Valby near Copenhagen (Am. Mus. Nat. Hist. 75.0-5128B).

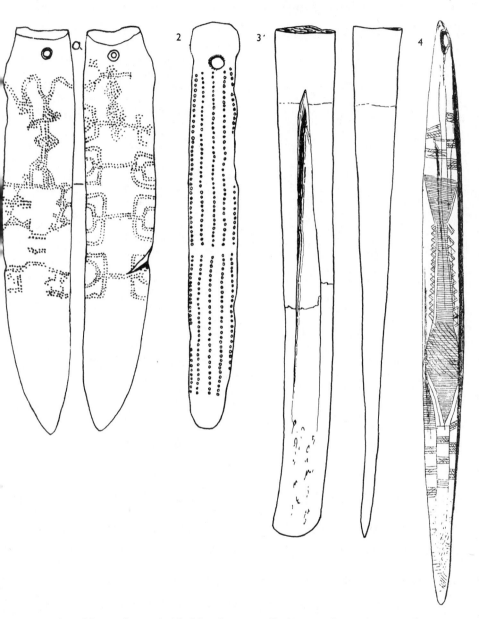

Fig. 18. 'Knife', spatulate tools (2), (3) and stout needle from northern Europe, made from bones including elk radius and ulna and red deer tibia. (1) Probably from Fünen, Denmark (2/3). (2) Limhamn, Scania (4/5). (3) Bohuslän, west Sweden (1/2). (4) Travenort, Holstein (11/10).

Table 7. *The principal kinds of artifact made from parts of the skeletons of the chief food animals from the Boreal period in south Scandinavia and north Germany.*

Parts of skeleton	Elk	Red deer	Roe deer	Aurochs	Wild pig
Antler	Mattocks	Mattocks Hafts, handles Axe/adze blades Barbed spears Harpoons	Fish-hooks		
Teeth	Beads	Beads		Beads	Beads Adze blades Knives, scrapers
Ribs		Barbed spears Fish-hooks			
Humerus				Mattocks	
Radius	Spatulate tools			Mattocks	Picks
Ulna	Spatulate tools	Picks		Picks	Picks
Tibia		Knives			
Metatarsus, Meta-carpus	Mattocks Barbed spears	Barbed spears Slotted points Spatulate tools 'Knives' Fish-hooks	Barbed spears	Mattocks	Tubular handle
Cubitus	Daggers	Daggers			

blanks, serve for making barbed points and a variety of other tools. The various forms of barbed point are discussed later (pp. 129 ff.). In the meantime attention may be paid to three other tool-forms made from portions of long bones. To judge from the number with symbolic decoration these were tools of high status and some at least were much used (p. 157), but their functions remain problematic. On morphological grounds three groups may be noted:

(*a*) Pointed forms with expanded heads and bone edges sharpened, presumed to be 'knives' (Fig. 18, 1). These resemble analogous objects inset with flint bladelets on either edge, a type that first became important in the later Boreal and early Atlantic.

(*b*) Spatulate forms with expanded or thickened heads (Fig. 18, 2, 3). An example from the Träbo bog, Östergötland (Larsson, Cnattingius and Lindell 1938) was recovered from early Ancylus lake clay and others came from the later Boreal Scanian site of Agerød I. Possible uses for this tool in removing bark from trees has been discussed by Lidén (1938).

(*c*) Stout 'needle' forms tapered at either end, the blunter of which was perforated (Fig. 18, 4), used possibly for netting or plaiting. Plain examples came from Sværdborg (Broholm 1931, fig. 56) and Øgaarde (Mathiassen 1943, fig. 40, 9) both on Zealand.

Pig metapodials were of little use except for making such things as small tubular handles. Some bones like the cubital or elbow bones of elk and red deer only required some sharpening to make effective daggers with ready-made grips. Tibia were seldom used, but those of red deer were occasionally shaped to make flaying-knives. Ulnae of red deer, aurochs and pig, as well as the radii of the last two animals were converted into the blades of picks. Humeri and femora were as a rule too large, thick and awkwardly shaped to be attractive to the tool-maker, although humeri were occasionally used for making perforated mattock-heads and during the immediately preceding period the craftsmen of Star Carr evidently succeeded in breaking up an aurochs femur and making heavy scraping tools from the fragments. Back-bones were quite neglected, but the rib-bones of the larger mammals were sometimes split to provide material for barbed points and occasionally for fish-hooks. In the case of antlers and of animal bones other than the cubital bones of elk and red deer and the lateral metapodials of elk it was necessary to cut them up into blanks of suitable shape and size and then to go through a more or less elaborate series of operations before they could be converted into useful artifacts. Animal teeth on the other hand only needed to be perforated to make personal ornaments and in the present context it is interesting to note that the teeth of fur-bearing animals, like bear, fox, otter and wild cat, were used as well as those of dog, aurochs, elk and red deer. Again large teeth, like beaver incisors or boar tusks, could be adapted for implements with little or no modification.

The way in which beaver incisors were exploited is worth attention (Fig. 19). It suggests that prehistoric men, like recent primitive peoples, profited by observing the effectiveness of beavers in felling the trees

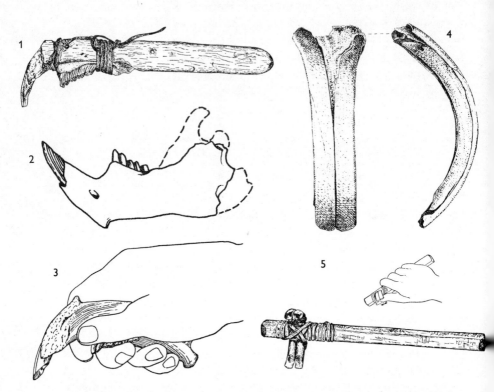

Fig. 19. The exploitation of beaver incisors by prehistoric and recent peoples. (1) Mandible modified in shape and mounted on wooden handle, Ingalik Indians, S.W. Alaska. (*After Osgood.*) (2) Mandible modified by removal of coronoid and condylar processes, Spjellerup bog, Zealand. (*After Hatting.*) (3) Mandible from Ulrome, Yorkshire, modified in similar manner, showing method of grasping. (4) Pair of incisors held together with resin, from Hohen Viecheln, near Schwerin. (*After Schuldt.*) (5) Pair of incisors lashed to handle and used for trimming wood by the Ingalik Indians. (*After Osgood.*)

needed for their lodges. Cornelius Osgood's study (1940) of the material culture of the Ingalik Indians of the lower Yukon river in south-west Alaska shows that beaver incisors were used in several ways. Set in their parent mandibles lashed to short wooden handles they were employed to scrape bark off roots needed for plaiting, very much as the Australian aborigines finished off their wooden artifacts by using opossum incisors set in mandibles attached to handles. Alternatively they were held directly in the hand or mounted at the tip of wooden handles for hollowing out cavities in wood. Yet another alternative was to mount the incisors in pairs on wooden handles and use them as draw-knives for trimming wooden products. Although no beaver mandibles have yet been found secured to their handles from the Stone Age in northern Europe there is ample evidence that the qualities of beaver incisors were recognised and exploited. Many beaver mandibles on prehistoric sites have been found to lack their coronoid and condylar processes. In some cases the fractures may have been caused by the weight of overlying deposits, but in some at least the fractures appear to have been the product of purposive design. A specimen from a late Bronze Age site at Ulrome in Yorkshire, England (Clark 1971) shows clear signs of trimming where the bone processes have been removed, as well as signs of wear on the incisors themselves; in this case also signs of friction on the mandible can most easily be explained by supposing that it was held in the hand and used for such purposes as working wood. When single incisors showing signs of wear are found in archaeological contexts it can hardly be inferred whether these were hand held or whether they have become detached, but a find from Hohen Viecheln shows that sometimes at least they were mounted in pairs, though not necessarily in precisely the same way as among the Ingalik Indians.

Animal hides and pelts. Since clothing must have been needed more particularly during the Boreal winters and since there is no evidence for weaving at this time, it is fair to assume that animal hides and pelts must have been used for this purpose. The extent to which large herbivorous animals were taken for food and the numbers of fur-bearing animals represented in the refuse from settlements shows plainly enough that plenty of these materials were available. Again, there is a wealth of scraping equipment. This includes not only convex flint scrapers, which in many cases, to judge from their wear, were probably used also for finishing wooden artifacts, but also bone tools with polished concave working edges of the kind known to have been used for working skins among Eskimo communities (cf. Clark 1934, fig. 73 and Fig. 18, 2–4 of the present work).

Wood. One of the most important uses of wood was to provide boats and the paddles needed to propel and steer them. Since the coastal sites dating from the Ancylus Lake phase are now mainly submerged, it follows that evidence for water transport is most likely to survive from the sites of lakes or from rivers. Tangible proof that dug-out canoes were being made during Boreal times on the north European plain comes from its western extremity in the form of the three metre example from Pesse, Drenthe, dated to the seventh millennium B.C. by means both of pollen analysis and of radiocarbon analysis (Gro 486: 6315 ± 275 B.C.). Wooden paddles (Fig. 20) are available from many sites in this geographical zone, notably from Star Carr (Clark et al. 1954, fig. 34), Duvensee (Schwantes 1939, Abb. 101, 102), Amosen (Andersen, K. 1951, fig. 5) and Holmegaard (Broholm 1931, fig. 35).

It is unfortunate that archaeologists have not always been sufficiently scrupulous in securing identifications of the timbers used by early man. The precise manner in which the properties of different substances were appreciated and utilised is after all a topic of central importance for the study of primitive technology. On the other hand thanks to pollen analysis and to the careful study of microscopic traces botanists working the field of Quaternary research have provided us with remarkably full information about the woods available at different times and places, and under primitive conditions it is reasonable to suppose that people occupying a more or less densely forested territory would have restricted their choice to timbers growing in their immediate habitat. From another direction we are fortunate that Scandinavia has been exceptionally well studied from the ethnographic point of view, so that we are reasonably fully appraised of the functional qualities and potentialities of the timbers available in the region.

Probably the most promising activity for testing in this regard is archery. Since this was vital to the survival of peoples who depended on hunting the kind of animals available in this area during the Post-glacial, it can be assumed that care would have been taken to secure the most suitable timber for making bows and arrow-shafts. The bows used in south Scandinavia at this time, which were self-bows having shaped grips and tapered limbs, were approximately of man size like the long bows of mediaeval England. By common consent the best wood for bows in temperate Europe at least is yew (*Taxus baccata* L.), a material used in England already from Neolithic times (Clark 1963, 51). On the other hand this tree, which today reaches as far as latitude 61° N in Sweden (Firbas 1949, 270), apparently did not flourish in northern Europe until the peak of Post-glacial warmth (Godwin 1956, 275). The most suitable timber available during Boreal times in south Scandinavia was elm (*Ulmus* sp.) and this was used for the earliest bows found there,

Fig. 20. Wooden paddle rudders from Pre-boreal and Boreal settlements in northern Europe. (1) Duvensee, Schleswig-Holstein (early Boreal) (1/3). (2) Holmegaard (late Boreal), Zealand (3/8). (3) Star Carr, Yorkshire (late Pre-boreal) (1/3).

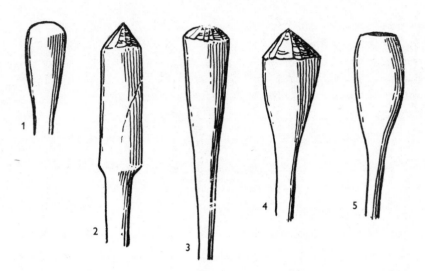

Fig. 21. Wooden bolt-heads for shooting birds or small furred animals from prehistoric and recent contexts. (1) Magleby Long, Denmark (Sub-boreal). (2) Holmegaard IV, Denmark (late Boreal). (3)–(5) Modern (Burjat, Wogul, Eskimo). (1/2)

namely two from Holmegaard and one from Muldbjerg in Denmark (Pl. III, p. 111) and one from Satrup, Schleswig-Holstein, the first two of Boreal, the last two of Sub-boreal age. In the case of arrowshafts there was a wider range of choice. The American toxologist Saxton Pope (1925) preferred birch for hunting arrows and pine for target work. It is of interest that shafts mounted with pointed flint heads from the Late-glacial (Stellmoor: fig. 3) and early Boreal (Loshult, Scania and Vinkelmose, Jutland: Pl. III, nos. 5 and 3–4, p. 111) were made of pine, whereas the blunt-ended bolt from Holmegaard IV (Fig. 21) was of birch wood. From the later phases of the Boreal when there was a wider range of choice we find (Clark 1963, 72) shafts of hazel (Hohen Viecheln) and Guelder rose (*Viburnum opulus*: Holmegaard). A point worth noting is that bows and arrow-shafts alike were cut from substantial timbers rather than branches.

Another good indication that the craftsman of the time had a clear understanding of the properties of timber that practically concerned them is given by the choice of root-wood for fashioning hafts for flint axes, objects which had to bear an exceptionally heavy strain. Examples include a specimen from the Elbe–Trave canal near Mölln (Fig. 16, 1) (Schwantes 1939, Abb. 97) and ones from Gammelby, near Flensburg (Schwabedissen, *Offa*, 1949, Abb. 9, 1) and Hohen Viecheln (Schuldt 1961, Taf. 141). The choice of wood for handles might be instructive if more information were available. In the meantime it is worth noting that early Post-glacial man at Star Carr (Clark *et al.* 1954, p. xv) had anticipated modern craftsmen by hardening the head of a wooden handle in the fire.

Bark and its by-products. Another material of great traditional importance to Scandinavian craftsmen has been tree bark (Clark 1952, 207–12). One of the key properties of bark seized upon very early was its resistance to water. For people who pitched their summer encampments in swamps its ability to insulate against damp was as precisely noted in respect of the finds of Holmegaard IV and Ulkestrup on Zealand (see p. 104). It may be that, as Lidén (1938, 22) has suggested, the chisel-like bone tools, which in some cases show signs of intense use, were employed for detaching the sheets of pine and elm bark needed for such purposes. Birch-bark on the other hand could readily be unwound from the trunks and there was evidence from Star Carr that it was stored in rolls* (Clark *et al.* 1954, pl. xxi). Bark also had a quality of buoyancy that was exploited from very early times in the east Baltic area for supporting nets (see p. 224). Birch bark by reason of its pitch-like content was also of particular value for torches, such as could well have been used for night-fishing from canoes.

It could well have been through observing beads of resin oozing from birch bark torches that this material (*Birkenteer*) first came to the notice of early man. This substance readily obtainable from birch bark by a process of distillation (Clark 1952, 209) was much exploited in prehistoric Europe and continued to serve down to modern times for medicinal as well as for industrial purposes, being used for treating skin complaints and among other things for preparing Russian leather (Merck's *Warenlexikon*, 5th ed., 54). It was already in use at Star Carr (Clark *et al.* 1954, 167) for fixing microliths and barbed antler spear-heads to their shafts. During the full Boreal period and later it continued to serve these purposes and in addition proved especially valuable for fixing blades into slotted equipment. For such purposes and doubt-

---

* Similar rolls from Mullerup were tentatively interpreted as net-floats by Sarauw (1903, 191).

less also for such subsidiary tasks as emphasising decorative designs engraved on antler or bone objects (Malmer and Magnusson 1955) it was found useful to lower the melting temperature by adding bee's wax and animal fat (Lidén 1938, 25–8; 1942, 99–100; Grewingk 1882, 25 f.). Whether oak bark – and indeed to judge from Lapp practice also birch and willow bark (Clark 1952, 219, n. 86) – was used for tanning leather cannot yet be tested, but the importance of hides at this time has already been emphasised (p. 123). A major content of certain barks, notably lime and willow, was bast fibre capable of being worked into threads of the kind needed for binding spearheads to their shafts and also for plaiting nets and bags.

Techno- and social territories. The archaeological material available from Pre-boreal and Boreal times in south Scandinavia and proximate regions shows that men used remarkably similar equipment for coping with their material needs over the whole extent of the north European plain as far east as the river Nieman. Quite evidently local circumstances and temporal seasons determined which elements in the repertoire were deployed to solve immediate problems. This does not alter the fact that social capital both technological and symbolic was remarkably homogeneous over a geographical zone broadly equivalent to that of the techno-territory occupied during Late-glacial times by communities whose flint technology is symbolised in the archaeological literature by tanged points. Two underlying reasons may be advanced for this fundamental homogeneity. Historically there can hardly be any doubt that, despite local displacements at a time of marked environmental change, the social capital of the communities occupying the north European plain and its Scandinavian projections during early Post-glacial times derived to a significant degree from Advanced Palaeo-lithic sources many of them thousands of years old. This applies not merely to technology, but also, as will be shown (p. 148), to the reper-toire of symbolic art engraved on Maglemose artifacts. One may go further and explain the closeness of the relations between the Maglemose and Kunda repertoires centring respectively on the west and east Baltic in precisely these terms: since they both drew on the same stock of ideas held in common over a territory extending from south-west Europe to Siberia, it is hardly surprising to find both for example using barbed bone points or making use in their symbolic art of closely similar elements. The differences which appear in the archaeological record between the two provinces can reasonably be explained in some measure from the circumstance that common social resources had to adapt to distinct ecological systems: it was for instance the wealth of first-class flint in the west that lent a special character to the most commonly surviving component of Maglemose assemblages, just as it was the lack of this which led to the widespread use of less tractable materials for small tools and in the case of heavier equipment to the use of edge-ground and polished stone ones. Within the territory of south Scandinavia and adjacent parts of north Germany the early Post-glacial population reacted to environmental constraints and oppor-tunities, which though subject to obvious local variations operated within a broadly uniform range.

If the Maglemose techno-territory is reasonably well defined in the archaeological record the same can hardly yet be said of the subsidiary social territories which must surely have existed. All one can do at the moment is to indicate one or two of the most promising media. One such is likely to comprise a category of artifacts at once numerous and pervasive and subject to potentially idiosyncratic treatment. Barbed points of antler or bone offer some promise in this regard. A first need is to distinguish between variations due to differences in function and ones which reflect alternative solutions to the same problem, since it is in such choices that we find the best indications of social definition.

On *a priori* grounds no great difficulty should exist in distinguishing between two major functional groups, namely harpoon-heads and spear- (or arrow-) heads, since the tasks for which they were designed ought clearly to be reflected in their morphology. In the former the tang would only need to be sufficiently developed to hold the head while the shaft was being propelled and the emphasis would rest on devices needed to secure the line, whether these took the form of perforations, grooves, protuberances or any combination of these. Again, since the barbs of harpoon-heads were designed to hold the victim while it struggled at the end of the line they would have to project from the stem sufficiently to present a hook-like profile, to be stoutly made and therefore to be widely spaced. Spearheads (or for that matter arrowheads) on the other hand were designed to be perma-nently fixed to the shafts while in use. The tangs would in this case be the prominent feature: in the case of arrowheads they might be pointed so as to fit into the head of the shaft without impairing the flight, but in spearheads one might expect to find the tangs longer and broader in order to give great purchase to binding. Again, the barbs, being intended only to hold the weapon in place and so impede the victim, could be finer, more closely set and less prominent. These suppositions are in fact supported by two kinds of observation. First there is the possibility of testing the function of heads by finding direct evidence of the way they were mounted: in the case of harpoon-heads the possibility of recovering the line is remote; but at least one object interpreted as a spearhead has been found with shaft and mounting intact (Fig. 22, *left*) and in several cases impressions of the binding and/or traces of the resin used to secure the mount have been observed (Fig. 22, *right*), invariably on objects conforming to the category of spearhead on morphological grounds. Further confirmation comes from observing barbed points in association with skeletons of victims which escaped in antiquity bearing the heads of weapons in their bodies. Here the point to note is that the weapon heads recovered with seal skeletons on at least four occasions invariably had arrangements for securing the line and stout, widely spaced and prominent barbs. It is a matter of observation that the barbs of objects classified on the criteria indicated are spaced, almost without exception, at intervals of over 2 cm and that spearheads invariably have theirs more closely set (Fig. 23).

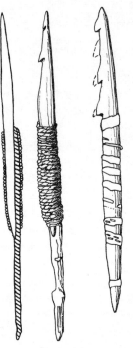

Fig. 22. Barbed bone spearheads from south Scandinavia with indications of mounting (1/2). (*left*) Spearhead secured to a hazel-wood shaft by thread, Ulkestrup IV, Denmark. (*right*) Spearhead with traces of resin between former binding threads, Råbelövsjön, Nosaby, Scania (SHM 13900).

It appears from the associations of the two classes that the Late-glacial to Post-glacial transition was marked by a strong swing in hunting land mammals from harpoons to spears and arrows. This was already apparent at Star Carr where there was only one harpoon-head (Clark *et al.* 1954, fig. 50, p. 86) as opposed to 190 barbed spear- and arrowheads. The Zealand settlements appear to have yielded no harpoon-heads as against many hundreds of the latter. Yet harpoon-heads did not entirely die out in south Scandinavia at this time as shown (Fig. 24)

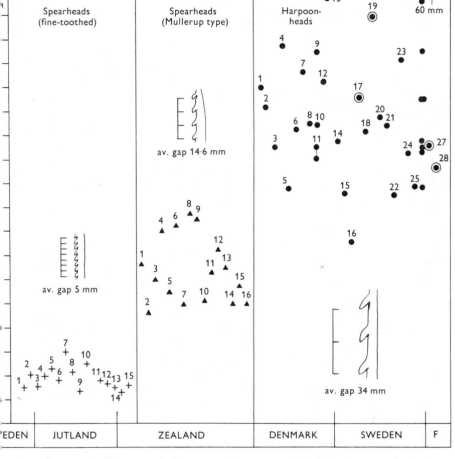

Fig. 23 Diagram illustrating differences in the spacing of barbs as between finely toothed and medium-spaced spearheads and harpoon-heads from Denmark and Sweden (Boreal–Sub-boreal). See Appendix B. [Note: Harpoon-heads enclosed by circles denote examples found with seal skeleton.]

by one found with three spearheads at Løjesmølle on Zealand (Clark 1936, pl. v) and another from Hästefjorden, Dalsland, dated to Zones V and VI by pollen-analysis (Thomasson 1937; Fries 1965b; Nilsson *in lit.*); and it is not so surprising therefore that harpoon-heads came back into favour with the great development of seal-hunting in the later Stone Age of Scandinavia. The number of harpoon-heads available from early Post-glacial times is far too small to provide a useful basis for detecting idiosyncracies of style or pattern. The abundance of other kinds of

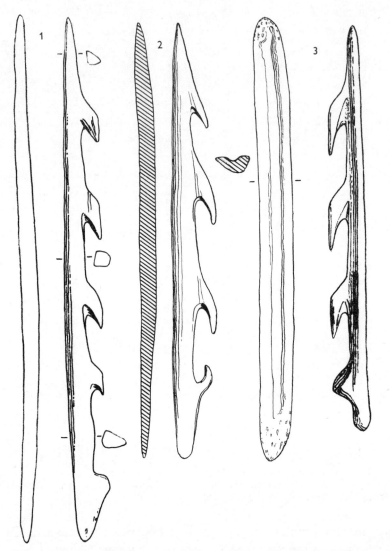

Fig. 24. Barbed harpoon-heads from south Scandinavia (Boreal). (1) Tjørnlunds
Raamose, Finderup, Jutland (NM A 22763). (2) Hästefjorden, Frandefors, Dalsland,
Sweden (SHM 4011). (3) Løjesmølle, Zealand. (1/2).

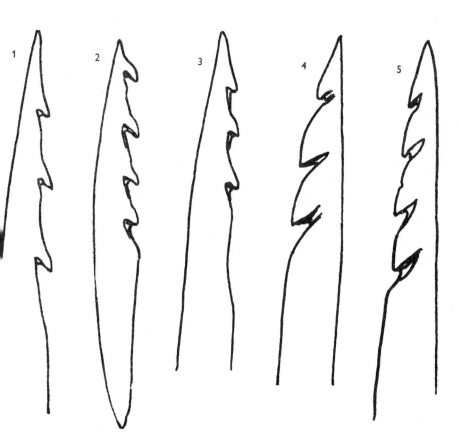

Fig. 25. Barbed bone points with medium-spaced barbs from Boreal sites in Denmark and north Germany. (1) Mullerup, Zealand. (2) Holmegaard, Zealand. (3) Løjesmølle, Zealand. (4), (5) Hohen Viecheln, Mecklenburg. (1/1)

barbed point encourages the hope that these may yet provide the necessary insights. A distinction frequently noted in the literature is that between finely toothed and medium-barbed spearheads, that is in terms of measurement between ones with barbs spaced at intervals (between tip and tip) of between 0·5 and 0·8 cm and those spaced at between 1·1 and 2·0 cm. Unfortunately there is insufficient evidence on whether we can treat these forms as the outcome of socially or technically determined choices. Finely barbed points have yet to be found in vital relationship to victims, but it may be significant that ones with medium-spaced barbs have been found with victims as widely disparate as elk

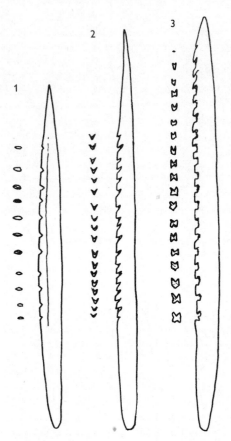

Fig. 26. Finely toothed points showing methods of forming notches by cutting directly into the blank, or obliquely, or in a double or criss-cross direction. (*left*) Ljungby, Scania; (*middle*) Hohen Viecheln; (*right*) Leman and Ower Banks, North Sea. (1/2)

(Taaderup) and pike (Kunda). Within Denmark the two forms are broadly complementary in spatial distribution. The type with medium-spaced barbs (Fig. 25) having the particular profile first noted at Mullerup on Zealand are concentrated on that island, though with outliers on Fünen and Lolland, whereas finely toothed ones, whether shaped by cutting transverse, oblique or criss-cross notches (Figs. 26, 27) are mainly found in Jutland. Finely barbed points are widely distributed in north Germany and Scania as well as further afield. Medium-barbed points found elsewhere in the west Baltic area have barbs of

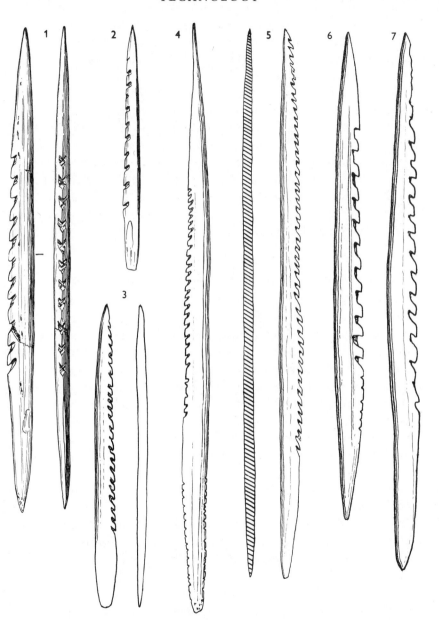

Fig. 27. Finely toothed spearheads of antler or bone from northern Europe. (1) Hornsea, Holderness, England (Hull Museum); (2) Béthune, Artois, France (St Germain M. 17532); (3) Undsted bog, Jutland (Århus M.); (4) one of five from a bog near Emmersbœk, Jutland (Hjørring M. 13819); (5) Bothildenslunds bog, Scania (SHM 13675); (6) Szirguponen, former E. Prussia; (7) Kunda, Esthonia. (1/2)

135

smoothly convex or angular profile. It is possible that more intensive typological study, not forgetting the need for greater precision in dating the various forms, may yet yield some further clues towards the definition of social territories.

There is little doubt that, as Malmer and Magnusson (1955, 119) were right to emphasise, symbolic art of the kind engraved mainly on antler and bone offers in principle the best scope for detecting stylistic nuances of the kind best suited to defining areas of intensive social interaction. On the other hand in the present state of research the corpus of material is too restricted and in many cases insufficiently documented for this purpose. As with so many other elements of Maglemose assemblages it serves at present mainly to emphasise the high degree of homogeneity prevailing over the whole techno-territory.

SUBSISTENCE

The lack of settlement sites with surviving organic refuse from the Pre-boreal means that we are not yet able to define the pattern of subsistence in any detail for the beginning of the Post-glacial period. Important clues to some of the main sources of animal protein have nevertheless been provided by certain stray finds. These show for one thing that, although, as we know from Star Carr, red deer were already important, the Pre-boreal was also particularly favourable for elk. The reason is not far to seek. Young and open forest with areas of swamps and small lakes provided ideal conditions for these animals which are especially fond of browsing leaves, twigs, buds and bark of aspen, willow and birch, as well as oak, hazel and *Sorbus* and also relish a variety of aquatic and semi-aquatic plants. It is hardly surprising that elk should have made a tentative appearance during the Allerød in Denmark, where it occurred for instance at Gentofte (Troels-Smith 1955, fig. 117) and with the flint assemblage at Bromme (see p. 84), as it did also in Britain at this time (Clark 1972a, fig. 14). Elk returned in force during the Pre-boreal when the environment was especially favourable. It was the gradual replacement of the open pioneer forest by the denser cover of the warmth-demanding trees that brought worsening conditions. The presence of extensive areas of marsh and lake allowed the elk to flourish though on a reduced scale during Boreal times, but it was the onset of the deciduous forest, more probably than the effect of hunting, which must nevertheless have exerted its toll,

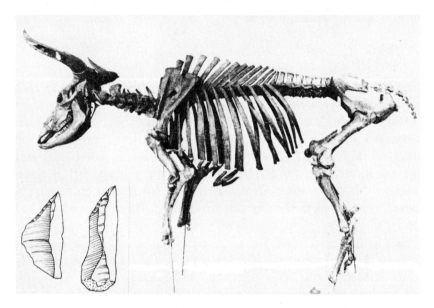

PLATE IV. Skeleton of aurochs (*Bos primigenius*) of Pre-boreal (Zone IV) age from Vig, Zealand. Two of the three flint arrow armatures from the breast are illustrated. (1/2)

that spelled its doom as a significant food resource. The dominance of mixed oak forests that prevailed during Zones VII and VIII seriously impaired conditions for the elk even though finds from the Ertebølle and Gjessinggaard middens, from Brabrand, Bundsø and Dyrholm show that it managed to hang on in parts of Denmark into Sub-boreal times.

Another stray find to throw significant light on the use of resources at this time is the aurochs (*Bos primigenius*) skeleton recovered almost intact in 1905 under 2·2 m of peat and 0·7 to 0·9 m of mould at Jyderup near Vig (Pl. IV) in north-west Zealand. Analysis of the macroscopic plant remains from the overlying peat published in the original report showed that the animal perished before the pine had reached its maximum and subsequent pollen-analysis confirmed that it was of Pre-boreal age (Hartz and Winge 1906; Degerbøl and Fredskild 1970, 12–13). The find is of interest from two points of view. In the first place it highlights the presence of aurochs from the very beginning of the Post-glacial. This has been brought out more fully by Degerbøl and Fredskild's recent study (1970) of the sub-fossil finds of this animal from Denmark. According to these authors we find the following distribution in time for Denmark as a whole, taking account only of specimens capable of being dated by pollen analysis:

Forest zones	III	III–IV	IV	V	VI	VII	VII/VIII	VIII	IX
Numbers of finds	1	1	14	20	22	1	3	23	1

Taken at its face value this table suggests that aurochs first appeared already during the closing phase of the Late-glacial, that it flourished during the Pre-boreal and Boreal as it certainly did also in Scania (Isberg 1962), declined sharply during the Atlantic period at the peak of the deciduous forest, recovered during the Sub-boreal and barely survived in the Sub-atlantic. A point obscured by lumping together the finds from Denmark as a whole is that, although the aurochs was particularly common on Zealand during Zones IV–VI, it had completely disappeared from this island by the close of Boreal times. This was probably due to a combination of factors: the increased density of the deciduous forest meant that the animals had to concentrate on open marshy areas, where hunters could more easily take them. That man played an important role is suggested by the fact that in Jutland the aurochs became important again in Zone VIII, a fact to be explained in part by the more open vegetation in some areas of the peninsula and in part by the fact that the territory could easily be reinforced from the south. The second reason why the Vig aurochs is of interest is that it throws light on the methods by which this animal was hunted early in the Post-glacial period. To judge from its wounds, this particular aurochs had been shot on two separate occasions, since the wound in the second rib had already healed to some extent before the lethal shot which pierced the ninth rib and apparently penetrated the lung. The intactness of the skeleton – only the metacarpals were missing – is hardly consistent with butchery and argues that the animal got away from its hunter and collapsed in the swamp. The force with which the flints had penetrated the ribs argued that they had been propelled by bows as armatures of arrows. Two microliths and a small flake were indeed recovered from the region of the breast arguing for at least a third shot. What is of exceptional interest is that the microliths were, as Mathiassen long ago recognised (1937, 149), of the same type as those represented in the more or less contemporary Jutland site of Klosterlund. The aurochs must have been a formidable animal to hunt and kill but other parallels to Vig can be cited: for instance a shoulder-blade from Grænge on Lolland (Zone V) showed the mark of a wound (Andersen, A. and Møller 1946, figs. 5 and 7) and another wound was found in a vertebra of a complete skeleton of a young one at Onnarp in Scania (Isberg 1962, 428–30; Welinder 1971, 39 and 176).

The picture is rather fuller for the Boreal period, since from this time we have a number of settlements with organic refuse. One limitation is that all these sites are found on the island of Zealand. This is to some extent offset by the availability of comparable material from north Germany and (though from a slightly earlier period) from England. Nevertheless, since the resources exploited were local, it is highly important that waterlogged sites be located and excavated as completely as possible from other parts of south Scandinavia. The fauna from the Zealand sites goes some way to confirming the seasonal nature of the settlements inferred from their location and flimsy construction. Summer occupation is suggested by the presence of many young mammals and birds, notably young of the crane, a summer guest, which raises its brood in Denmark (Winge in Friis Johansen 1919, 262); and also by the fact that roe deer were killed while still carrying their antlers. The frequent occurrence of quantities of empty hazel nutshells argues that occupation extended into the autumn. The situation in Zealand appears then to be the opposite of that encountered at Star Carr in England where occupation of bog sites centres on the winter. This is hardly surprising. The behaviour of human predators is inevitably closely linked with that of the animals on which they mainly depend for their protein and the seasonal movement of herbivorous animals is conditioned to a significant extent by topography. There is a pronounced contrast in this respect between a flat territory like Denmark, and more particularly Zealand, and one with the marked relief seen in northern England.

Analysis of the animal remains (Appendix C) brings out two basic and closely interrelated differences between the Late-glacial pattern of exploiting animal resources and that which obtained during the early Post-glacial period in Denmark and north Germany. Instead of concentrating to a significant degree on reindeer, men drew in the first place upon the much wider range of animals that became available as glacial gave place to temperate climate; and among these they showed no marked or invariable preference for any particular species. The principal weapons used included the bow and arrow, the spearhead and much more rarely at least on inland sites, the only ones available in this region during the early Post-glacial, the harpoon or if not this at least the spear with detachable head secured by a line. Bows, which as we have seen (p. 124) were made from single staves of timber with shaped grip and tapered limbs, were somewhere near the size of a man. They fired wooden bolts with blunt heads for securing birds or small furred animals and arrows inset with microliths as tips and barbs. There is no evidence that barbed points served as arrowheads, as they apparently did at the English site of Star Carr in respect of one group (form D) characterised by pointed tangs too short to permit of mounting as spear heads. On the other hand their pointed resin-coated bases suggests that narrow bone points with flint insets fixed in lateral slots may (see p. 173) have been mounted as arrowheads.

The only animals from sites of Boreal age to show clear signs of the kind of genetical change associated with a certain stage in domestication is the dog (*Canis familiaris*), almost invariably present on the Zealand sites, as well as at Star Carr and Hohen Viecheln. When some of the bones from Star Carr originally identified as those of wolf were first recognised to belong to dog (Degerbøl 1961), the point was made that the animal concerned was 'a true dog, and not a tamed wolf in the first generation of taming'. The recognition of dog-remains at the mammoth-hunting station of Mezine in the Ukraine (Pidoplichko 1969, 99 and 162, fig. 33) shows indeed that this animal was domesticated from the wolf already during the Late-glacial period and can hardly therefore be considered as derived from communities based on farming. Indeed there seems no reason why dogs should not have been domesticated from wolves more than once over the latter's extensive territory.

At this point it is worth mentioning that fragmentary remains of human skeletons were found both at Mullerup and Sværdborg, the former including an adult and child and the latter more than one individual of between 16 and 18 years; an ulna with one extremity missing came from Øgaarde; and Vinde-Helsinge yielded the upper part of an ulna and a metacarpal bone. What these occurrences portend is still unknown. There is no positive evidence of the kind available from Atlantic times in Denmark for the practice of cannibalism. There are evident signs that the ulna from Vinde-Helsinge had been scraped, but this could have happened a long time after death and may have resulted from use of the bone as an implement (Degerbøl in Mathiassen 1943, 183).

Table 8. *Changes in the proportions (%) of basic food animals during Pre-boreal and Boreal times in northern Europe. Data from Fraser and King in Clark 1953, ch.* III; *Gehl in Schuldt 1961, table p. 43; and Degerbøl in Mathiassen 1943*

	Forest zones	Roe deer	Red deer	Elk	Aurochs	Pig	Samples
Øgaarde (2nd occ.), Denmark	VI	13·9	51·4	2·8	13·2	18·8	144 astragali
Hohen Viecheln, N. Germany	V	50·0	36·9	3·1	5·1	4·8	1,382 bones
Star Carr, York-shire, England	IV	23·9	58·0	8·0	6·5	3·6	138 indi-viduals

Published information is not yet available in sufficient quantity to provide definitive information about changes in the proportions of the main food animals during the early Post-glacial period on the north European plain. It may yet be worth tabulating (Table 8) the information from three sites ranging in age from late Pre-boreal (IV) to late Boreal (VI).

Among noteworthy features is the decline of elk and the increase in swine, both functions of the spread of mature deciduous forest. Roe deer and red deer, which were also favoured by forest conditions, were taken in proportions which appear to reflect no consistent pattern in time, a conclusion emphasised by the fact that at Sværdborg roe deer and pig were the most important animals (Winge in Friis Johansen 1919, 261-3). Earlier publications seldom provide information about the culling policy pursued at this time, but we know that in respect of roe deer at Hohen Viecheln (Gehl in Schulde 1961, 48) the emphasis rested on young animals: thus of 23 roe deer mandibles, 4 belonged to kids, 6 to second year animals, 9 to animals between the third and fourth and fifth to seventh years, 3 to ones between seven and nine years and none whatever to animals over twelve years; and the high proportion of young mammals was specifically noted at Sværdborg (Broholm 1931, 30). In the case of elk and aurochs evidence has already been cited that adult animals were hunted, but for what this is worth none such is available in respect of red deer, roe deer or swine. Analysis of the skeletal material from Hohen Viecheln shows that roe deer must have been carried back to the site complete, but in the case of the larger animals only the neck vertebrae were present, showing that they must have been butchered elsewhere. In the case of the two largest, elk and aurochs, the absence of skulls argues that the heads may have been left on the kill sites.

The other mammals taken at this time were of prime value for their pelts, a commodity much needed during the Boreal winter, but in most if not all cases they were also valuable as sources of meat as well as for raw materials for artifacts or personal ornaments. The fur-bearing animal most often present and sometimes strongly represented is the beaver. Although this animal was evidently a recognised resource, the fact that remains from Star Carr were consistent with the killing of a complete family of beavers hardly suggests a consistent or systematic policy of conservation. Records of the meat consumed between September 1960 and May 1961 by Algonquin Indians engaged in trapping for the Hudson's Bay Company (Leeds in Vayda 1965, 35 n. 5) indicate that beavers provided c. 2/5 of the meat consumed and these animals also yielded fat of high nutritional value. Other fur-bearing animals to occur on the main Zealand sites included badger, fox and marten. Of more sporadic occurrence were brown bear, lynx, otter, wild cat and wolf. For killing small fur-bearing animals (and perhaps for birds) blunt-ended wooden arrows or bolts were used in order to minimise damage to the pelts (Fig. 21).

Although some thirty species of bird have been identified from sites of this period none of them are present in numbers sufficient to indicate highly specialised fowling activities. The remains are chiefly interesting for the way in which they reflect seasonality and the character of stations occupied mainly during the summer. By far the great majority are inland species, mostly water birds like various bitterns, ducks, cranes, geese, divers, grebes and swans, but also including some marine and coastal ones such as cormorants and gulls. Ground game birds of the kind most easily snared during the winter are extremely scarce, though there is a record of grouse from Sværdborg. The presence of the white-tailed or sea eagle on the main Zealand sites of this period, as well as on later prehistoric sites in Scandinavia proper, may well have been due primarily to the value of their pinion feathers for fletching arrows (Clark 1948c, 128).

The only fish of much economic importance caught at this time in the west Baltic area was the pike (Clark 1948a, 57–60), a fish of which

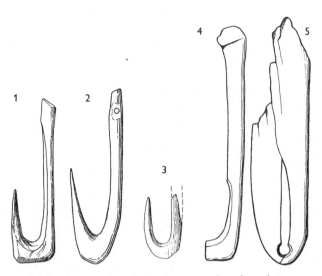

Fig. 28. Bone fish-hooks from Boreal sites in Denmark and north Germany. (1), (4) Sværdborg, Zealand; (2) Havel lakes, Germany; (3) Øgaarde; (5) Mullerup. (2/3)

Isaac Walton remarked that its flesh was 'too good for any but anglers, or very honest men'. The fact that it occurs so invariably on Boreal sites with adequate bone samples and in such quantity – the original excavations at Sværdborg for instance yielded 80 upper and 64 left lower jaw bones – argues that it was systematically harvested. Analysis of the 32 individuals represented at Hohen Viecheln (Schuldt 1961, 72) shows that only 3 were under 3 lb, 15 were between 3–8 lb, 10 between 8–15 lb and 4 between 15–20 lb in weight. This argues strongly against net-fishing and suggests that the fish were caught individually either on hook and line or by spearing. Fish-hooks, which at this time had no barbs, were a novel feature, but their comparative rarity (Fig. 28) and the abundance of barbed spear-points suggests that the latter method was preferred. This agrees with the known habits of the larger pike – the 'grass pike' of Swedish peasant lore – which often spawn in the late spring in shallow water on flooded land under situations which make them peculiarly vulnerable to the noose or the fish spear. Even the largest pike – the so-called 'leaf-pike' which spawn in deeper water – can be taken by spearing from a boat as they lie sunning themselves near the surface or by enticing them by means of flaming torches (Scheffer 1674, 107). Convincing proof that pike were indeed speared by Mesolithic

143

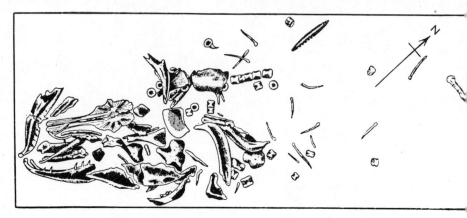

Fig. 29. Remains of pike (*Esox lucius*) with barbed point in the region of the
back from a Boreal deposit at Kunda, Esthonia. (*After Indreko*)

man in northern Europe is given by two finds from Kunda, Esthonia,
one of a barbed point sticking directly into the skull of a pike, the
other of a point in position in the back of a metre-long pike (Fig. 29)
(Indreko 1934, 283; Thomson, P. W. 1926). Another large fish probably taken in the same manner, though much more rarely was the
sheat fish (*Siluris glanis*) which must have reached Zealand during the
mainland period (Degerbøl and Iversen 1942). A specimen of Ancylus
Lake age from Bred in west Fünen measured *c.* 1½ m long. The sheat
fish – the last survivors in Denmark were caught in the Søro lakes
between 1797 and 1799 – hibernates in deep lakes and only comes to
the surface to spawn when temperatures reach *c.* 18°/20° C, a level
probably not attained in Denmark until the summer. Thus both the
main fish caught at this time are consistent with the Zealand sites being
occupied from late spring into the summer.

The Post-glacial environment offered a richer or at least a more
varied source of plant food than did that of the Late-glacial period.
Unfortunately, no systematic attempt has been made so far to recover
this. Only traces of macroscopic size are likely to be noticed in the
normal course of archaeological excavation and since the Boreal period
was marked by a powerful spread of hazel it is not surprising that
hazelnuts have frequently been recorded, sometimes as at Duvensee and
Ulkestrup occurring in sufficient numbers to form perceptible layers.
Another source of plant food known to have been exploited by the
Boreal population of Zealand are seeds of the yellow water-lily (*Nuphar*

Table 9. *Marsh and open-community plants represented at Star Carr with an analysis of their occurrences in the intestines of bog corpses of the Danish Roman Iron Age and also in the diet of European peasants during the nineteenth and twentieth centuries*

Star Carr (Mesolithic)	Tollund Grauballe (Danish Roman Iron Age)		Recent (19th–20th cent. Europe)
Phragmites communis	.	.	×
Menyanthes trifoliata	.	.	×
Chenopodium album	×	×	×
Polygonum aviculare	.	× ⎫	×
P. persicaria	×	× ⎭	
Rumex sp.	×	×	×
Galeopsis tetrahit	×	×	.
Stellaria media	×	×	.
Urtica dioica	.	.	×

lutea) (the white endosperm of which is known to have been of high nutritive value), a cache of *c.* 250 cc of which was found immediately below the archaeological layer at Holmegaard (Broholm 1931, 19). A fuller picture is available from the plant residues recovered from the mud containing the animal refuse and artifacts at Star Carr, dating from the late Pre-boreal. Although it can hardly be proved that any or all of these were in fact eaten by man, it can hardly be a coincidence that of the thirteen open-community plants represented no less than six among those were washed out of the intestines of a Danish bog corpse dating from the Roman Iron Age and that a seventh is known to have been in common use in modern times. Again, dried rhizomes of two of the numerous marsh plants *Phragmites communis* and *Menyanthes trifoliata* were being eaten in the form of pounded meal by Swiss peasants as late as the nineteenth century. Three of the open community plants, *Urtica dioica, Stellaria media* and *Chenopodium* sp. flourish on the nitrogen arising from settlement refuse and may well have been one reason, even if only a subsidiary one, why frequent returns were made to the site. In connection with plant food it may be suggestive that what appear to be mattock-heads made of antler or bone are a leading element of equipment and that towards the end of the period perforated stones recalling those used by Bushmen for weighting digging-sticks began to come into use. On the other hand the few possible rubbing-stones from Duvensee (Schwabedissen 1944, Taf. 105, 1–3) only emphasise the extreme rarity of stone equipment for preparing plant food.

PSYCHIC NEEDS

Disposal of the dead. A necessity universally recognised among men from the Late Pleistocene onwards has been to separate the dead from the living in a formal manner. For a number of reasons very little information is available about the disposal of the dead during the early Post-glacial in Europe and such evidence as we have was found accidentally and poorly recorded. Among peoples living in such small groups there was no question of marking graves by the kind of monumental structures associated with some quite primitive agricultural communities. Again south Scandinavia lacks the caves and rock-shelters that in some other territories provide likely sites for finding early burials. Such evidence as we have for burials dating from Boreal times in our area has been found accidentally and suffers from the attendant drawbacks. Even so the recovery of a skull and bones in the course of digging peat at Koelbjerg, Odense, Fünen, dating from pollen Zone V is most easily explained in terms of a burial. If the remains had been in a contracted position it is surely likely that this would have been observed because of its divergence from modern practice. Undoubted evidence for extended inhumations was found at Stångenäs, Bro sn., in the west Swedish province of Bohuslän by gravel diggers quarrying a shell-bank in 1843. Two skeletons were found, their heads close together and their bodies at an angle of 125°. The shell-bank itself has been assigned to the Boreal period (Hägg 1924). The question is whether the bodies were buried while the bank was forming as Sven Nilsson appears to have thought or whether they were inserted later. From a morphological standpoint the Stångenäs skull is markedly more long-headed than those of Neolithic date in this area and in this respect stands closer to the Mesolithic series, which however spans the Atlantic as well as the Boreal period. There remain a number of fragmentary finds of Boreal age from Danish settlement sites which seem hard to explain if inhumation was systematically and invariably practised: bones relating to an adult and a child came from the Mullerup site and several individuals between 16 and 18 years of age were represented in the finds from Sværdborg; broken ulnae came from Øgaarde and Vinde-Helsinge and the last mentioned also yielded a metacarpal bone; and mention should be made of a calvarium found stray in the Ravenstrup bog. Certain marks on the ulna from Vinde-Helsinge have been explained as the outcome of casual use rather than as evidence for cannibalism (Degerbøl in Mathiassen 1943, 168–9, 183).

Personal adornment. Another feature common to existing groups of mankind and which appeared in the context of the first art as one of the attributes of the Advanced Palaeolithic was the conscious adornment of the person by means of ornaments. The fact that no burials, the richest source of such objects, have been excavated under scientific conditions means that such finds as we have are stray beads and pendants in many cases from actual settlements. Animal teeth perforated through the roots have always been favoured among peoples who drew much of their protein from hunting and, as already noted (p. 121), some species including a number of fur-bearing animals were drawn upon for this purpose during Boreal times. Already during the final stages of the Pre-boreal, sections of tubular bone, in this case taken from a large bird, were being used for beads as well as small stone pebbles perforated from one face (Clark *et al.* 1954, pl. xx). Amber lumps were perforated or grooved presumably to serve as beads or pendants. From the full Boreal period plain amber pendants are known from a number of settlements on Zealand, including Sværdborg, Lundby and Verup. Examples ornamented by parallel rows of pits drilled into the surface include stray finds from Kongsted mose, Aamosen (*DOI*, 228) and Ringkjøbing, Jutland (Clark 1936, Appendix vi, no. xxxvii) as well as two unprovenanced finds from Denmark ornamented with anthropomorphic designs (Fig. 34, 8, 9) which may possibly have served as amulets rather than merely as ornaments.

Symbolic art. Symbolic art in the form of engravings on antler and bone was executed in three main techniques (Appendix D). The commonest was incision, mostly very fine, but sometimes, and more especially during the early phase of the ensuing Atlantic phase, more deeply cut and in some cases intended to hold a resin inlay. A second method of defining patterns was to drill regular pits into the surface (*Bohrornament*) of the material. Rather less commonly found are designs formed by lines made up of small angular dots formed by an acutely pointed implement. The motifs represented comprise a number of variants of elementary geometric patterns, including shading, barbed lines, ornamented bands, chevrons, lozenges, squares, rhombs and opposed triangles; more complex mesh and chequer patterns; theriomorphic representations; and schematic delineations of men.

A considerable proportion of geometric designs, including examples of each of our five main groups, were already known in other parts of Europe during the Late-glacial period. As was long ago pointed out (Clark 1936, 178–9) many of the more elementary patterns, including c, e–h, i1, j1, k, q1, s, x1–2, y2 of Fig. 37, were already employed by the Magdalenians of France. On the other hand as more material is becoming available from the U.S.S.R. it is becoming evident that this territory must also be considered as a significant potential source of inspiration for northern Europe. For instance, even from preliminary information about the designs on mammoth ivory objects from the rich burials of Sounguir near Vladimir, it is evident that some of the commoner designs engraved on antler and bone pieces from 'Maglemose' assemblages (e.g. motives b, e, f, q1) formed part of the Late-glacial repertoire in this part of Russia. Even the hexagonal mesh design known from Denmark and especially from south-west Sweden is to be found finely engraved on a mammoth tusk (Fig. 32) from Elisavichi in the Desna basin (Nougier 1972, Pl. 2, 5). Other pieces from Sounguir, notably a perforated disc and the cut-out silhouette of a horse, are decorated by arrangements of pits in drilled technique precisely as on objects from 'Maglemose' and 'Kunda' assemblages of Boreal age. Pit ornament had indeed long been known from Late-glacial contexts as far afield as Siberia as witnessed for example by a spiral design from the Mal'ta site (Ozols 1971, Abb. I). In the west European caves on the other hand it is rare and the occurrence on a bone from the Abri Lartet in the Gorge d'Enfer, Dordogne (Marshack 1972, fig. II) belongs to a remote period near the very beginning of the Advanced Palaeolithic sequence.

Reference to the mesh design reminds us that technology and design may be closely interconnected in societies in which individuals performed many different tasks. It is under such circumstances only to be expected that handicrafts like net-making and plaiting would provide potential sources of design patterns. Since no traces of nets or plait-work have survived from Boreal contexts in the west Baltic area (unlike the east Baltic, see p. 223), the suggestion that net-like designs on engraved objects were inspired by netting or plaiting can by its nature be no

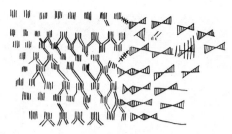

Fig. 30 Engraving on roe deer antler from Horsens Fjord, Jutland (1/1).
(*After Broholm*)

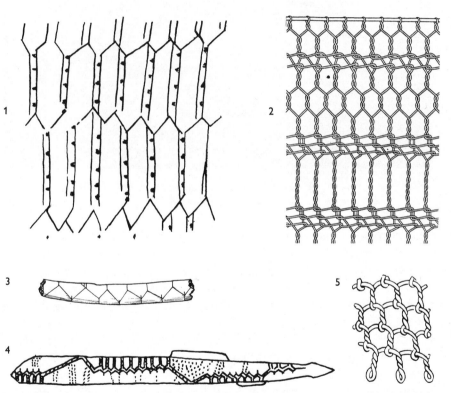

Fig. 31. Hexagonal mesh designs and later representatives of possible prototypes:
(1) engraved on bone 'chisel' from Bohuslän, west Sweden; (2) *sprang* type plait
from Bronze Age burial at Borum, Denmark. (*After Hald*); (3) engraving, Mullerup,
Zealand (early Boreal); (4) engraved on slotted point from Kongemose, Zealand
(early Atlantic); (5) twisted plait of lime bast from Ordrup bog, Denmark (sub-
Boreal).

149

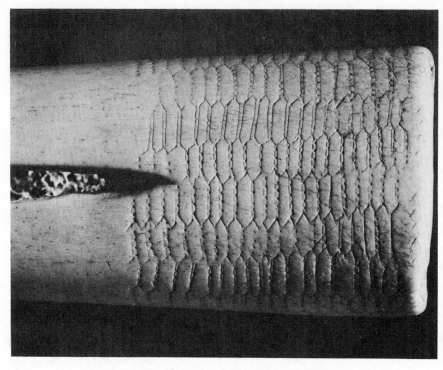

PLATE V. Fine mesh engraved on upper end of bone chisel
from Bohuslän, Sweden (2/1).

more than a hypothesis. Yet it is one worth offering. An imperfect
pattern engraved on a piece of roe deer antler (Fig. 30) from Horsen's
Fjord, Jutland, suggests a knotted net with squarish mesh of the kind
known from this period at Korpilahti in south-east Finland. On the
other hand the other net designs (Fig. 31) of which that engraved on
a socketed bone chisel from Bohuslän, Sweden (Pl. V) is the most
outstanding example, show an elongated hexagonal mesh and recall
much more the kind of knob-less plait-work represented by the hair-net
in the Danish Bronze Age oak-coffin burial from Borum-Eshoj and
comparable with the *sprang* work still surviving in parts of Norway.
A particularly interesting feature of this work is the way the long
strands were strengthened by binding, a feature which seems to be
reproduced in the engraving on the piece from Bohuslän, as well as on
a slotted implement from Kongemose, Denmark. The high antiquity

of this design is shown by the engraving on mammoth tusk from the Palaeolithic site of Elisavichi, U.S.S.R. (Fig. 32). Whether the chequered pattern found most notably (Fig. 33) on the perforated antler object from Kalundborg on Zealand and on a more restricted scale on the needle from Travenort, Schleswig-Holstein, and overlying one of the cervids engraved on the antler mattock head from Ystad (Fig. 35) was suggested by plaiting is rather more speculative, since no work of this kind is so far known from this early period in northern Europe. The earliest record so far documented takes the form of traces of plaited floor-coverings of a simple plain design on the floor of clay huts at the mid-seventh millennium B.C. settlement of Jarmo, Iraq. Tangible traces first appeared in the European records from the early third millennium in the form of impressions on the bases of hand-made pots (Vogt 1937, 6 f.).

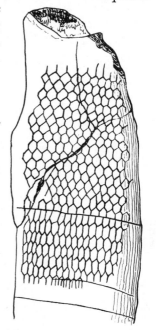

Fig. 32. Hexagonal mesh design engraved on mammoth tusk from Elisavichi in the Desna basin, U.S.S.R.

Engravings of animals are rare. Apart from an enigmatic form on a slotted bone implement from Langeland, they include finely incised fish and serpents from Skalstrup, Zealand, a cervid from Grabowo, Szczecin, Poland, and two finely engraved cervids (Pl. VI; Fig. 34), one incomplete, from Ystad, Scania, all three on perforated mattock-heads made from the bases of red deer stag antlers. In no case do the animal forms share the natural vitality of the best Magdalenian representations and it is perhaps diagnostic that the head of the finest outline, that of the more complete cervid on the Ystad antler, has been incorporated, although in a later phase of engraving, in a chequerboard design.

More or less highly stylised anthropomorphic figures are slightly more numerous (Fig. 35). They appear in each of the three techniques used in this art group and in the case of those executed on antler or bone pieces they are normally accompanied by one or more geometric motifs, most commonly chevrons (r) and barbed lines (e). In many cases the figures are shown individually, even if several are combined

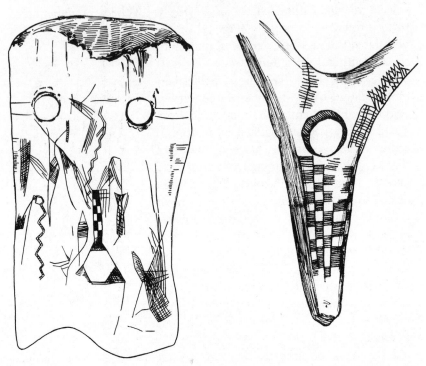

Fig. 33. Perforated red deer antler from Denmark ornamented with chequer and other designs (*left*) Skalstrup, Zealand (5/16). (*right*) Kalundborg, Zealand (1/2).

into an overall net-like design as on the well-known bone piece from Fünen (Clark 1936, fig. 57, no. 5), but in two cases a clear relationship is established between two or more figures. This applies to two figures engraved on the antler from Veksø mose, Zealand, one of whom is depicted as a potent male (no. 3) and even more to the enigmatic scene depicted on an aurochs metapodial from a Zone VI level at Ryemarksgaard, Zealand. This shows five figures and on the right three vertically disposed chevrons (no. 1), the left-hand figure shown frontally or dorsally, jubilant with arms extended, the others, three shown from the side and apparently walking and a fourth seen like the first from front or back, depicted without arms and in more sober mood. Heads are either omitted or represented in the case of amulets by perforations or rendered perfunctorily as triangles or lozenges.

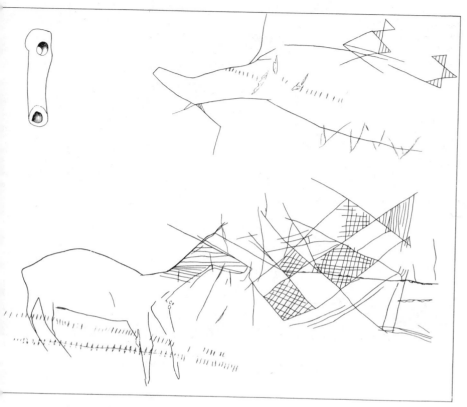

Fig. 34. Three periods of engraving on red deer antler mattock-head
from Ystad, Scania (2/3).

The more frequently used elements in the repertoire of this art group
are widely distributed in south Scandinavia and the territories round
the southern part of the Baltic from north Germany across northern
Poland. This applies both to specialised techniques like pit ornament
and to the main incised motives. To take two examples only, the site
of Hohen Viecheln, near Schwerin, yields antler and bone artifacts
ornamented by examples of the first five groups listed above. Sites
from even further afield in the territory of the state of Poland, as it
existed before the Second World War, also display a number of the
motifs used in south Scandinavia (see Table 10). The early inhabitants
of south Scandinavia and contiguous territories engraved or drilled
the various elements of their repertoire of graphic symbols, whether

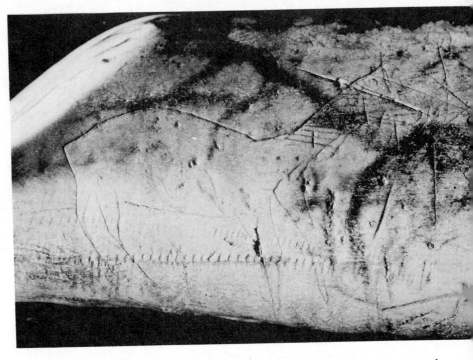

PLATE VI. Outline of red deer and geometric designs finely engraved on stag antler mattock-head from Ystad, Scania, Sweden.

geometric, anthropoid or theriomorphic on most kinds of antler or bone artifact that presented convenient surfaces. Mattock-heads made from the bases of red deer antler were among those most commonly chosen, but perforated bone mattock-heads and picks were also ornamented. Other artifacts of normal use rather commonly chosen were slotted knives and spears, as well as netting needles and chisels and antler or bone handles. A distinct category comprises red deer antler staves as a rule perforated near the base and polished smooth after removal of the tines, which can most probably be interpreted as in a certain sense cult objects. Some of the best-known finds from Jutland have been ornamented by pit-ornament in all-over net-like designs, but it is noteworthy that many antler beam pieces from north Germany and Poland carry rich incised ornament. Perforated amber lumps which could well in some instances have served as amulets also carried orna-

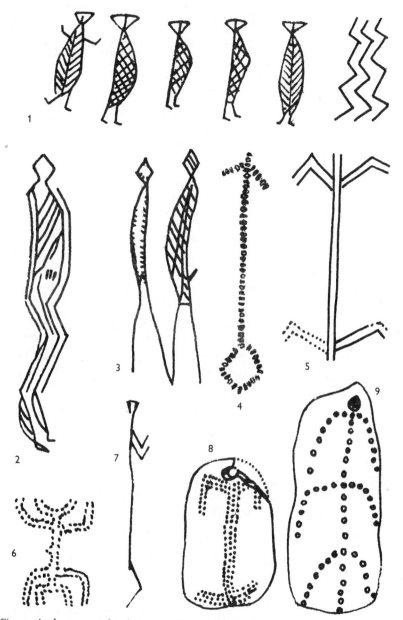

Fig. 35. Anthropomorphic designs on objects of antler, bone and amber from Denmark: (1) Ryemarksgaard, Zealand; (2) Jordlose bog, Zealand; (3) Veksø bog, Zealand; (4) Refsvindinge, Fünen; (5) Stensby, Zealand; (6) Fünen?; (7) Koge Sonakke, Zealand; (8), (9) Denmark.

Table 10. *The occurrence of symbolic designs engraved on Maglemose antler and bone artifacts from Poland (1918–39)*

Motives	Biskupin	Grabowo	Nitki	Ostrołęka	Podjuchy	Woźniki
c	.	.	.	×	.	.
e	.	.	.	.	×	×
g	.	×	.	.	.	.
jı	×	.	.	.	.	.
k	×	.	.	.	×	.
qı	.	.	.	×	.	×
r	.	.	×	.	.	.
x2	.	×	.	×	.	.
y3	.	.	×	.	.	.
Theriomorph	.	×	.	.	.	.
Anthropo-morph	.	.	.	.	×	.

ment, mostly commonly by drilling, but also by incision and including anthropomorphic as well as simple linear patterns.

Close examination of some of the more complex examples shows that in some instances objects have been engraved over periods of time, as Alexander Marshack (1972) has observed in respect of Advanced Palaeolithic examples from the French caves. The antler base mattock-head from Ystad is a case in point (Pl. V; Fig. 35). This appears to have been engraved at two main periods separated, to judge from the worn appearance of the earlier work, either by a longish period of time or by a period during which the object underwent intensive use and handling. During the first period two converging rows of short incisions at right-angles to the main axis and later scored in one case by an irregular line were engraved on a part later overlaid by the sharply incised legs of the more complete cervid and elsewhere a zig-zag line, almost worn away in one instance, was subsequently intersected by the much fresher back-line of the less complete cervid. The finely engraved outlines of the two cervids are so sharp that the mattock-head must have been discarded or deposited in the peat within a comparatively short time: even so two periods of work can be distinguished in this later phase since the head of the more complete animal has been incorporated in an irregular chequer pattern. In connection with the wear observed on the first phase attention may be drawn to the way in which the fine net design on the well-known bone chisel from an

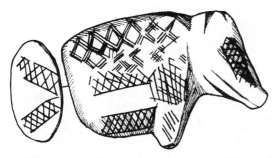

Fig. 36. Animal figure carved from amber, Resen mose, Skive, Jutland (2/3).

unknown locality in Bohuslän has been worn away in places (Pl. V, p. 149). The position of the wear and the smooth polish on the surface of prominent parts suggests that the tool was held in the hand and used vigorously over a period of time, something which recalls Osgood's observation, quoted in connection with our earlier discussion of the use of beaver mandibles as tools, that among the Ingalik Indians favourite tools might be passed from father to son. Another ornamented piece that seems to have been engraved over a period of time is the well-known star-shaped perforated stone club from Bråttjarr farm, Stala parish, Orust Island, Bohuslän. Although a stray find this object may be included in this discussion because it includes elements of several of the commonest designs from this art group (b2, e, f, q1, and r) as well as the mesh pattern. Although the designs incised on the stone surface are difficult to interpret in detail sufficient palimpsests occur to make it plain that not all the work was done at one time: for instance barbed lines (e) can be seen plainly to overlie multiple linear chevrons (r) and elsewhere these chevrons are visible underlying in part multiple transversely shaded bands (j1). The existence of palimpsests and the fact that in the case of the Ystad example there could even have been a considerable interval of time between the two main periods of engraving argues that the engraving was more than merely decorative and was far away from idle 'doodling'. Quite evidently there must have been some symbolic meaning in which people evidently shared in daily life as well perhaps in relation to cult activities.

Although no specimens have yet been recovered from dated contexts there is a strong possibility that certain small amber carvings (Fig. 36) of animals may belong to this art group. These include an elaborate

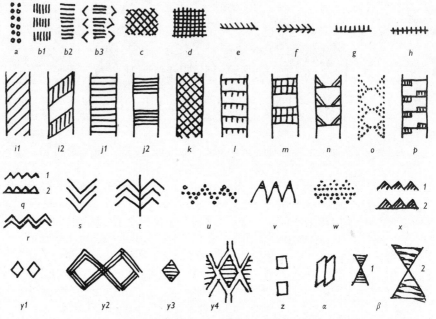

Fig. 37. Geometric designs in the Boreal repertoire of the
west Baltic area. See Appendix D.

carving of an elk's head found during drainage work at Egemarke,
Holbæk, Zealand and evidently designed to be mounted on a model.
Since elk was extinct on this island during Atlantic times this carving
must have been made at an earlier date or alternatively have been
imported. The fine zig-zags (motive q1) engraved on its surface
appeared at Mullerup already in Zone Vb, although it is fair to point out
that it was a favourite motif of ceramic ornament during the middle
Neolithic. An indeterminate figure (bear or wild boar?) from Resen
mose, Jutland, is engraved with a lozenge pattern (y2) again consistent
with a Børeal age. A carving of an aquatic bird in similar style from
Engesvang bog near the Bølling Lake in Jutland, reminds of a significant
component of the food quest.

Enough has been said to indicate that this art group, at any rate
in respect of engravings, forms part of a coherent tradition rooted in
South Scandinavia and the territory immediately west and south of the
Baltic, though stemming from much more ancient Advanced Palaeo-

lithic sources. The chronological boundaries are less easy to define with precision. Analysis of designs engraved on pieces from the Zealand settlements and from other pollen-dated find-spots in Denmark, as well as from Hohen Viecheln, Schwerin, shows that it was already firmly rooted by the latter half of the Boreal and that some elements were certainly older. Thus of the 37 varieties of geometric designs distinguished on Fig. 37, no less than 23 came from deposits firmly dated in respect of pollen-analysis, radiocarbon dating or both, and of the remainder:

7 occur on the same objects (nos. 17, 23, 67 and 79) as dated designs.

3 are executed in pit ornament (no. 10), itself employed at Sværdborg.

2 occur (nos. 1, 61) with the net design already present at Mullerup.

1 occurs on a perforated bone pick (no. 9) of a type dated to Zone VI.

The only design (y4) which cannot be inferred to have been present during at least the late Boreal, either by direct dating or by association with dated designs or implement forms, is in itself merely an elaboration of the shaded lozenge (y3) which occurs on objects with dated designs (e.g. nos. 23 and 84).

On the other hand there is evidence that patterns and techniques used during Boreal times continued in use during the succeeding period. Thus motifs b2, i1, q2 and x2, as well as what may be a schematically drawn flat-fish, were engraved on a perforated antler mattock-head from layer 3 at Ølby Lyng, Zealand, dated by radiocarbon (K 1098 : 4120 ± 130 B.C.) to the latter part of the fifth millennium B.C. There are also indications that pit-ornament had a long life: for instance a bone fragment with rows of pits from layer 3 at Norslund, Jutland, dates from late in the Atlantic period. Another sign of the continued vitality of the art is the appearance of a new style in the context of the Kongemose find dating from the beginning of the Atlantic. More than this, it is a fact that nearly all the motifs employed in the later Stone Age decorative art of Scandinavia as a whole were introduced to the region during its earlier Stone Age.

5

Atlantic settlement in
south Scandinavia

CHRONOLOGICAL FRAMEWORK

The old dichotomy: Maglemose/Ertebølle

During a period of archaeological research still embalmed in many text-books it was common form to contrast, as though they were self-contained, two distinct entities namely the Maglemose and Ertebølle 'cultures', the first corresponding broadly to what was described in the previous chapter of this book, the second finding its classic exposition in the volume summarising the investigations of the second commission appointed to examine the phenomenon of the Danish kitchen-middens (Madsen *et al.* 1900). Among the more evident differences to point the contrast were a number of typological character: microliths abounded in the Maglemose and were virtually absent from Ertebølle sites and conversely with chisel-ended arrowheads; a new form of red deer antler mattock perforated through the stump of a tine to form a socket appeared in the Ertebølle; barbed spearheads of antler or bone, a leading feature of the Maglemose, were absent from Ertebølle sites; and whereas pottery was absent from Maglemose sites it was present in Ertebølle ones in the form of jars with pointed bases and smoothly everted rims and shallow oval vessels interpreted as lamps. In addition topographical and economic considerations have been brought into play: the Maglemose was commonly dubbed an inland 'mere' culture, the Ertebølle a coastal and specifically kitchen-midden or shell-mound culture.

Before discussing the form of economy and land-use practised during Atlantic times in Denmark, it needs first to be emphasised that the equipment recovered from Ertebølle and of other contemporary sites on the Litorina shore of the northern parts of the country reflects only one phase of its Atlantic settlement. This after all is very much what was shown to be true in the last chapter of the assemblage from Mullerup which reflects on the middle phase of a long tradition extending from the Pre-boreal to the close of the Boreal period. And secondly that, as was pointed out long ago (e.g. Clark 1936, 161), there were in reality significant elements in common between Maglemose and Ertebølle assemblages, elements we can now recognise as reflecting an underlying continuity of tradition. In respect of flint-work it was noted that each included axe, adze and pick blades, something after all not so surprising in view of the fact that the Post-glacial inhabitants of south Scandinavia were confronted by an environment dominated by forest trees. This basic fact was not impaired by certain differences for instance that the ratio of flake to core tools was higher in the Ertebølle assemblage, or again that the blades of core adzes and axes tended to be heavier in the later period, something perhaps connected with the change-over from birch and pine to tougher and often thicker deciduous trees. Similarly, the addition of the new socketed form does not detract from the fact that perforated mattock-heads made from red deer antler were common to both. Projectile points slotted in either edge to receive flint insets were another component common to Atlantic and late Boreal assemblages, as also were barbless fish-hooks made of bone.

One way of accounting for similarities of this kind in assemblages of widely differing age would be to infer some degree of historical continuity between them. The most likely way of testing this hypothesis would be to examine the evidence of assemblages of intermediate age and this is precisely what research since 1936 has made it possible to do. When I wrote *The Mesolithic Settlement of Northern Europe* there were already certain clues. The most important of these were provided by Erik Westerby's excavations (1921–3) at the coastal site of Bloksbjerg north of Copenhagen. Deposits containing Ertebølle and younger material (layers A–C) were found to overlie ones (layers D–E) with finds differing equally from those known from Boreal sites; and Westerby was already able to cite (1927) close parallels for these, notably finds made in constructing the Free Harbour at Copenhagen. Westerby's work focused attention on the gap in the archaeological record between Sværdborg and Ertebølle. On the other hand it was a discovery in Quaternary research that first provided a framework into which new finds could be fitted. Johs. Iversen's stratigraphical investigations at Søborg Sø (Fig. 38) and above all his study of fluctuations in the proportions of chenopods and diatoms at this locality demonstrated the highly important fact that the Litorina Sea transgressed the land

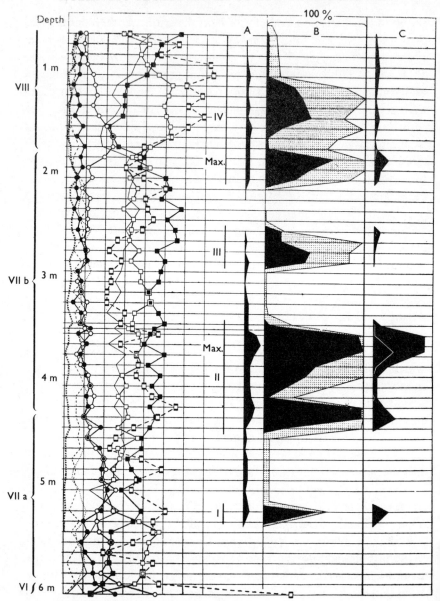

Fig. 38. Diagram illustrating fluctuations in the level of the Litorina Sea as witnessed by changes in the frequencies of salt-demanding organisms in the profile investigated by Iversen at Søborg Sø, Zealand. A. Proportions of Chenopodiaceae pollen in relation to total tree pollen. B. Diatom diagram based on plankton forms: salt-demanding forms in black, neutral in stipple and freshwater open. C. Percentages of salt-demanding Epiphytdiatoms in relation to total Epiphytforms. The percentage of most pronounced salt-demanding forms is shown by a white line.

above modern sea-level on four major occasions, not to mention that two of these were double events marked by minor regressions (Iversen 1937). The crucial significance of this demonstration for archaeology lay in the fact that the Ertebølle middens dated from the third transgression: in other words a period of time comprehending the first and second transgressions intervened between the end of the later Boreal and the Ertebølle material long known to archaeologists. By careful sectioning of foreshore deposits at points occupied by early man therefore the possibility opened up of obtaining a stratigraphic sequence of archaeological levels and thus to establish on a secure basis the relationship if any between Maglemose and Ertebølle phases of settlement.

The existing framework

Denmark. Research was in the meantime bringing forward an increasing body of archaeological material to fill the gap. Already in 1933 Westerby had recorded finds from the important site of Gislinge Lammefjord and in 1938 Vebæk published his investigation of closely similar material from the site of Carstensminde some 130 m out from the eastern shore of Amager Is., south of Copenhagen. The fact that the Carstensminde assemblage was covered by *c*. 3 to 4 m of water at high tide, and compared with finds earlier dredged from the Free Harbour at Copenhagen, as well as in a general way with that from the lower, pre-Ertebølle levels at Bloksbjerg, suggested to Vebæk that it reflected the type of equipment used at the earliest period from which coastal sites are available for study in Zealand. For this reason he assigned such finds to what he termed the Early Coastal Culture, a term which as it turned out helped to delay a correct understanding of their significance.

The first and most ambitious attempt to link different phases of coastal settlement to the several transgressions of the Litorina Sea was made by Therkel Mathiassen (Mathiassen *et al.* 1942) at the site of Dyrholm in north-east Jutland. By observing carefully the precise context of the sequence in shore deposits of materials washed out of or discarded from successful phases of occupation, Mathiassen was able to show that the site was occupied during an early phase of the second or high Atlantic transgression as well as during those of the late Atlantic and Sub-boreal transgressions (Fig. 39). In interpreting his results allowance has to be made for the fact that the refuse layers and more especially those from the second and third transgressions were closely bunched on the landward side: as Troels-Smith (1967, 519) for instance

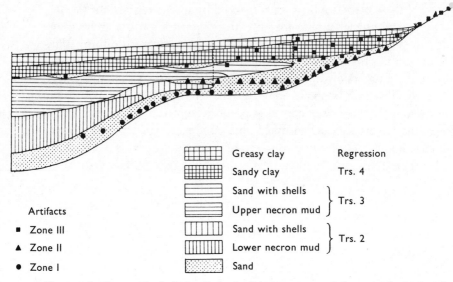

Artifacts

■ Zone III

▲ Zone II

● Zone I

Greasy clay

Sandy clay

Sand with shells

Upper necron mud

Sand with shells

Lower necron mud

Sand

Regression

Trs. 4

} Trs. 3

} Trs. 2

Fig. 39. Section at Dyrholmen, Jutland, showing traces of the second, third and fourth Litorina transgressions in the succession of foreshore deposits.

has pointed out, the handful of sherds from the earliest refuse layer can reasonably be discounted since they occurred exclusively in that part of the section where the earliest refuse layer was directly overlaid by the second which contained pottery in large quantities. This by no means lessens the service performed by Mathiassen in demonstrating for the first time the context of three phases of settlement in the stratigraphic record of Litorina transgressions. In considering the material from Dyrholm I Mathiassen drew attention to parallels at Carstensminde and Gislinge Lammefjord and soon afterwards he was to find yet another in the material from Vedbæk Boldbaner (Mathiassen 1946 b). The remaining gap was finally closed for Zealand by the discovery of an assemblage at Kongemose in Aamosen sealed in peat and mud (*gyttja*) and dating according to pollen-analysis to the close of Zone VI (Jørgensen 1956), a site important not only for its age, but also from the fact that it was situated in a quite definitely inland habitat.

The sequence of stages antecedent to Ertebølle, based in part on the relationship of cultural deposits to successive transgressions of the Litorina Sea and in part on pollen-analyses, is wholly consistent, as will shortly be shown, with the typological development of the associated

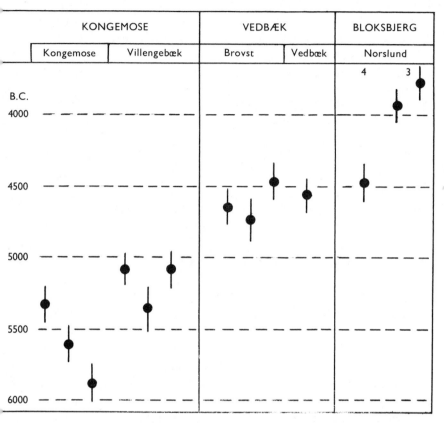

Fig. 40. Table showing radiocarbon ages (years B.C.) of Kongemose, Villengebæk, Vedbæk and Bloksbjerg (D–E) phases of settlement in Zealand.

Kongemose: K 1588, 5330±130; K 1528, 5610±120; K 1526, 5890±140. Villingebæk: K 1369, 5090±120; K 1368, 5330±120; K 1486, 5080±130. Brovst: K 1614, 4640±130; K 1661, 4730±150; K 1660, 4470±130. Vedbæk: K 1303, 4560±110. Norslund: (level 3) K 3780±120; K 3930±120; (level 4) K 4470±130.

cultural material. It has also been confirmed in the most striking manner (Fig. 40) by the application of radiocarbon analysis (Tauber 1971). The sites chosen by Troels-Smith in his masterly summary of the situation published in 1967 – Kongemosen, Vedbæk Boldbaner and Bloksbjerg (D–E) – all happen to be situated on Zealand, but it is highly important to our argument that each stage was equally represented in Jutland, that some can certainly be recognised in south Sweden and that taken together they find an equivalent in the Oldesloe 'culture' of Schleswig-

Holstein. The Jutland sites, like those of Schleswig-Holstein and Scania underline Jørgensen's point that industries of this kind occur equally in the interior as on the coast, a fact which totally invalidates the term Early Coastal Culture applied to them during an earlier phase of research. In respect of the occurrences in the interior of Jutland, it is necessary to begin by discussing Mathiassen's concept set forth in his paper of 1937 of an inland Gudenaa 'culture' rooted in Klosterlund and persisting through the remaining part of early Post-glacial time, finally to run parallel to a coastal Ertebølle 'culture'.

The material dealt with by Mathiassen in his well-known paper was collected by a number of amateur archaeologists from over 360 sites at favourable points mainly at the junctions of rivers and lakes in the Gudenaa catchment area of central Jutland. From their nature – mainly picked up on the surface of cultivated fields – the finds consist almost entirely of flint implements. There was no means of dating them other than typology. And, worse still, the very fact that they came from strategically situated sites means that one can almost assume them to represent mixed assemblages belonging to two, three or more periods of settlement. It is precisely because of this that Mathiassen found it impossible to attribute these Gudenaa assemblages to either Maglemose or Ertebølle groups: sites that yielded microliths for example also produced rhombic and transverse arrowheads; and others with certain Ertebølle features could not be attributed to this group on account of containing microliths or even on account of coming from inland sites. Again, Mathiassen did not fail to observe (1937, 123–4) that material from some Gudenaa sites showed affinities with that from Lammefjord and the lower levels at Bloksbjerg, but here, again, the inventories showed elements quite alien to these: for instance sites 5 (Havstrup Sø) and 117 (Rye Bro) had both 'Maglemose' and 'Ertebølle' components, site 109 (Salten Sø) had 'Maglemose' ones and site 279 (Præstkær) 'Ertebølle' ones, as well as in each case featuring such forms as rhombic and oblique arrowheads.

By treating each surface site as though it was a chronological entity Mathiassen was driven to invent a new 'inland culture' which starting from Klosterlund persisted into Neolithic times. If on the other hand one begins with the assumption that the assemblages from each 'site' are likely to represent mixtures from a series of occupations, then the most economical way of explaining Maglemose, Kongemose/Vedbæk/ Bloksbjerg (D–E) and Ertebølle components is to attribute them to a

Table 11. *Summary of the relation of some key occupation levels in Denmark during Atlantic time and the transition to Sub-boreal time*

C^{14} B.C.	Climate	Litorina transgressions	Zealand	Jutland
3200	Sub-B	4	Barkær; Sølager III Muldbjerg; Sølager II	Dyrholm III
3800	AT (Late)	3	Bloksbjerg (A–c); Sølager I; Ølby Lyng; Kolind III; Benthines Bro, Ø. Jolby Bloksbjerg (D–E)	Ertebølle; Dyrholm II; Norslund 1–2; Hankholm (late) Norslund 3–4; Brovst (upper)
5000	AT (High)	2	Vedbæk Boldbaner; Carstensminde; Gislinge Lammefjord Kongemose; Villinge- bæk	Dyrholm I; Brovst (lower)
5600	AT (Early)	1		Hankholm (middle)
	BO 2			

series of occupations. In this case Jutland would have been occupied by people whose material equipment ran parallel to that used at successive periods of Atlantic time in Zealand. This is precisely what careful stratigraphical excavations in inner Jutland have begun to confirm, notably at the site of Hankholm where Søren Andersen (1971, 23) has successfully established three well defined cultural levels separated by sterile layers and attributable to successive occupations by people whose equipment compares with that known from Maglemose, Kongemose and Ertebølle. Mathiassen's own excavations at Dyrholm, a coastal site at the time of its occupation, had already established an occupation comparable with that at Vedbæk Boldbaner in Zealand and in recent years has revealed at Brovst, Hjørring, north Jutland, one comparable with this same assemblage overlaid by an upper level analogous to Bloksbjerg (D–E). The flint assemblages alone are enough to show that the technology of the Atlantic populations of Jutland and Zealand between them underwent the same broad course of development (Table 11). Owing to the character of most of the key sites much less is known of the organic component of the technology of the inhabitants of Jutland at this time, but it is significant that slotted bone points came from the Kongemose level at Hankholm, from Kolindsund, and from the Bloksbjerg (D–E) level at Norslund (3). In the same connection it is worth citing the ornamented two-edged slotted bone knife handle from the basal layer at Flynderhage (Andersen, S. 1969).

Schleswig-Holstein. Parallels to the phases of settlement that intervened and established continuity between the late Maglemose and Ertebølle in Denmark may be found in Schleswig-Holstein to the south, and to the east in Scania. Research on this topic in the former region is still extremely backward. The so-called 'Oldesloe stage or culture' compares rather closely with the now generally discarded 'Gudenaa culture' of Jutland with which it forms a geographical continuity: evidence for it was gathered by collectors from the surface of low eminences along the course of the River Trave; it is confined to lithic material; and this material exhibits a mixture of types which can at least as readily be explained in terms of admixture from a number of phases of occupation as by hypothesising a highly catholic 'culture'. What is certain is that several sites have yielded rhombic arrowheads of a type current in Denmark during the Kongemose and Vedbæk phases but which had passed out of use by the time of the lower occupation at Bloksbjerg: among examples witnessed by illustrations in Schwabedissen's book of 1944 may be cited: Oldesloe, Naherfuhrt and Grande 1, all in Kr. Stormarn, and in addition Satrup in Schleswig-Holstein Kr. Another point worth emphasising is that the Schleswig-Holstein sites were exclusively in the interior, linked with inland waterways.

Scania. If the situation in Scania is already rather more rewarding, this is due in very large measure to the highly original and creative researches undertaken by Carl-Axel Althin (1954). Notable advances in Danish prehistory and not least those resulting from systematic application of radiocarbon analysis have modified the cogency of some of Althin's comparisons. The fact remains that he was among the first to appreciate that collections from sites of the so-called 'Gudenaa culture' were in reality mixed assemblages, the product of visits over long periods of time. He fully realised the need to establish an independent Scanian sequence (see Table 12).

Here, again, the presence of rhombic arrowheads provided a useful clue. When they first appeared in the upper peat at Agerød I, they were

Table 12. *Approximate synchronisation of Scanian and Danish phases of settlement during Atlantic times*

Althin's periods	Scanian assemblages	Danish periodisation
IIId	Elinelund, Malmö sn., site 6	Ertebølle
IIIb	Agerød, Munkarp sn., site V	Bloksbjerg (D–E)
IIIa	Häljarp, Tofta sn.	Vedbæk Boldbaner
IId	Agerød, Munkarp sn., site I: HC (upper peat)	Kongemose

still accompanied by a few microliths of late Maglemose character. On the other hand Layer 4a at Häljarp, which Taage Nilsson has equated (1967a) with the first Litorina transgression in Scania, yielded flints which Althin considered to be 'absolutely identical' to those from Cartensminde: they included a very high proportion of core to flake axes (20:1), micro-blades of the kind used for insetting slotted bone forms and accompanying handle-cores, end of blade scrapers and burins, and a long series (37 and 6 rough-outs) of rhombic arrowheads; and no microliths of Sværdborg type. In Agerød V rhombic arrowheads were greatly outnumbered by transverse ones, including a number with oblique edge. Finally, in the Elinelund site Althin was able to point to an assemblage in which arrowheads were exclusively of the transverse chisel variety, in which flake axes slightly outnumbered core ones and in which polished stone axes of Limhamn type and sherds of Ertebølle type were present.

Althin's investigation of the Scanian finds not only confirms the validity of the developmental sequence then in course of being established in Denmark. It was no less important for showing, in conjunction with results obtained in Jutland and Schleswig-Holstein, the true geographical context of the sites. Although Althin continued in his book to use the term Early Coastal Culture, he saw clearly enough that finds from the Atlantic period occurred just as much on rivers and lakes in the interior as in the coastal tract. Indeed if one concentrates on sites with rhombic arrowheads (Althin 1954, nos. 62, 152, 187, 193, 221 and 222) and excludes those lacking them (no. 61, 64), the distribution is even more markedly inland in south Scandinavia and Schleswig-Holstein (Map 11). Before discussing the question of continuity and change in the

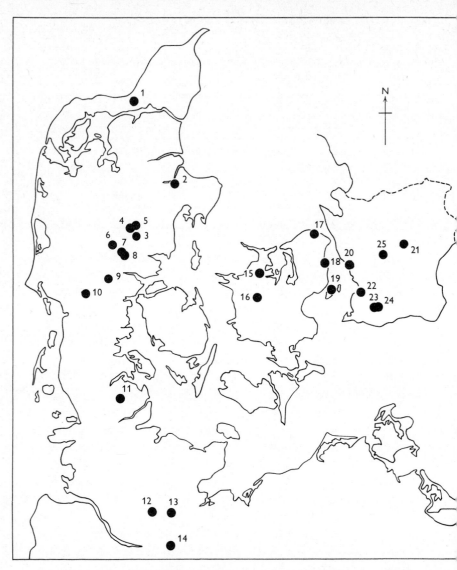

11. Map showing sites with rhombic arrowheads in south Scandinavia and Schleswig-Holstein.

Find-spots:

1, Brovst; 2, Dyrholm; 3, Hankholm; 4, Salten Sø; 5, Rye Bro; 6, Vester Mølle; 7, Havstrup; 8, Melhede; 9, Bindeballe/Lille Refsgaard; 10, Præstkær; 11, Satrup; 12, Naherfuhrt; 13, Oldesloe; 14, Grande; 15, Gislinge Lammefjord; 16, Konge-mose; 17, Villingebæk; 18, Vedbæk; 19, Carstensminde; 20, Häljarp, Tofta; 21, Store Mossen, Häglinge; 22, Malmø; 23, Svedala, site 4; 24, Bastanäbbet, Svedala; 25, Agerød V. Munkarp.

Sources: Althin, 1954; Andersen, S. (in letter); Berthelsen, 1944; Jørgensen, 1956; Kapel, 1969; Mathiassen, 1946; Troels-Smith, 1967; Vebæk, 1938.

material equipment of the people occupying south Scandinavia during the Atlantic time a word may be said on the implications of the relevant radiocarbon dates (Tauber 1971). The main point to emphasise is that these validate in a highly convincing manner the sequence established by other means (Fig. 40). Second and more specifically the dates obtained for the first phase are of particular importance for the relationship of Kongemose and Sværdborg. In the original publication Jørgensen argued (1956, 511) on the basis of pollen-analysis that Kongemose was contemporary with Sværdborg, a conclusion which would involve the existence in a very restricted area of two distinct 'cultures'. But radiocarbon analysis allows of greater precision in dating and leaves no doubt that, wherever the botanists decide to draw the line between Zones VI and VII, the phase of settlement represented by Kongemose is younger than that represented by Sværdborg.

TECHNOLOGY: CONTINUITY AND CHANGE

Sværdborg–Bloksbjerg (Fig. 41)

Among the many features indicating continuity between the Maglemose cycle and that of Kongemose and succeeding phases of settlement the following may be mentioned: the common presence of core axes and adzes and of 'flake axes' and the continuing predominance until the Ertebølle stage of the former; the continuance of the microlithic points and barbs, though only into the initial phase; the persistence down to the penultimate phase of slotted bone equipment and down to the end of burins, end scrapers, mattocks made from the basal ends of stag antlers, and elementary geometric symbols (see p. 159).

Slotted equipment. From among these something special needs to be said of the slotted bone equipment which played a role of particular importance during early Atlantic time. One form taken by this was the knife handle made from split metatarsal bones of red deer, slotted on either edge to receive flint bladelets held secure in resin (Fig. 42). Many of these are stray finds, but a good example appeared in the lower level at Bloksbjerg and a specimen from Monbjerg, Jutland, is ornamented in the style well known from Carstensminde. The other class of artifact to employ this method of sharpening the edge were projectile heads of two main classes (Fig. 43), one flat-sectioned with triangular to

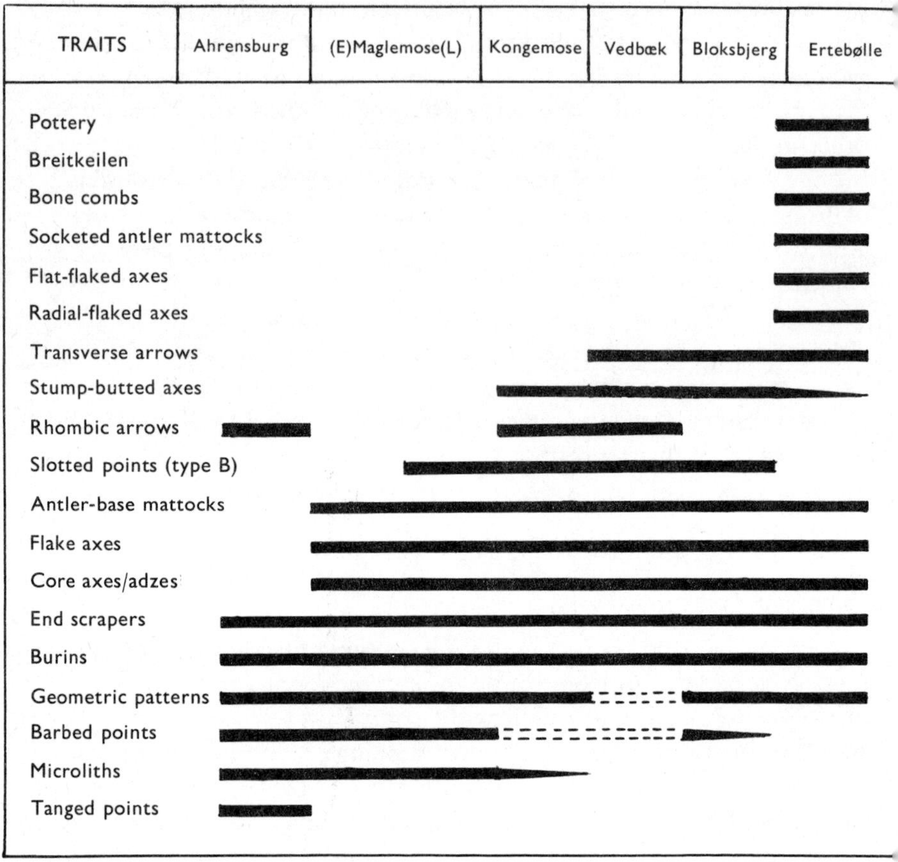

TRAITS	Ahrensburg	(E)Maglemose(L)	Kongemose	Vedbæk	Bloksbjerg	Ertebølle
Pottery						
Breitkeilen						
Bone combs						
Socketed antler mattocks						
Flat-flaked axes						
Radial-flaked axes						
Transverse arrows						
Stump-butted axes						
Rhombic arrows						
Slotted points (type B)						
Antler-base mattocks						
Flake axes						
Core axes/adzes						
End scrapers						
Burins						
Geometric patterns						
Barbed points						
Microliths						
Tanged points						

Fig. 41. Diagram illustrating the duration of certain material culture traits in Denmark from Late-glacial to the end of Atlantic times.

lozenge-shaped head, the other narrower and tending to have a more pointed head, the former commonly decorated, the latter plain. The first class, as we know from its occurrence at Mullerup, had already appeared in early Boreal, but it persisted until early Atlantic times at Kongemose. In Scania it occurs in the lower level at Sjöholmen (Thomas 1954), which must certainly overlap with Vedbæk Boldbaner, and in a less closely dated collection of finds from Råbelövssjön. The second is known in several forms as Lidén already showed (1942):

Type A. Points more or less cylindrical in section and symmetrically tapered at either end. These might be slotted on both edges (A1)

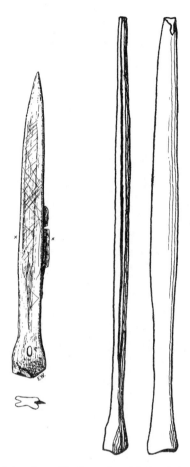

Fig. 42. Bone knife handles with flint micro-blades set in slots to give sharp
edges. (*left*) Bloksbjerg (D) Zealand; (*right*) Monbjerg, Jutland. (1/2)

or only on one (A2). No example has yet been found hafted, but
being pointed at either end it looks as though they were intended to
fit into a socket in the forepart of a shaft and traces of the resin used
to set them more firmly frequently appears at one end. Whether the
shafts were propelled by bows or dart-throwers will only be determined when complete shafts are found. The type seems to have
appeared for the first time in the west Baltic region in the Lower
and Upper Peats at Agerød: HC, Scania, which dates from the later
Boreal.

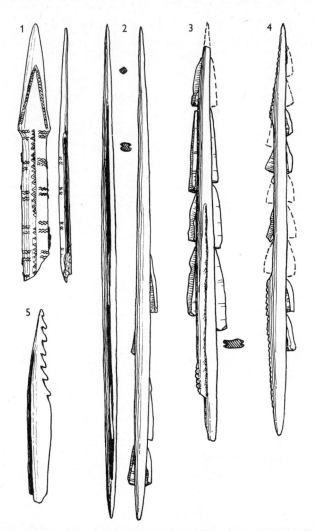

Fig. 43. Bone projectile heads inset with micro-blades of flint. (1) Flat form with decoration: Mullerup. (2) Narrow form, class A (Agerød class): South Scania. (3) Ditto, class B 1 (Sværdborg class): Scania. (4) Ditto, class B 2 (Bussjö class): Bussjö. (5) Ditto, class B 3 (Kunda class): Kunda. (1/2)

Type B. Points rather flatter in section and provided with notches or barbs. In B1, named after Sværdborg from its occurrence on that later Boreal site, the notches are confined to the lower end and *pace* Lidén may have been designed merely to engage the thread used to secure the head to its shaft. In B2 on the other hand the fine barbs appear on the forepart as well as on a more extended zone of the lower part and were pretty clearly relevant to the function of the weapon-head. A find of about thirty examples of this type, named after the Scanian find-spot of Bussjö, from Åmossen, Slågarp sn., also in Scania, has also been dated on the basis of pollen-analysis to the later Boreal (Nilsson, T. 1935, 531). A third type B3, named after the Esthonian site of Kunda (see p. 225), and known from the site of Alby on Öland has rather prominent barbs on one edge of the forepart, helping to confirm Lidén's insight that types B2 and B3 at least combine two concepts, those of slotting and barbing.

It has sometimes been claimed that the idea of slotting bone knife-handles and projectile-heads and insetting plain flint bladelets to sharpen them was a specifically north European invention of the Post-glacial period on the ground that this device appears to be absent from the rich repertoire of bone work in the Magdalenian. Yet, as Westerby long ago pointed out (1927, 113), it was deeply embedded in the Advanced Palaeolithic tradition established in Russia from the Ukraine to Siberia. Publication of more finds from the Soviet Union has made it even plainer that it was used both for knife handles and for projectile heads much earlier in these territories than it was in northern Europe: to quote only a few instances, slotted bone equipment is known from Advanced Palaeolithic deposits from Molodova V on the Dniester,[*] from Afontova Gora II on the Yenisei[†] and from Oshurkovo in Trans-Baikal.[‡] This suggests as a working hypothesis that the device was derived by the early Post-glacial inhabitants of northern Europe from the east. The fact that it appeared during Post-glacial times over a broad tract of the north European plain from Jutland to Esthonia argues that it was taken over on a broad front.

A concomitant of slotted equipment, more especially in respect of the delicate projectile heads, was the production of thin narrow micro-blades made so regularly that they could be inset without the need for secondary retouch. This in turn is reflected in the flint cores found in archaeological sites. Narrow micro-blades of the kind required for this purpose, as well as for the delicate elongated microliths with secondary

---

[*] Chernysh 1961, fig. 28, 8 and fig. 29.
[†] Auerbakh and Sosnovskij 1932, p. x, 5, 6.
[‡] Okladnikov, 'The Palaeolithic of Trans-Baikal', *American Antiquity* 26 (1961), 490, fig. 4a.

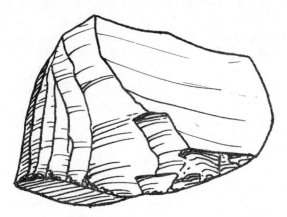

Fig. 44. Flint handle-core showing scars of micro-blades (1/1).

retouch characteristic of the later Maglemose tradition in Denmark, could be obtained during the final stages in the reduction of cores to conical form. Even more control could be exercised by the flint-worker when he was able to obtain a secure grip on the core and direct his technique to one end, something which could most easily be done by removing the microflakes from one end of what is often termed a handle-core, a type which first came into common use in the later-Boreal as at Holmegaard and Sværdborg, but which continued during much of Atlantic time down to the Bloksbjerg phase (Fig. 44).

Flint axes and adzes. One of the main threads of continuity is provided by the core axes and adzes and the side-blow flakes which beginning in the Pre-boreal lasted down into Sub-boreal times when they were replaced by polished flint and stone forms. Although the core tools tended to increase in size and regularity, no decisive change in the mode of production of either group occurred until the Ertebølle phase. Similarly the proportions of core and side-blow flake tools remained within much the same range down till this time (Fig. 45).

Stump-butted pecked stone axes (Fig. 46). A form which appeared for the first time in Denmark during the Kongemose phase was the stump-butted stone axe with more or less circular section, pecked into shape and ground to a smooth edge. Since Denmark was exceptionally well provided with flint, the appearance of this novel feature, which signi-

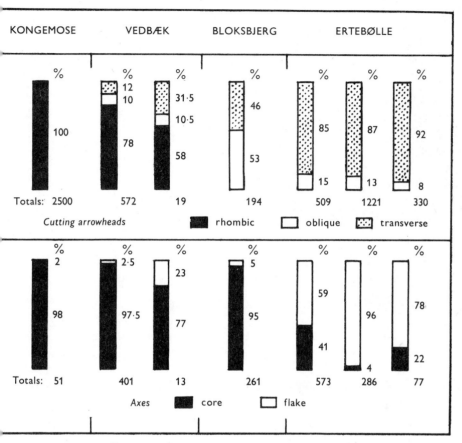

KONGEMOSE   VEDBÆK   BLOKSBJERG   ERTEBØLLE

Fig. 45. Diagram illustrating changes in proportions of different forms of cutting arrow and flint axe during Atlantic time. [Note. The Vedbæk samples are in each case respectively from left to right from Vedbæk Boldbaner and Brovst (2 and 11) and the Ertebølle ones from Ertebølle, Vester Ulslev and Ølby Lyng.]

ficantly had only a short life there, calls for some explanation. The most likely hypothesis is that it was adopted temporarily as a result of contact with a region nearer the Scandinavian shield, where stone was the native material normally used for axes. One does not have to look further afield than Scania and Bohuslän for immediate sources. At Agerød 1: HC pecked stone axes of this type were already being used in later Boreal times (Althin 1954, Pl. 12, 1 and Pl. 14, 1) alongside tools made from the flint so readily available in Scania. Further north on the Swedish west coast similar axes are known from an assemblage

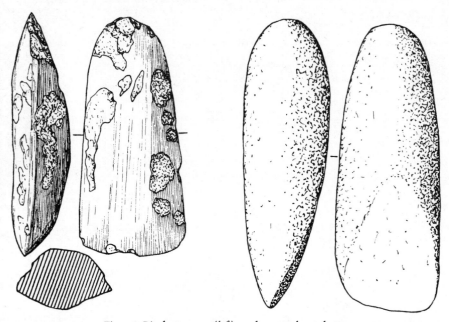

Fig. 46. Limhamn axe (*left*), and stump-butted axe
(*trindokse, trindyxa, Walzenbeil*) (*right*) (1/2), (3/4).

of basically Maglemose lithic character at Sandarna near Göteborg
(Alin, Niklasson and Thomasson 1934, fig. 29). Here again one may
invoke contact with the Scandinavian shield, contact which was first
made possible as isostatic recovery opened up access to the interior.

Rhombic and transverse arrowheads (Fig. 47). More striking because more
fundamental and quantitatively much more significant was the change
in the flint components of arrows. In place of tipping and barbing by
means of microliths which in late-Boreal times at sites like Holmegaard
and Sværdborg had developed into delicate elongated forms, we find
varieties of cutting arrows made from sections of large regular blades
struck from block cores. In a sense this change was part and parcel of
a broad technical change from the use of flakes and micro-blades to true
blades for a variety of tools other than axes and adzes; from the
Kongemose phase down to and including the Ertebølle we find not
merely cutting arrows made from sections of blades, but such common
forms as scrapers, burins and awls made on the ends of blades so regular

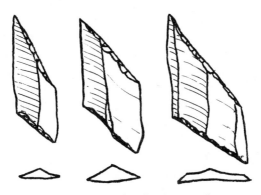

Fig. 47. Flint arrowheads of rhombic form, Häljarp, Scania (1/1).

and symmetrical as to recall the blade and burin industries of the Late-glacial period. It is logical therefore to discuss the change in arrowheads and in the underlying lithic technology in terms of a reversion to the style of flint-work prevailing during that time. Before entering into a historical discussion it is worth emphasising the functional connection between cutting arrowheads and the production of broad blades with regular flake scars. One might take the position that it was the change in arrowhead type from a piercing to a cutting variety that precipitated a reversion to the production of regular blades. In this connection it needs to be remembered that even microlithic arrow-armatures depended for their effect partly on cutting and partly on penetrating and there is no inherent improbability in the possibility of fashion swinging from emphasis on one or the other. On the other hand the view might be taken that the most important change was a reversion to an advanced blade technique and that the production of flake arrows made from sections of regular blades was facilitated by this. In any case the two go together and unless we suppose the changes to have been spontaneous it is natural to look to some external stimulus.

Could it be that the Atlantic blade tradition stemmed ultimately from that prevailing in south Scandinavia and adjacent parts of Germany during the Late-glacial? Therkel Mathiassen (1946a, 196–7) argued in so many words that such a connection existed and even that rhombic arrowheads might well have developed from tanged points of Ahrensburg type. In fact, as shown earlier in the present work (Fig. 5), rhombic arrowheads were already present alongside tanged points in some Late-glacial sites, notably at Stellmoor in Schleswig-Holstein. Typologically the link between the two is impressive. Yet as the present writer noted long ago (1936, 145), the blade component even of the Ertebølle phase resembled the intervening lithic industries of Pre-boreal and Boreal age; and the point was developed earlier in the present work (p. 99) that there was a marked break in continuity brought about by the disintegration of the Late-glacial environment. One way of reconciling these facts would be to suppose that continuity was nevertheless maintained in the coastal territories submerged in the course of early Post-glacial times by the eustatic rise of sea-level. So long as it was held that a marked dichotomy existed between inland and coastal 'cultures' this hypothesis might well have seemed plausible, even if incapable of verification. Today, when, as argued earlier in this chapter (p. 166), we no longer have a right to attach the term Early Coastal Culture to the early Atlantic settlement of Denmark or to treat the Sværdborg and Kongemose sites as if they were contemporary, this no longer applies. The alternative is to consider a territory through which the Later-glacial reindeer hunters withdrew at the time when ecological zones underwent their northward shift and where as a result their lithic traditions might be expected to have survived into the Post-glacial era, namely the east coast of the northern part of the Kattegat or further north in the Norwegian Østfold (cf. Freundt 1938). The hypothesis that the stimulus for a resumption of the Late-glacial mode of blade production and of the use of four-sided and in particular of rhombic arrowheads that stemmed ultimately from tanged points may have come from an area of survival on the northern periphery fits in well with the idea that the temporary adoption of the pecked stone axe was inspired by contact with the Scandinavian shield.

Although the rhombic arrowhead itself does not seem to have outlasted the Vedbæk stage in Denmark, the use of the cutting arrow made from sections of regular blades lasted down to the period of the middle Neolithic. In the course of time it passed through a number of phases of development (Fig. 45). Already during the Vedbæk stage one begins to find arrowheads with oblique or transverse cutting edges and by the Bloksbjerg phase these account for the total production of cutting arrows. Again, as between oblique and strictly transverse arrowheads it is noteworthy that whereas in the Vedbæk and Bloksbjerg phases the former existed in a ratio of from around one in three to around one half, during the Ertebølle phase it had sunk to around one in ten.

Table 13. *The range in the relative proportion of core and flake 'axes' in Danish Ertebølle assemblages*

	Core	Flake	Sample
Bloksbjerg (A–C)	163 (66%)	84 (34%)	247
Ertebølle	236 (41%)	337 (59%)	573
Klintesø	37 (19%)	158 (81%)	195
Dyrholm II	93 (14%)	571 (86%)	664
Brabrand	49 (9%)	467 (91%)	516
Vester Ulslev	11 (4%)	275 (96%)	286

Bloksbjerg (D–E) *to Ertebølle*

Many of the basic components of the tool-kit of the inhabitants of Denmark and Schleswig-Holstein remained the same from the beginning of the Post-glacial settlement. These include flint axes and adzes of core type, side-blow flake axes, end-scrapers and burins and mattock-heads made from the bases of red-deer antler. The persistence of the groove and splinter technique down to this period, as witnessed by finds in the Satrup bog, Schleswig-Holstein (Schwabedissen 1958, Abb. 10) is a further noteworthy instance of continuity. On the other hand some of the basic components underwent significant changes and some entirely new ones were added. Indeed as our diagram (Fig. 41) brings out the interface between the Bloksbjerg and Ertebølle phases was notably more sharply defined than any other of Atlantic time. Before discussing the meaning of this something may be said about changes in forms which continued.

Flint work. Two changes may be noted in respect of heavy equipment. On one hand the proportions in which core and side-blow flake axes occurred underwent a marked change. The tendency was for flake axes, once of subsidiary importance, to predominate markedly over core axes and adzes (Table 13), even though at particular sites this was nothing like so marked: at Ertebølle itself core axes and adzes continued to amount to two-fifths and at Bloksbjerg (A–C) even to two-thirds of the total, whereas at Dyrholm II they only accounted for 14%, at Brabrand 9% and at Vester Ulslev only 4%. A second feature which separated the Ertebølle assemblage from previous ones was the appearance of secondary flaking to improve the appearance of the two main types.

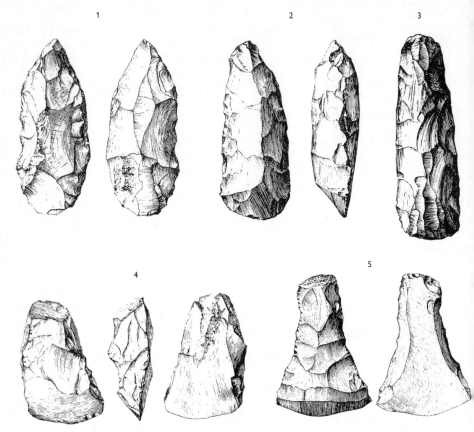

Fig. 48. Core adzes and pick and side-blow flake 'axes' of flint: (1), (4) core pick and flake axe: Sværdborg (late Boreal); (2) core-adze: Kvistrup, Øsby; (3) core-adze with radial flaking: Hallebygaard (late Atlantic); (5) side-blow flake 'axe' with flat flaking: Godsted (late Atlantic). (4/11)

In the case of core-tools this took the form of radial flaking from the cutting-edge, and in that of flake axes of flat-flaking on one face (Fig. 48). Again, the proportions in which the three main forms of cutting arrows occurred had been undergoing progressive change in the course of Atlantic time, but the Ertebølle phase witnessed a particularly sharp change when transverse arrowheads rose to overwhelming predominance. Meanwhile, as the very existence of this type of arrow-head implied, skill in the production of regular blades with more or less parallel flake scars (Fig. 49), a skill reintroduced into or revived in

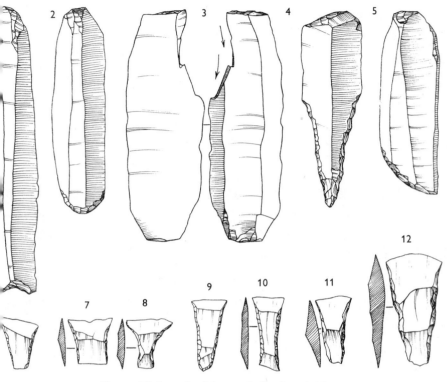

Fig. 49. Blade tools of the Ertebølle phase (2/3).

south Scandinavia at the onset of Atlantic time, continued unabated as it did through the ensuing millennium.

Antler and bone work. Although the old type of perforated mattock-head made from the base of a stag antler persisted, a new form came into use made from a section mid-way up the antler and perforated through the stump of the trez tine which formed a useful socket for the handle (Fig. 50). A significant feature of this socketed type of mattock-head is that it is found widely distributed on the north European plain in the context of pottery-using peasant communities from the Omalian, the Belgian version of the Danubian, to the Funnel-neck Beaker using groups of south Poland and the Danubian peasants on the Dnestr. Other innovations included bracelets cut from discs removed from shoulder-blades, and small toothed combs.

183

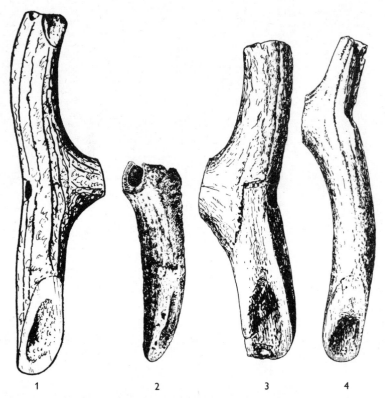

Fig. 50. Socketed mattock-heads of red deer antler from Ertebølle, Omalian and Jordansmühl contexts. (1) Kolding Fjord, Jutland. (*After Danmarks Oldsager*, I.) (2) Place Saint-Lambert, Liège. (*After Hamal-Nandrin.*) (3), (4) Graves xxxiv and xxxii, Brzesc Kujawski, Poland. (*After Jadżewski.*) (1/3)

Pottery (Pl. VII and Map 12). The most radical and significant innovation in the field of material culture was undoubtedly pottery. The ware named after the Ertebølle midden took two main forms that were frequently found together, namely large vessels with pointed base, swollen body, and lightly everted rim, which could have been used as in Ghana for boiling shell-fish (Noe-Nygaard 1967), and smaller shallow oval vessels commonly interpreted as lamps. The large jars, which like the lamps were thick-walled, were built up by the coil technique and the outer surface was sometimes smoothed by rubbing with flat pebbles. Decoration was confined to oblique or transverse impressions on the top of the rim. There can be no question that this

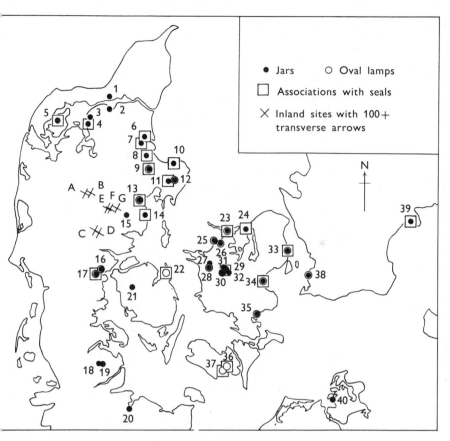

12. Map showing distribution of Ertebølle ware in south Scandinavia and north Germany.

Find-spots: 1, Brovst; 2, Sebber; 3, Bjørnsholm; 4, Ertebølle; 5, Benthines Bro; 6, Havnø; 7, Aamølle; 8, Gjessinggaard; 9, Dyrholm; 10, Meilgaard; 11, Kolind; 12, Nederst; 13, Brabrand Sø; 14, Norslund; 15, Skanderborg; 16, Gudsø Vig; 17, Kolding Fjord; 18, Werschau; 19, Rüder moor; 20, Ellerbek; 21, Assenbølle Mose; 22, Langø; 23, Klintesø; 24, Sølager; 25, Ordrup Næs; 26, Faareveille; 27, Drøsselholm; 28, Hallebygaard; 29, Øgaarde; 30, Magleø; 41, Kildegaard; 32, Tingbjerggaard; 33, Bloksbjerg; 34, Ølby Lyng; 35, Strandegaard; 36, Godsted; 37, Vester Ulslev; 38, Limhamn, Järavallen; 39, Siretorp; 40, Jasmund Bodden, Lietzow.

Sources: Andersen, S. and Malmros 1965; Andersen, S. 1969a; Bagge and Kjellmark 1939; Becker 1939; Kjellmark 1905; Madsen et al. 1900; Mathiassen 1935, 1942 and 1943; Nykjøbing Mus.; Petersen 1971; Schwabedissen 1966; Schwantes 1939; Westerby 1927.

NOTE. Flint assemblages with many transverse arrows from: A, Skygge; B, Klosterlund; C, Havstrup; D, Melhede; E, Salten Sø; F, Rye Bro; G, Siimholm (Mathiassen 1937).

185

form of pottery is an integral part of Ertebølle equipment. It is known from a substantial number of sites in Denmark, as well as from a smaller number in Schleswig-Holstein and Scania. The extreme care taken during the excavation of the original Ertebølle midden with respect to the location of sherds leaves no doubt about its stratigraphic position: sherds occurred in 635 locations at all levels but were notably scarce in layer 1, rather more frequent in layer 2, only becoming abundant in layers 3 and 4 and continuing down to the bottom. The fact that sherds like worked flints diminished sharply in the basal layers is explained by the fact that the midden occupied a progressively larger area in the course of time. The point has been emphasised because the Ertebølle midden has been investigated with particular care for radiocarbon dating. The results at the same site (Fig. 51) show that the bottom five or six 20 cm spits containing the mass of the sherds date from between 3,600 to 3,800 B.C.; and results from other radiocarbon-dated sites with Ertebølle–Ellerbek pottery from Denmark and Schleswig-Holstein confirm that this pottery spanned the greater part of the fourth millennium B.C. In other words it overlapped broadly with the Rössen phase of the Danubian peasant culture which extended from the Rhineland to the Lower Oder.

Perforated stone axe blades (Fig. 52). Another novel feature to appear at this time in south Scandinavia and Schleswig-Holstein is the heavy perforated stone tool of broadly 'Danubian' aspect, first effectively recognised by Glob (1939: cf. Lomborg 1962; Schwabedissen 1966). Two leading forms may be singled out for discussion, namely the perforated shoe-last celt (*durchbohrte Schuhleistenkeil*) of D-shaped section and the flat-faced axe of subtriangular form perforated in line with the working edge (*Breitkeil*). A few isolated examples of the former penetrated Schleswig-Holstein, but since the only specimen at Copenhagen has no provenance it remains uncertain whether the type also reached Denmark in prehistoric times. The *Breitkeil* on the other hand, a type at home in the Rössen and Stichband manifestations of the Danubian tradition, evidently came into widespread use in Schleswig-Holstein, Jutland, the main Danish islands and Scania. In the case of so elementary a form it would be hazardous to set an upper limit to its

PLATE VII. Ertebølle pottery from Denmark. (*upper*) Milled rim sherds, body of large jar and pointed bases from Ertebølle. (*lower*) Oval lamp from Gudsø Vig. (1/3)

187

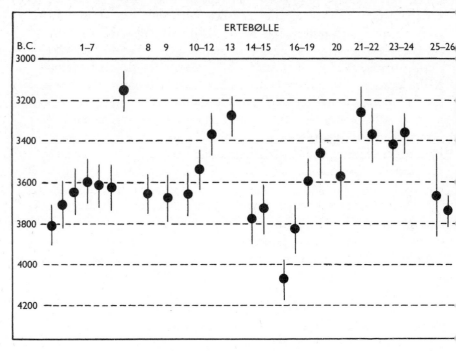

Fig. 51. Radiocarbon dates for Ertbølle–Ellerbek assemblages:

Jutland

Ertebølle, Ålborg   (above o.g.s.)
(7) *K 1535: 3160±100 (125–7 cm)
(6) K 1534: 3630±110 (102–4 cm)
(5) K 1533: 3620±110 (84–5 cm)
(4) K 1532: 3600±110 (67–8 cm)
(3) K 1531: 3650±120 (44–5 cm)
(2) K 1530: 3710±120 (22–3 cm)
(1) *K 1529: 3810±100 (5–7 cm)
Brovst, Hjørring
(8) *K 1613: 3660±100 (upper level)
Haldrup Strand, Skanderborg
(9) K 1612: 3690±120
Ringkloster, Skanderborg
(10) K 1654: 4470±100 (upper)
(11) K 1653: 3540±100 (middle)
(12) K 1652: 3660±110 (lower)
Flynderhage, Århus
(13) *K 1450: 3280±100
Norslund, Århus
(14) K 990: 3780±120
(15) K 991: 3730±120

Zealand

Salpetermosen, Frederiksborg
(16) K 1235: 3460±120
(17) K 1234: 3830±120
(18) *K 1233: 4070±100
(19) K 1232: 3600±120
Sølager, Frederiksborg
(20) K 1723: 3570±110
Ølby Lyng, Højelese,
Copenhagen
(21) K 1231: 3370±130
(22) K 1230: 3260±130
Christiansholms mose,
Copenhagen
(23) K 729: 3350±100
(24) K 750: 3420±100
        Schleswig–Holstein
Rüde
(25) Y 441a: 3670±200
(26) Y 160: 3740±70
Ellerbek
(27) Y 440: 4110±200

★ Average of two runs.

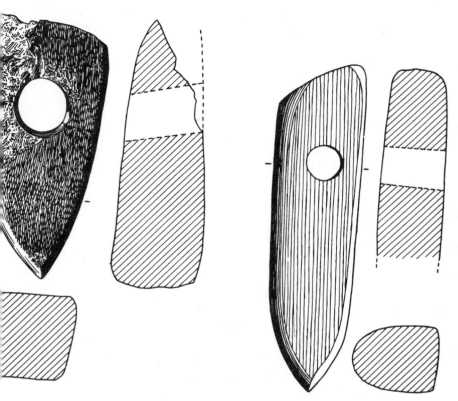

Fig. 52. Perforated stone blades of Danubian type from Schleswig-Holstein. (*After Sangmeister*). (*left*) *Breitkeil*; (*right*) perforated shoe-last adze blade (1/2).

period of use. On the other hand there seems no good reason for doubting that it first appeared in an Ertebølle–Ellerbek context: the fragment recovered by Glob in an Ertebølle context at Vester Ulslev, Lolland, has since been confirmed by the find on Forstermoor, Satrup, held by Schwabedissen to be the type-station of his Ellerbek stage in Schleswig-Holstein.

SUBSISTENCE

Territory. A point which needs emphasising as an antidote to notions embedded in the early literature is that it is becoming increasingly clear that the inhabitants of south Scandinavia during Atlantic times exploited the resources of the interior as well as of the coast. The earlier notion

189

that settlement was concentrated on the coast at this time stemmed from the circumstances of discovery. The shell-mounds or kitchen-middens, which as we now recognise date from the third and fourth transgressions of the Litorina Sea, were in fact the first traces of human settlement other than funerary monuments and stray finds to receive systematic treatment by Danish archaeologists. The stately publication *Affaldsdynger* which enshrined the labours of the second commission for the study of the kitchen-middens remained for a time the only repository of information about the human settlement of Denmark during the Atlantic period. Again, when Westerby and Vebæk began the process of unveiling earlier phases of Atlantic settlement, they concentrated on sites which happened to be situated on the coast of Zealand, so that the Ertebølle or kitchen-midden phase of settlement was visualised as the successor of a newly recognised Early Coastal Culture.

As we have earlier noted it was not until a similar assemblage was recovered from the inland bog site of Kongemose that the appellation Early Coastal Culture was first seen to be inadequate to describe a phase of settlement which existed in the interior as well as on the coasts of Zealand. The concept was further weakened as the true nature of the 'Gudenaa culture' of inland Jutland as the product of many phases of settlement extending over a long period was recognised, since the lithic material from a number of sites in the interior of Jutland approximates to that of so-called Early Coastal Culture sites. An analogous transformation occurred with respect to the Ertebølle or kitchen-midden 'culture'. Systematic investigation of sites of Atlantic age in the great bog system of Aamose in the interior of Zealand brought to light quantities of finds, ceramic and antler, as well as lithic, identical with that earlier recovered from the coastal middens. Again, as a glance at the schedules in Mathiassen's original account of the 'Gudenaa culture' shows (1937, 10–35), several flint assemblages from the interior of Jutland were marked by features diagnostic of that originally found in the coastal middens of Ertebølle type. In listing assemblages from the Gudenaa basin containing a hundred or more transverse flint arrowheads figures are also given for flake and core axes, which where the sample is large enough confirm their basically Ertebølle character (Table 14).

The Danish evidence is amply complemented by that from Schleswig-Holstein. In this territory, where the Litorina shores, like those of the Ancylus Lake further north, are submerged below modern sea-level,

Table 14. *Sites with flint inventories of Ertebølle character in the Gudenaa basin*

Site nos.	Names	Numbers of transverse arrowheads	Core axes	Flake axes
5	Havstrup S.E.	630	17	27
6	Melhede	102	5	9
39	Siimholm	122	1	1
116	Salten Sø	186	28	21
117	Rye Bro Sø	734	78	119
217	Klosterlund	157	6	5
223	Skyge	497	4	0

traces of Atlantic settlement have always and necessarily come from inland sites. The original finds from Ellerbek, although only recovered from the present Kiel Fjord by means of dredging, came from sites originally situated by the margins of fresh-water lakes. More recent systematic investigations further north have brought to light pointed-based jars and antler and flint work typologically similar to that from the Danish coastal middens from the sites of Rüde and Forstermoor in the Satrup bog (Schwabedissen 1958, 1966). So closely similar is the material from the Schleswig-Holstein sites to that from the Danish shell-mounds that Schwabedissen even proposed to reserve the term Ellerbek for the inland aspect of the culture known from its coastal finding-places as Ertebølle. What is at any rate clear is that the inhabitants of south Scandinavia were exploiting inland as well as coastal resources throughout Atlantic time.

Meat-diet. This is no less evident from the composition of faunal material from coastal settlements (see Appendix E). Whether one turns to sites like Villengebæk or Vedbæk dating from the earlier part of the Atlantic time or to the numerous assemblages from sites of late Atlantic times, the most striking conclusion to emerge is that the main source of protein came from terrestial mammals. The only species invariably represented were red deer, roe deer and wild pig, but aurochs was present at each of the seven Jutish sites. Elk were absent from sites of whatever phase of Atlantic time on Zealand (see p. 137), but appeared at least occasionally on sites of this age in Jutland. Marine mammals certainly contributed significantly to the supply of meat and fat but even so were markedly inferior quantitatively as sources of food. Common, Greenland and ringed-seals, as well as killer-whales and dolphins, were evidently caught from time to time, but only the grey seal and porpoise made really considerable contributions. Most, if not all, the fur-bearing mammals also yielded meat and served to exaggerate even more the contribution made from land-mammals. Of these, the wild cat (9 occurrences), pine marten (7) and fox (6) appeared both in Jutland and Zealand. The occurrences of other species reveal notable differences as between Jutland and Zealand; brown bear and lynx (each 2), wolf and badger (each 4) were only found on Jutland sites. Fish were predominantly caught in salt water and it is worth noting that only cod (7) and flounder (6) were very frequently represented. Another way of bringing out the leading part played by terrestrial species in supplying animal protein is to observe the relative importance of different species at particular sites: thus at the site of Ølby Lyng on the east coast of Zealand the main terrestrial food mammals accounted for c. 82% of the faunal material as against only 12·3% of marine mammals (seals 10·6% and porpoise 1·7%). On the other hand, of the six species of fish, represented by some 3,864 fragments, cod accounted for c. 95·7% and flounders c. 4%, and the birds were overwhelmingly marine (Møhl 1971).

The conclusion is irresistible that, while on coastal settlements the men of this time depended primarily for meat and furs on land-mammals, they at the same time exploited the special opportunities offered by sea-mammals, notably seals – and in particular grey seals – and porpoises, as well as by sea-fish, above all cod and to a lesser degree flounders, and birds. In respect of fishing it is likely that the hook and line were used for cod and bone hooks have been found on Ertebølle sites, barbless as in those from the Boreal period. Funnel-shaped basket traps or weels (Pl. II, right lower, p. 107) had already come into use at an early phase of Atlantic time, as shown by the specimen recovered from Villingebæk (Kapel 1969), probably for taking eels.

A feature of the food-quest which first becomes obtrusive in the archaeological record during the third transgression of the Litorina Sea was the consumption of shell-fish and more particularly of *Ostrea edulis*, *Mytilus edulis*, *Cardium edule*, *Nassa reticulata* and *Litorina littorea* on a scale sufficient to result in the accumulation of substantial shell-mounds. Why this should have happened at this particular period and not for instance during earlier phases of marine transgression is one of many problems still unsolved. What is perhaps of more immediate importance is the part played by shell-fish in the diet of the time. One way of coming to grips with this problem is to form some estimate of the calorific value of the shell-fish represented in the middens. Short of special investigations in the field only approximate indications can be obtained. It is not possible from the information provided in *Affalds-dynger* even to estimate precisely the volume of shells in the well known Ertebølle midden. Nevertheless it is known that the midden extended over a length of 141 m; that its maximum breadth was 20 m but that over its southern half it was only between 6–8 m across; and lastly that its maximum thickness ranged from 1·55 m in the southern half and 1·9 m in the north, but that over much of its length it scarcely reached 1 m and that everywhere it thinned drastically at the margins. Taking all these indications together one arrives at an approximation of *c.* 1,500 cubic metres for the volume of mollusc shells in the Ertebølle midden. What does this imply in terms of food? For this it is reasonable to turn again for a very approximate order of magnitude, to work done in New Zealand on middens composed mainly of oyster, mussel, cockle and scallop shells. Careful estimates made by Shawcross (1967) on a midden at Galatea Bay indicate that the $18 \cdot 7 \pm 5\%$ cubic metres of shell-mound would have yielded between 1,400,000 and 4,100,000 calories in all. If it is assumed that an average biological family living in the temperate zones requires *c.* 11,400 calories daily, this would mean that it could have subsisted on shell-fish alone for somewhere between 123 and 360 days. If these estimates are applied to the 1,500 cubic metres estimated for the Ertebølle midden, one arrives at a range of between *c.* 7,653/8,427 days at the lower to *c.* 20,918/23,037 days at the upper end of the scale. Now it is known that the Ertebølle midden was mainly formed over a period of *c.* 200 years. If it is further assumed that the shell-fish were exploited annually – and the sections shown in *Affalds-dynger* betray no signs of prolonged stabilisation – then we could say that a single biological family could have satisfied its calorific needs solely from eating shell-fish for a period of between 38/42 days and 105/115 in the average year. On the assumption that the middens related to small groups rather than to single biological families one would arrive at figures of the following orders: 3-family group: from 12/14 days to 35/38 days; 4-family group: from 9/10 days to 26/29 days.

Put another way, and making the further assumption that the middens were occupied on the average for 180 days per annum, it can be seen that shell-fish would have accounted only for between 6·6% to 21% of the diet for this period of a 3-family group and 5% to 16% of a 4-family unit. On the analogy of the New Zealand middens we arrive at the conclusion, whichever end of the range we care to adopt, that shell-fish played only a subsidiary role even at the time of the year when people were settled within range of the shell-mounds. As in so much traditional prehistory, terminology and the body of ideas associated with this rests on the accident that a particular category of site happens to be visually prominent.

Settlement and seasonality. When the middens came under closest scrutiny (1893–7) investigation was restricted to the actual mounds. No systematic attempt seems to have been made at the time to test ground within easy discard distance of the refuse mounds for evidence of dwellings, but trials subsequently made at Vegger and at Ertebølle itself have been used to suggest that shelters may have been placed on shallow terraces cut into the banks immediately overlying the middens (Simonsen 1951). Excavations in the actual midden at Ertebølle suggested on the other hand that the mound grew largely as the result of open air encampments on the actual site (Madsen *et al.* 1900, 9–28, 71–7). Many traces of fire-places were found and it is significant that on average 1·8 charcoal samples were collected for each square metre. Again, it is of great interest to observe that some 20,308 animal bones were recovered for the 314 square metres investigated, an average of between 64 and 65 a square metre. The fact that pottery was recovered from 635 locations, on the average 2 for each square metre explored, argues that seasonal dwelling-places at least can hardly have been far off. On the other hand if these were as close as Simonsen's hypothesis argues, well within reach of the stench of the shell-midden, it is difficult to see why cooking-places were scattered throughout the midden. Judging from the fact that fitting sherds from the same pot have been found in three separate spits, it looks as though the surface of the midden was undulating at the time of successive encampments or expeditions, a conclusion which finds support in the indications of local heaping of shells in these sections. The abundance of pottery on the other hand argues that the people who exploited the middens must have lived not too far away even if only seasonally.

Since it became more evident that the people responsible for the shell-mounds also exploited the resources of the interior and certainly established settlements there, the possibility arises that the middens related to a seasonal exploitation or to seasonal exploitations. So far as the biological indicators provided by food-refuse from the actual middens go, a number of clues point to the spring as at any rate one time of resort. This applies especially to the sea-food which attracted people to the coast. Thus grey seals are hunted in the Kattegat in March and April and during the historic period this was also the time of one of the two main seasons for catching porpoises. Again cod were taken in these waters from late winter to early spring. Guillemot, which seem to have been taken in quantity at Ølby Lyng, collect for breeding in February/March. The abundance of fur-bearing animals in the middens is consistent with the winter or early spring, as is the presence of red deer antlers broken out of the skull. As for the shell-fish themselves these are of maximum value immediately before their summer breeding season. The marine and coastal resources available in the spring must have been a source of considerable attraction at a time of the year when food is traditionally scarce.

There are a number of signs that communities quite far inland were in contact with the coast. For instance a piece of whale bone comes from the upper level of Ringkloster 14 km as the crow flies inland from the apparently contemporary site of Flynderhage on an estuary south of Aarhus and, even more striking, there is the record from an earlier phase of the Atlantic of a grey seal, represented by bones suggesting that a complete animal was in question, from the site of Øgaarde some 16 km inland from the closest inlet of the Litorina Sea.

The fact that, to judge from certain items in their technology (see p. 187), the inhabitants of Denmark, Scania and Schleswig-Holstein were evidently in some form of culture contact with the farming populations of Danubian antecedents in northern central Europe raises the question whether or how far the south Scandinavians adopted elements of farming economy from the same source. Much the richest body of information is provided by the large and extensive bone material. Although coastal sites in particular are likely to be complicated by the effects of secondary occupation, there is no good evidence that the material from primary Ertebølle sources provides any remains of animals showing genetic features of the kind commonly associated with effective farming other than the dog, a domestic animal already of long standing in northern Europe. The large and extensive body of *Bos* material from Ertebølle sites recently studied in detail by Degerbøl and Fredskild (1970) includes two main sizes of adult. This has been interpreted by some as indicating the co-existence of 'wild' and 'domesticated' forms, but Degerbøl prefers the more economical explanation that it is a product of sexual dimorphism. Having reviewed the total material Degerbøl concludes categorically that the earliest domesticated cattle in Denmark are those from the Atlantic–Sub-boreal (VII–VIII) transition of Øgaarde I, although not ruling out of court the possibility that close relations falling short of those accompanied by genetic change may have developed much earlier. It is a fair comment on this last possibility, however, that *Bos* failed to survive the Boreal–Atlantic transition in Zealand. This would be difficult to explain if any such close relation had in fact existed.

Even more decisive evidence is provided by remains of sheep/goat from the Danish middens. In this case there can hardly be any question that when these animals appeared in the west Baltic area they must have been introduced in an already domesticated form. It may therefore be useful to examine the pattern of occurrence of sheep/goat in deposits respectively of late Atlantic and Sub-boreal age. The results for the fourteen assemblages set out in Table 15 indicate unequivocally that sheep/goat formed no part of the economic system of the Ertebølle phase of settlement.

Evidence for plant food is exceptionally meagre for the Atlantic phase of settlement in south Scandinavia as a whole. The best hope for rectifying this lies in the investigation of inland bog sites. In this connection great interest centres on the site of Forstermoor, Satrup, Schleswig-Holstein in view of Schwabedissen's interim reference (1966, 416) to the occurrence of pollen of *Plantago lanceolata* and of cultivated cereals. Although Schwabedissen treats this as a type site for his Satrup stage, it is interesting to note the occurrence, alongside pointed based pots, of thin-walled beakerlike vessels. When radiocarbon dates are available and the site fully published it will be possible to decide whether in fact this assemblage does not equate with the Atlantic–Sub-boreal transition and compare rather with the phase of settlement discussed in the beginning of chapter 6. Even if, as seems not at all unlikely, cultivated cereals can be shown to have been among the traits acquired during late Atlantic time from Danubian sources, there is no indication that they contributed in any substantial way to sub-

Table 15. *The absence and presence of sheep/goat from archaeological deposits of late Atlantic and Sub-boreal age in Denmark*

Sites	References	Absent	Scanty and superficial	Present
Sub-boreal (Early Neolithic)				
Ørum Aa	Madsen *et al.* 1900, 146	.	.	×
Aalborg	Madsen *et al.* 1900, 160 f.	.	.	×
Leire Aa	Madsen *et al.* 1900, 172	.	.	×
Kolind IV	Mathiassen *et al.* 1942	.	.	×
Late Alantic (Ertebølle)				
Ertebølle	Madsen *et al.* 1900	×	.	.
Faareveille	Madsen *et al.* 1900	×	.	.
Aamølle	Madsen *et al.* 1900, 103	.	×	.
Havnø	Madsen *et al.* 1900, 111	.	×	.
Klintesø	Madsen *et al.* 1900, 132	.	×	.
Dyrholm	Mathiassen *et al.* 1942	×	.	.
Kolind I–III	Mathiassen *et al.* 1942	×	.	.
Norslund	Andersen and Malmros 1965, 109	×	.	.
Benthines Bro	Nykjøbing Museum	×	.	.
Ølby Lyng	E. B. Petersen 1970	×	.	.

sistence. One of the striking facts about the massive assemblages of material equipment available from settlements of this time is the absence of equipment for harvesting or grinding cereals.

PSYCHIC NEEDS

Disposal of the dead. Evidence continues to be sparse but such as it is it suggests a continuance of the rite of individual inhumation. As a rule the body was extended. In the case of the burial found in the course of harbour works at Korsør Nor, Zealand, underlying a clay deposit dating from Zone VIIb, the skeleton lay on its back on a layer of bark and was covered by sheets of bark strengthened by wooden slats (Nørling-Christensen 1945). There were no personal ornaments, but a flint flake lay among the bones and may have been deposited with the dead man. Among objects from the harbour excavations was a slotted handle with flint insets. A burial of comparable age found under the culture layer at Vedbæk Boldbaner (Mathiassen 1946*b*, 33 and fig. 8) also testified to the custom of placing the dead in an extended position on the back and in this case no grave goods were found. In the case of burials from the Danish shell-mounds it is difficult to be sure whether they belong to the time when the midden was actively formed or whether they were not inserted at a later date. For what they are worth two records may perhaps be quoted. The excavators themselves certainly considered that the extended inhumation buried in the eponymous site of Ertebølle was covered by an undisturbed accumulation of shells (Madsen et al. 1900, 77–80) and again that the extended skeleton in the Aamølle midden (Madsen et al. 1900, 100) protected by boulders and covered by a shell layer showing no apparent signs of disturbance belonged to the same period as the middens themselves. In neither case were personal ornaments or other possessions observed.

A notable exception to the rule of extended burial without or with only minimal grave goods is provided by the individual found in a seated position in a round pit some 1·2 m deep at Backaskog, Scania, accompanied by a slotted point of type A and a bone chisel (Althin 1950). The sex of the individual has been the subject of some debate (Gejvall 1970). To judge from the goods it should date from the close of the late Boreal or from an early phase of the Atlantic period.

Reference may conveniently be made at this point to the human skeletal material found broken and scattered throughout the site at Dyrholm. According to Degerbøl (in Mathiassen et al. 1942, 105–22) at least nine individuals were represented. Some of the bones had been gnawed by dogs, but what is more significant is that they showed the same evidence of butchery as the bones of wild animals. Long bones had been split and strips removed from the lower edge of mandibles presumably for the extraction of marrow. Again clear signs were visible on the skulls and other bones of cutting by flint knives. The treatment of the bones and their mode of occurrence leave little doubt of the practice of cannibalism. Whether this should be taken as an indication of hunger or whether it testifies to the satisfaction of a psychic need is something for which the existing evidence hardly supplies an answer.

Personal ornaments. The complete absence of personal ornament from the burials just discussed and the extreme rarity even of the simplest beads from settlements suggests that the inhabitants of south Scandinavia either eschewed personal decoration during Atlantic time or went in for feathers, paint or ornaments made from plant substances for which an archaeological record could hardly be expected.

Symbolic art. During the initial Kongemose and Vedbæk phases symbolic art was not only carried on vigorously, but developed a number of marked characteristics, particularly in respect of applying patterns to slotted knife handles and antler mattock-heads: these were commonly engraved more deeply than in former times, sometimes in the form of overall designs (Vebæk 1939, fig. 7) and lozenge patterns were particularly favoured. In the later stages engraved designs were not only scarcer, but tended to be applied in perfunctory engraving. In respect of the Ertebølle middens it is possible that the scarcity of symbolic art is linked in some way with the nature of the sites and the economic activities associated with them. It is always possible and indeed highly probable that some stray specimens with engraved or pit designs in fact belong to this phase of settlement. The bone fragment with pit ornament from level three at Norslund (Andersen and Malmros 1965, 70, fig. 3) is suggestive in this respect.

6

The Older Stone Age Colonisation
of the Fennoscandian Shield

Since the entire territory of the Fennoscandian shield was at one time buried under the ice-sheet, it follows that land only became available to land mammals including man himself as an outcome of the process of melting. It is hardly necessary to labour the point that human settlement was peripheral to the contracting ice-sheet. The case of south Scandinavia has already been dealt with. Our concern here is with territory that first became available only in part at the close of the Late-glacial but in large measure in the course of Post-glacial time. Here the location and accessibility of the earliest areas of settlement were a direct outcome of the history of the formation and contraction of the ice-sheet itself. As explained in an earlier chapter (p. 37), although glaciation began on the high mountain background of Scandinavia, its centre and in consequence the area of maximum isostatic displacement came to focus on the western side of the present Gulf of Bothnia. In the mean time the influence of the Gulf Stream ensured that even during the period of Late-glacial settlement in south Scandinavia the Atlantic and Arctic coasts of Norway were free of ice. On the other hand human bands preying on reindeer herds displaced from their former grazing grounds by the spread of temperate forest were barred from middle Sweden, since this was still covered owing to continued isostatic depression by the waters first of the Yoldia Sea and then of the Ancylus Lake. The only way of gaining access to the ice-free area of the Fennoscandian shield at the end of Late-glacial times was by skirting west and/or possibly east of the glaciated area. It was only as isostatic recovery progressed sufficiently for middle Sweden and Finland to emerge as extensive land areas that colonists, by now adapted to forested environments, were able to initiate the settlement of the bulk of Fennoscandia.

Table 16. *Successive phases of Stone Age settlement at the upper and lower ends of Oslofjord showing heights (m) of contemporary strand-lines above modern sea-level according to W. C. Brøgger (1905)*

Archaeological fossils	Oslo	Outerfjord
Nøstvet axes	+70	+42
Stump-butted axes	+55	+36
Thin-butted axes	+25	+19
Boat axes	+15	+10

Chronological framework

Nøstvet phase. As was the case in much of Scandinavia the younger phase of the older Stone Age settlement was the first to come to light. The initial discoveries symbolised by a particular form of narrow core axe of quadrangular or triangular section were made at Sigersvoll, Lista, Vest Agder in 1877 and at Nøstvet, Akershus in 1879. Because of its greater proximity to Oslo no doubt, the site of Nøstvet was chosen by W. C. Brøgger (1905) to designate the new phase of settlement. Its antiquity was suggested by the fact that in the Oslo region Nøstvet axes normally occurred above the *Tapes* strand, whereas objects relating to later phases of settlement might occur at levels which implied more advanced stages in the isostatic recovery of the land (Table 16). Stone axes of Nøstvet type have since been found over much of the coastal tract of southern Norway as far north as the southern frontier of the Trøndelag.

Fosna–Komsa phase. The first suggestion that Norway was inhabited before the Nøstvet phase and possibly as early as the beginning of Post-glacial times came in 1909 with Nummedal's discovery of assemblages of worked flints at fairly high levels in the region of Christiansund in the ancient west Norwegian province of Fosna. The same investigator next located similar traces on the east side of Oslofjord at levels above those associated with Nøstvet settlement. In 1925 he extended his researches to Finnmark where he discovered near the foot of Mt Komsa stations with analogous though not identical lithic artifacts at levels indicating that the coastal tracts of this northernmost territory were occupied at a time when isostatic recovery of the land had reached only a comparatively early stage. The attention of the outside world was first seriously engaged when Nummedal joined with Johs. Bøe in describing, illustrating and discussing, though not quantifying except in the most rudimentary way, the material from more than sixty stations in the province in time for the Oslo Congress of 1936. Since then the number of sites with Komsa material has been more than doubled: in particular many new sites have been recognised on the south shore of Varanger Fjord (Odner 1966) and it was early established that sites existed east of Finnmark in the territory of the Soviet Union (Zemljakof 1940). Knowledge of the geographical extent of sites with Fosna material has likewise been enlarged: an occurrence has been noted on the coast of Hordaland helping to bridge the gap between Oslofjord and the province of Fosna (Freundt 1948) and the latter has itself been extended northwards to the islands and coasts of the Trøndelag (Marstrander 1956). Even more suggestive in some respects, sites have been recognised at intervals along the coast of Nordlund (Freundt 1948) in what was formerly a wide gap between the Fosna and Komsa provinces. Again, until comparatively recently it had always been assumed that the early lithic sites in each of these areas were confined to ancient coast-lines. So far as Finnmark is concerned this still appears to be true, but within the Fosna zone assemblages of comparable, although not identical character, have been located deep in the mountainous interior, as for instance on the Hardangervidda (Bøe 1942; Hagen 1960–1; Johansen 1969) and in the south Trøndelag (Marstrander 1956).

As with Brøgger in respect of the Nøstvet finds in the south, so was Nummedal's interest in the Fosna–Komsa assemblages stimulated by the height at which they occurred above modern sea-level. Whereas assemblages from the younger Stone Age in northern Norway occurred below the *Tapes* strand, equivalent to an early phase of the Atlantic in south Scandinavia, the assemblages first noted by Nummedal occurred exclusively at higher levels. Indeed they have been observed to occur in Finnmark as high as the *Portlandia* Late-glacial strand which at the head of fjords is approximately 50 m above the *Tapes* level. Since the sea has always been a main source of protein for the inhabitants of Norway it is safe to assume that the coastal tract held great attractions for settlement. How far it is safe to assume that men lived as close as possible to their main source of food – in which case in a territory of progressive land emergence occupation sites could be dated more or less precisely in terms of their relative heights above sea-level – is a matter for discussion. The obvious way of testing this is to observe the relation of actual structures to successive strand-lines. The rare and invariably incomplete nature of the data relating to Fosna and Komsa settlements means that this test can hardly be applied in their regard: on the other hand when such structures first appear in quantity, as they do in the later Stone Age settlement of the south coast of Varanger Fjord, it is significant that rows of dwellings can be seen to adhere rather closely to successive strand-lines as though the inhabitants were living as near as possible to their main food-resource. This is after all what might be expected. Men do not as a rule expend more energy than they need to achieve their ends. Yet, although as a generalisation one may agree that the makers of the lithic assemblages from Norwegian coastal tracts are likely to have camped as close as they conveniently could to the shore, this is by no means to say that the location of individual encampments was determined primarily by this single factor: shelter and visibility were requirements which might under certain conditions have run counter to mere propinquity. It follows that, although the heights of assemblages in relation to ancient strand-lines provide a legitimate general guide to their age in relation to other assemblages, the age of particular sites cannot legitimately be inferred purely by reference to their relation to strand-lines; nor is it possible to accept as a certainty that individual assemblages are necessarily homogeneous in age, since it is theoretically possible that artifacts from the same site relate not merely to different visits, but to visits that might conceivably have been made, if the location was particularly favourable, over a long period of time.

The general absence of stratification makes it extremely difficult to relate assemblages directly to the geological sequence. In respect to coastal finds in Fosna province only one firm clue exists in the form of a heavy tanged flake, corresponding closely in form to those known from the Bromme–Lyngby–Segebro province of south Scandinavia, recovered from *Pholas* clay at Christiansund (Nummedal 1921; Clark 1936, fig. 24, 2), the locality where traces of the earliest settlement of Norway were first located. This appears to offer a firm indication that south Norway began to be occupied at least as early as the middle phase of the Ancylus Lake, that is by around the first half of the seventh millennium B.C. At this point reference may be made to the sites from three main localities on the Hardangervidda, namely Lærdal at the

Table 17. *List of early radiocarbon dates relating to lithic assemblages from the interior of southern Norway*

Lærdal	B.C.
Sulemarki VII (*c.* 1420 m)	T 671: 5970 ± 120
Osen II (c. 1120 m)	T 664: 6340 ± 120
	T 665: 5500 ± 110
	T 666: 5170 ± 120
Vukleåni	T 667: 5580 ± 100
	T 668: 5460 ± 100
	T 669: 5170 ± 110
Finsevatn	
Finseøya (*c.* 1200 m)	T 223: 5700 ± 150
Vesle Beruosen	T 130: 4150 ± 140
Vrålsbu II	T 131: 4910 + 140
Gyrinosvatn	
Gyrinos III (*c.* 1100 m)	K 710: 5910 ± 120
	T 215: 6200 ± 200
Gyrinos IV	K 711: 3750 ± 120

Radio carbon dates from the south Trøndelag, although still rare, also point in the same direction:

Albusetra A	T 442: 4150 ± 120
B	T 443: 6580 ± 360

head of Sognefjord, Finsevatn above the head of Hardangerfjord and Gyrinosvatn near the centre of the Hardangervidda, which have yielded radiocarbon dates (see Table 17).

Collectively these analyses show beyond question that the coastal zone of south Norway was occupied already by the earlier part of the seventh millennium and the mountainous interior at least seasonally during the sixth if not at the close of the seventh millennium B.C. Precisely when the colonisation of south Norway began has yet to be determined, but lithic assemblages from round about 100 m above modern sea-level on the coast of the east Östfold* suggest that this strategic region was already occupied by around 7000 B.C.

Dating evidence other than what can within limits be inferred from location in relation to old strand-lines is extremely rare in Finnmark. The only clue, though one of high potential importance, is that provided by the discovery of apparent artifacts on the *Portlandia* strand at Bossekop

* E.g. from Holsten, Muleröd and Åneröd represented in the University Museum of Antiquities at Oslo.

at the head of the Alta Fjord some 69·2 m above present sea-level, which according to Bøe and Nummedal (1936, 193) show signs in some instances of having been subjected to water-rolling. This opinion, recently confirmed by Odner (1966, 155) is also shared by the present author as the result of visual inspection. Since this strand-line is situated high up on a terrace (Bøe and Nummedal 1936, pl. vi *upper*), rolling can hardly have been effected by drainage streams or torrents. It can only therefore have resulted from wave action when the sea was at least within reach of the *Portlandia* strand. *Pace* Freundt (1948, 1–7) this strand must surely correspond with the Yoldia Sea phase of the Baltic. Before accepting as a certainty that man had infiltrated the perimeter of Fennoscandia at this time a more abundant and unambiguous body of evidence would be welcome, for it has to be admitted that the mere process of rolling tends to diminish if not obliterate the visual indications that lead one to infer or reject human workmanship.

The next question is whether individual assemblages can be accepted as necessarily homogeneous in age. The problem is even more complex in this case because Fosna and Komsa assemblages are found on or close to the modern surface, so precluding stratified sequences. It has already been argued that one cannot accept assemblages from particular sites as necessarily relating to a single period of settlement. This is important because in terms of south Scandinavian criteria the Norwegian coastal assemblages (Fig. 53) appear to contain elements of widely disparate age. Discounting typologically 'primitive' elements on the ground that these are of too widespread occurrence on sites where artifacts were manufactured from locally abundant material to be significant, one is nevertheless confronted by components, some of which compare with ones that flourished during the Late-glacial and others at an advanced stage of Atlantic time, a span of four or even five millennia. As Freundt implied, if one insists on the homogeneity of the assemblages and at the same time accepts as axiomatic that cultural innovations must necessarily have come from the south, one is logically compelled to date them by their 'latest' component in south Scandinavian terms. Strictly speaking this would mean correlating the whole phenomenon with the Ertebølle phase of the Danish Stone Age when the side-blow 'axe' with surface flaking made its first appearance in the south Baltic. But such an extreme view is contradicted by the geological dating of coastal sites and by radiocarbon dating of those on the Hardangervidda. Plainly the 'late' elements (in south Scandinavian terms) must either

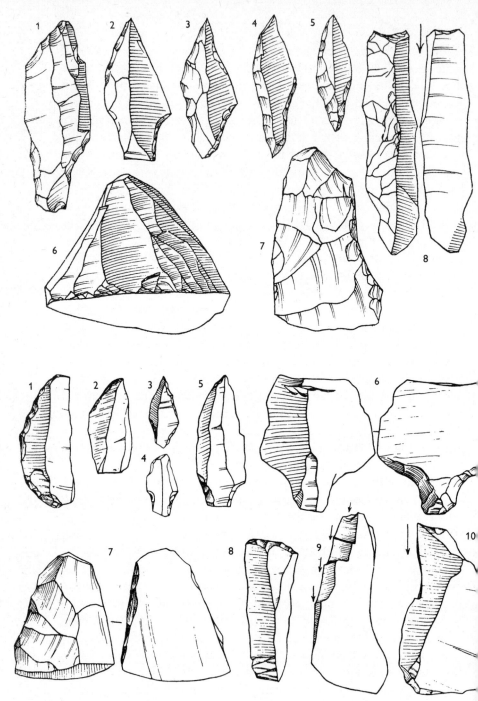

Fig. 53. Flint and stone implements from (*above*) Fosna and (*below*) Komsa assemblages from the Norwegian coastal zone. Fosna: (1/1), except 3, 6, 7 (1/2) and 8 (2/3). Komsa: (2/3), except 5–8 (4/9).

have spread along the coasts of Norway as secondary impulses or the Ertebølle flake 'axe' technique was independently developed in the north. The side-blow flake 'axe' was in itself a relatively early trait in the south, appearing already in the Pre-boreal and early Boreal, and there seems no *a priori* reason for ruling out of court the possibility that the flat-flaking technique might have been invented independently in the north and south. Whatever may turn out to be the case in this regard, the existing data invite the suggestion that the earliest settlement of Norway occurred at a very early stage of the Post-glacial but that from time to time it received impulses and reinforcements from the south.

The question whether the Fosna and Komsa finds represent manifestations of a single spread and if so from which direction this came, whether from the south or the east, or whether they represent two distinct spreads, one from west Sweden and ultimately from south Scandinavia, the other from north-west Russia has been much discussed: Bjørn considered there was a single spread from the extreme north to the south; Bøe and Nummedal (1936) derived the Fosna assemblages from the south and the Komsa ones from the east; Freundt (1948) on the other hand derived both from the south; Luho (1956b) returned very much to the position of Bøe and Nummedal; but Odner (1966) held to the essential unity of the two and returned in some respects to the position of Freundt. Anders Hagen (1967) took much the same position, but found it inadequate to consider the Komsa assemblages as merely 'an integral part of the Fosna complex'. This is important. The character of any intensive archaeological assemblage depends not only on its source, in other words on inheritance, but also on the environment it penetrates. In the case of the earliest Norwegian assemblages the social aspect of the new environment can by the nature of things be ignored since the territory was previously unoccupied. We are left with the natural resources and characteristics of the Finnmark environment. So far as technology is concerned a main difference was that whereas in Fosna flint was the most important material for lithic artifacts, in the case of Finnmark materials were more varied and included quartzite and greenstone as well as hornstone quartz and the more tractable dolomitic flint; no doubt it was the availability of the first two in unlimited quantities that lent the appearance of greater coarseness to the Komsa assemblages noted by Hagen and other writers.

In considering the historical antecedents of the earliest settlement of Norway Bøe and Nummedal (1936, 243 f.) already emphasised the similarities that existed between the tanged point component of the Fosna assemblages and those of south Scandinavia and north Germany. Freundt (1948, 31–3) gave added point to these analogies by focusing attention on assemblages in the intermediate zone of Oslofjord and the northern part of the west Swedish coast. A point worth emphasising is that this component of the early assemblages from Norway and west Sweden between them combine idiosyncratic traits characteristic of each of the social territories recognised for the Late-glacial period in south Scandinavia and the south Baltic hinterland. Thus tanged points made on heavy flakes in Bromme/Lyngby/Segebro style occur at Christiansund (Clark 1936, fig. 24, 2) and also in the far north at Vedbotneidet and Storbukta (Bøe and Nummedal 1936, pls. LXXXI and LXXXVI, 372). Delicate tanged points and associated forms of Ahrensburg type occur on the coastal sites of Fosna and Komsa and not least on the Hardangervidda (Fig. 54). And, lastly, points with tangs or bases with inverse retouch of the kind known from Poland are well seen at west Swedish sites like Djupedal (Fredsjö 1953, fig. 2, 5) and alongside Ahrensburg points at Hensbacka. As hinted earlier (p. 180) this strongly suggests the break-up of earlier cultural configurations and the general northward shift of populations that might have been expected to follow the transformation of the old Late-glacial landscape. Despite the vestigial character of the available clues the hypothesis is at least worth framing that initially men followed the reindeer, the last substantial wild herds of which still survive on the Hardangervidda. On the other hand, as will be emphasised in the following section, those who occupied the coastal tracts can only have done so and remained viable by adapting to fishing, wild-fowling and the hunting of sea-mammals. Further, if remote and disconnected tracts of the Norwegian coast up to and including Finnmark were settled from the south, this can only have been achieved by people well adapted to this way of life and equipped with boats. Whether the entire settlement including that of the Murmansk coast proceeded from the south by the western route or whether this was complemented by a similar movement from the east can only be tested when far more is known about the prehistory of the extreme north-east of the U.S.S.R.

Whereas the Fosna and Komsa assemblages can be equated in their origins with the actual colonisation of virgin territories and can there-

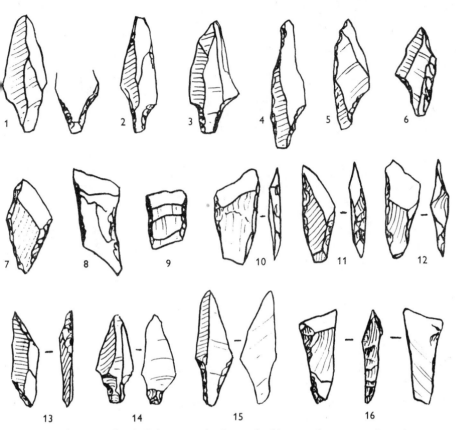

Fig. 54. Flint arrowheads ((7) quartzite) of tanged, oblique and transverse form from the Hardangervidda, S. Norway. (1)–(9) Sumtangen (Bøe 1942); (10)–(12) Gyrinos (Hagen 1960–1); (13)–(16) Finseøya (ibid.). (1/1)

fore be linked with the spread of people, the mechanism responsible for the spread of Nøstvet traits in the south of Sweden is more debatable. As we have known since the discovery of the initial phase of settlement represented by the Fosna–Komsa assemblages, the Nøstvet assemblages mark no more than an enrichment, a secondary accretion to the cultural capital of Norway. Whether this proceeded by way of an additional movement of people or by a spread of ideas may never be decided. What seems reasonably sure is that the enrichment like the original colonisation reached southern Norway by way of west Sweden.

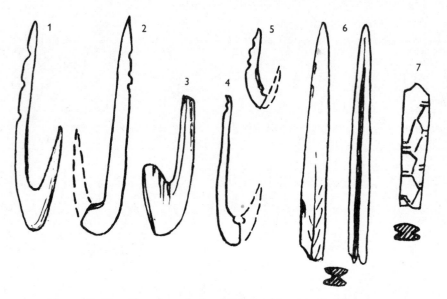

Fig. 55. Bone artifacts from the basal (Nøstvet) level in the Viste cave near Stavanger (1/1).

Technology

Our knowledge of the technology of the older Stone Age inhabitants of Norway is severely restricted by the physical conditions prevailing at the settlement sites. The archaeological assemblages lie in almost every case at or close to the modern surface. This means that only artifacts of flint or stone have any change of surviving in the prevailing climate; animal materials and wood which must have provided the main elements in material culture are at present totally lacking for the Fosna–Komsa phase and for the Nøstvet phase the evidence is mainly confined to the lowest level in the cave of Viste near Stavanger (Fig. 55).

Attention must needs therefore be focused on lithic industries as constituting almost the sole source of information about technology. Whereas the early inhabitants of Denmark, and parts of south Sweden had access to ready supplies of flint of cretaceous origin the material occurred in Norway only in the form of small nodules transported by natural agencies during the Ice Age. Although in southern Norway supplies were adequate for the early Fosna settlers and continued to serve during the younger Stone Age for such small objects as arrowheads and scrapers, flint of the size and quality needed for axes first reached Norway as the southern part of the country became incorporated in an exchange net-work that comprehended north Jutland, something which did not happen until the younger Stone Age. The early inhabitants of Finnmark had indeed to depend even for small equipment on the locally abundant quartzes and quartzites, except in so far as these could be supplemented by hornstone and by dolomitic flint derived from local rocks of Cambrian age. Similarly the makers of Nøstvet axes in south Norway had to depend on stone for these tools, though in this case there is evidence that supplies of particularly favourable stone were carefully organised and redistributed by means of social net-works. For instance the finely grained greenstone forming Hespriholm off the south-west coast of Norway was quarried on this islet, trans-shipped to the island of Bømloy which was large enough to support a permanent population and there reduced to axe-blades that were ultimately redistributed over much of the coastal zone of Jæren on the mainland.

Since Brøgger was mainly concerned with the type-fossils needed to document the process of land emergence in the course of isostatic recovery, our knowledge of the total assemblages of which the Nøstvet axes were a prominent feature is still very defective. Even the elementary task of recovering and analysing total assemblages from a sufficient number of sites unrifled by surface collecting has yet to be accomplished. It can however, be said that the Nøstvet axe, characteristically of triangular or rectangular section (Fig. 56), was frequently accompanied by side-blow flake 'axes', the latter appearing in the proportion of c. 1:4. Again, pecked and edge-ground stump-butted axes appeared at least in younger Nøstvet assemblages. Quite evidently Nøstvet techno-logy was well adapted to the felling and utilisation of forest trees. Another component of the Nøstvet tool-kit was the microblade intended for arming slotted equipment and the handle-core (Fig. 44) from which such could most conveniently be struck (Gjessing, G. 1945, 6).

Useful confirmation of this last trait is afforded by the meagre material from the lowermost level at Viste which is nevertheless precious for its yield of bone components: this contained not only Nøstvet axes and microblades, but also fragmentary bone points slotted on either side. In addition it yielded barbless bone fish-hooks including ones made by each of the two techniques in use in south Scandinavia during Boreal times.

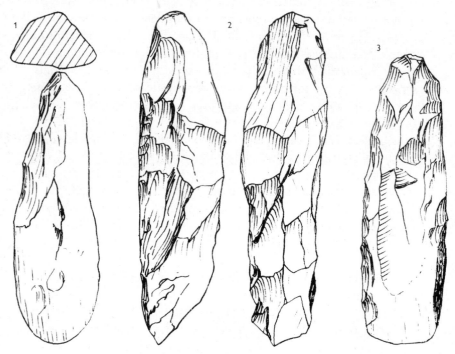

Fig. 56. Nøstvet (2), (3) and Lihult (1) stone axes (4/7).

Shelter and subsistence

The makers of the earliest lithic assemblages of Norway appear to have lived on open sites, whether on the shore or as in the case of the Hardangervidda on the mountains of south Norway. There is no indication that they occupied caves or rock-shelters, the first evidence for which dates from the Nøstvet phase in south Norway. Nor again are there signs that rectangular huts with thick stone-faced earthen walls of the kind known from the younger Stone Age on Træna island off the coast of Nordland (Gjessing, G. 1943) or from the south shore of Varanger Fjord in Finnmark (Simonsen 1961) had yet been taken into use. The only actual traces of living emplacements, for which we have above all to thank Knut Odner (1966, pls. III–XVIII), comprise stone set hearths and shallow round floor depressions. The most reasonable hypothesis is that the earliest inhabitants of Norway occupied skin tents of the kind used in modern times over much of the circumpolar zone and of which significantly there are indications from the Late-glacial period in Schleswig-Holstein. This form of shelter was well adapted both to the environment and the economy of the people. It agrees with the absence of stone axes or adzes and reflects the abundance of animal skins available to hunters.

The absence of animal bones from Fosna and Komsa sites means that we are deprived of direct evidence of the animals on which the people must have depended for much of their protein and the same applies to traces of plant food. We have therefore to depend on inference from the position of sites and on the direct evidence available from later periods. One of the most striking facts about the distribution of Fosna and Komsa sites is that they are mainly concentrated on locations open to the influence of the Gulf Stream, that is on islands, the outer coasts and the mouths of fjords, something particularly well seen (Map 13) in the case of the Trøndelag (Marstrander 1956). In this connection it is interesting to observe how many sites were situated on islands, a point which taken in conjunction with the sporadic distribution of sites on the Norwegian coast as a whole, indicates the high importance of boats. Although no trace of these has survived from this early period the presumption is strong that skin boats of the type depicted on the rock-engravings of the younger Stone Age (Gjessing, G. 1936, 197) had already been taken into use. Before leaving the topic of distribution one difference between the Fosna and Komsa distributions is worth noting: whereas in the Trøndelag area the heads of fjords appear to have been quite neglected, in Finnmark a significant number of sites are found at the heads of the deeply indented Alta and Porsanger Fjords (Map 14). Moreover, as Noel Broadbent (1971) has recently emphasised, these include some of the sites most prolific of artifacts, notably in the case of Bossekop I, II, Stenseng I and Tollevik.

The concentration of Fosna–Komsa sites on the coasts and islands argues that the sea was already the main source of protein, as we know from analysis of bone assemblages that it was during the younger Stone Age and in the case of south-west Norway at least by the Nøstvet phase. The relative closeness of the continental shelf means that the coastal waters and in the case of salmon the rivers of Norway are and have always been favoured spawning grounds: important food fish, above all bottom-feeders like cod, ling, halibut, haddock, pollack and whiting and the anadromous salmon, all came in their seasons within easy reach of man with even elementary equipment. The presumption

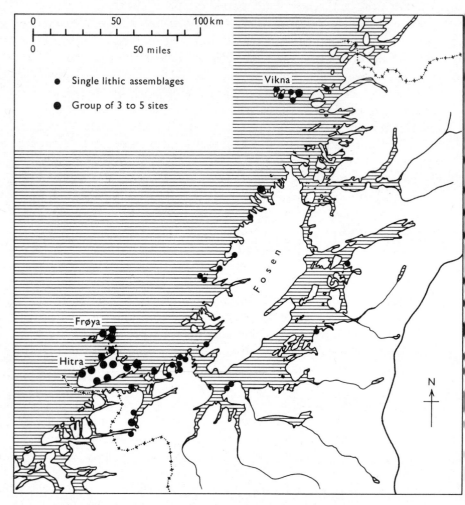

13. Map showing the distribution of Fosna lithic assemblages in the Trøndelag. The coastline shown corresponds with Tanner's d strand (mid-7th millennium B.C.). (*After Marstrander*)

is therefore a strong one that the line fishery documented by bone fish-hooks and associated fish bones from the younger Stone Age of northern, western and south-western Norway (Clark 1948a, appendix II) was already established during the early phase of settlement as it certainly was in the last mentioned region during the Nøstvet phase (Fig. 55, 1–5). From the nature of the case the off-shore line fishery pre-

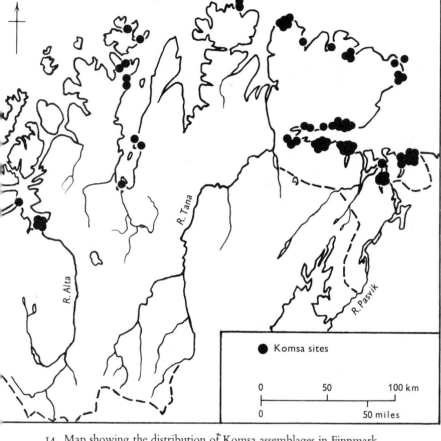

14. Map showing the distribution of Komsa assemblages in Finnmark.
(*After Bøe, Nummedal and Odner*)

supposed the use of boats which as we have seen must in any case be
inferred to account for Fosna–Komsa settlement on islands. Representations on some of the Nordland rock-engravings show pretty clearly
that the boats used were made of skin stretched over light frames and
in one case, that at Forselv (Gjessing, G. 1932, pl. xi) such a vessel is
associated with the outline of a halibut on a line.

Sea mammals, notably seals (Clark 1946) and toothed whales (Clark
1947), were other important sources of protein available and known to
have been exploited during the Stone Age. The cave of Viste for

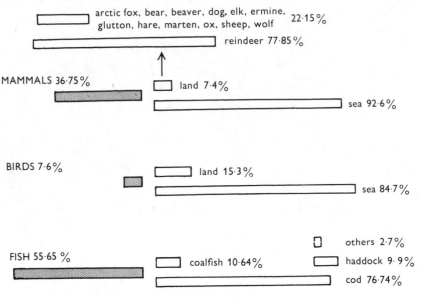

Fig. 57. Table analysing the animal bones from house foundations of the younger Stone Age on the south shore of Varanger Fjord. (*Based on Olsen*)

instance yielded three species of seal, grey, common and harp, and the first of these was certainly being taken during the Nøstvet phase. The earliest identified assemblage from northern Norway, that from the Varanger settlements (Fig. 57), yielded the same three species and in addition the ringed seal as well as walrus and six kinds of whale (killer, pilot, porpoise, sperm, white-beaked dolphin and *Hyperoodon ampulatus*) (Olsen 1967, 14). Another useful source of information from the younger Stone Age, the rock-engravings of Nordland, depicts seals at Rødøy and Valle, at the former associated with porpoise and a skin boat. As we know from recent usage among the Eskimo, but more relevantly perhaps from the coasts of Donegal and the western isles of Scotland (Clark 1946, 38), seal skins were particularly sought after for covering skin boats, partly on account of their resistance to floating ice. The engravings also show porpoises (Rødøy (2), Evenhus (II) and Valle), killer whales (Klubba (2) and Evenhus) and pilot whale (Strand) (Clark 1947, 102).

Sea birds provided another, though relatively insignificant, source of protein. The younger Stone Age settlements of Varanger Fjord (Olsen

216

1967, table 16) yielded bones of several species of auks, guillemot, eider-ducks and gulls and it is significant that water birds are depicted on the rock-engravings and represented in miniature sculptures from the younger Stone Age of Nordland. The fact that auks are represented in the Varanger deposits more than twenty times more often than gulls which occur in nature in approximately equal numbers suggested to Olsen that the former was pursued for some special reason, the most likely one being the superior value of their skins and plumage for lining skin garments as the Eskimo do today.

If the earliest food refuse from Norwegian settlements points to an overwhelming predominance of marine species, this is not to say that terrestrial sources of protein were neglected even on coastal settlements. Thus in the case of bird bones from the Varanger sites identified by Haakon Olsen, some 15% belonged to willow grouse, birds which came down from the mountains in the autumn, and up to modern times have commonly been taken in snares during the period of snow cover. In the case of mammals the proportion of marine species in the Varanger deposits was even greater, amounting to c. 92·6%. Of the land mammal remains over three-quarters – 2,513 out of 3,228 – belonged to reindeer. Of the rest it is interesting to note the occurrence of elk so far north, as well as a large number of fur-bearing species and a few domestic animals. Firm information about the early spread of reindeer into northern Norway is extremely thin, comprising as it does nothing more than that from the Varanger sites and certain rock-engravings, notably that from Bola on the Atlantic coast. On the other hand it is a fair presumption that reindeer penetrated Finnmark from north Russia as soon as the province became geographically accessible, even if at the moment the presence of this animal cannot yet be documented in adjacent parts of Russia at this time. Similarly no firm clues exist about the spread of reindeer into southern Norway. What is quite certain is that owing to the rapid rise of temperature in this territory the reindeer herds must very soon have been restricted to the higher ground of which the Hardangervidda is a conspicuous example. The earliest bone assemblages we have from the coast zone of southern Norway show no traces of reindeer. In the earliest level at Viste corre-sponding to the Nøstvet phase of settlement elk, wild pig and red deer are already established in a forested environment, though the last mentioned was still only of subsidiary importance by comparison with its predominant role during the younger Stone Age of south-west

Norway. It is significant that horse and ox were represented only in the uppermost layer at Viste dating from the closing phases of the younger Stone Age. On the other hand remains of dogs were found as early as the Nøstvet layer, just as in south Scandinavia they had been present from the beginning of the post-glacial settlement. That wild animals were taken for their skins as well as their meat is suggested by the large number of species of fur-bearing animals represented both in the Varanger Fjord and Viste sequences, at the latter polecat, otter, marten, bear, wolf, lynx, squirrel and beaver, though only the first-mentioned can be proved to have been taken during the initial phase of occupation.

We must await the discovery of adequate samples of organic refuse from the older Stone Age of Norway before hypotheses about the actual animals exploited can be checked – and if the Fosna–Komsa settlers invariably occupied tents this may be difficult to obtain since there were no earthen walls to collapse and cover the cultural deposits as there were for instance in the younger Stone Age settlements on Varanger Fjord. The same applies to the programming of the food quest with its implications for the permanence or seasonality of settlement. This is important because it rarely happens that there is only one way of exploiting a given set of opportunities and the one actually chosen needs to be determined for each particular case. For instance we do not know and in the present state of evidence cannot know whether or to what extent the earliest settlers of different parts of Norway shifted their home bases seasonally or stayed on the same sites, exploiting the various species in their seasons. What seems reasonably certain is that the coastal sites were occupied during the peak of the cod fishing, that is during the winter months. What would be interesting to establish is whether the Fosna–Komsa settlers abandoned their coastal winter sites to penetrate into the interior during the summer, as the younger Stone Age settlers of Varanger apparently did in pursuit of salmon. The absence of traces of inland Komsa settlement at this time in Finnmark might seem to argue against this, though it needs to be emphasised that this may at any time be contradicted by finding traces of inland settlement. Conversely, as already noted, traces of Fosna settlement in the interior of south Norway could well indicate seasonal exploitation of resources, though equally they might imply specialisation, with most groups living permanently on coastal sites but others living in the restricted highland habitats occupied by reindeer. What seems reasonably sure is that the earliest intruders into Norway were either already attuned to exploiting coastal resources, perhaps as a seasonal activity, as may even have been the case in Late-glacial Denmark, or alternatively that they adapted rapidly to exploiting coastal resources.

Psychic needs

No information of any kind is available about the way in which the earliest settlers of Norway satisfied their psychic needs. Indeed the only evidence we have from the whole of the older Stone Age in this country comes from the Nøstvet occupation level at Viste. This comprises a few symbolic designs engraved on bone. However sparse, these have one point of interest, namely that they are basically taken from the stock prevalent in south Scandinavia during Boreal times. They include the linear zig-zag (motif r), a variant of this in which one slope of each zig-zag is doubled, the shaded band (motif ii) and however fragmentary a trace of the mesh pattern (Fig. 55, 7).

FINLAND

Geographical setting

The territory of Finland took shape belatedly as in the most literal sense it rose above the waters (Map 15). During the period of the Yoldia Sea the country was restricted to a narrow peninsula extending in a southeasterly direction from the head of Lake Ladoga, together with a number of small discrete islands. It was not until the process of isostatic recovery had proceeded far enough for solid land-masses to appear above the level of the Ancylus Lake that the country offered an attractive field for colonisation. Throughout the Stone Age and indeed down to the early historic period main weight of settlement concentrated on coastal tracts and to a significant degree on the actual shore. This was especially true of the period before farming was introduced. By occupying this zone, which naturally shifted as the progress of isostatic recovery caused the waters of the Baltic to recede, communities were able to exploit both marine and inland resources, combining seal-hunting with the exploitation of elk and the trapping and shooting of a wide range of fur-bearing animals, not to mention fishing and the foraging of plant resources. At the same time the interior of the country, plentifully provided with lakes and reticulated by streams, although not

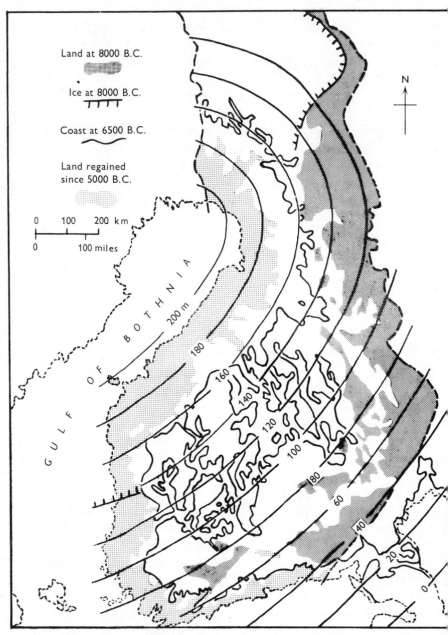

15. Map illustrating phases in the emergence of Finland. (*After Hyyppä*)

densely settled, was subject to a systematic seasonal exploitation, in particular during the period of snow cover when hunting and transport was assisted by sledges and in due course also by skis. The process of Post-glacial uplift which may at first have been as rapid as 10 m a century and is still of the order of 1 m along the Bothnian coast, had the effect of adding extensive flat areas of fine graded sediments of clay, loam and silt, a process that even today increases the area of Finland by something like a thousand square kilometres a hundred years. It was these potentially fertile soils that first attracted agriculturalists in prehistoric times and much of the farmland of the historic period has in fact emerged since the end of the Stone Age. Isotherms reflect the influence of the Baltic and its gulfs and help to explain why farming was largely confined to the south-west of Finland and the southern part of the coastal zone of Ostrobothnia. Floristically also it is significant that southern and south-western Finland was the only part of the country to fall within the north European mixed forest, the equivalent of the southern taiga of European Russia. Most of the country, apart from its northernmost parts was situated in the Boreal coniferous region, counterpart of the northern taiga of the Soviet Union.

To begin with, while the Ancylus Lake extended east of Lake Ladoga, southern Finland was most accessible from the south, but the northern part of the country was always open to the east from peoples of the northern taiga. Contact with east Sweden and Norrland across the Baltic and the Gulf of Bothnia is not likely to have been important until the progress of isostatic recovery on either side had materially narrowed the gap, though one should not forget the possibility of early movement round the head of the Gulf. Meanwhile in late Boreal times the closest reservoir of population was situated on the northern margin of the southern taiga extending from the east Baltic states to the lake region of western Vologda.

The Antrea find and its context in the settlement of the East Baltic

It is hardly a coincidence that the earliest site identified on Finnish territory (as this existed down to 1940), the find at Antrea, was situated at the northern end of the high ground extending west of Lake Ladoga from Leningrad in the direction of Viborg, the point at which the traverse of the Gulf of Finland was narrowest at the time (Map 16). The nature of the find itself suggests that we need not look beyond the food-quest for an explanation.

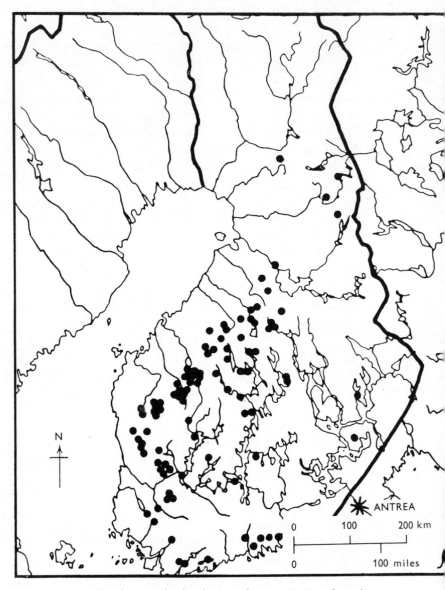

16. Map showing the distribution of Suomusjärvi perforated stone maceheads. (*After Luho*)

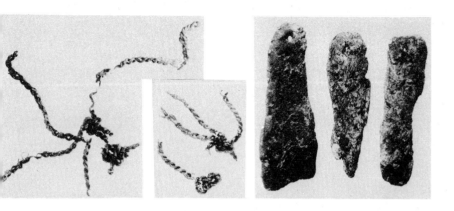

PLATE VIII. Remains of net of Boreal age from Antrea, near Viborg, formerly in Finland.

The most notable items comprised the remains of a seine-net resting on water-laid sediment (Pl. VIII), a net which to judge from the positions of the sinkstones and floats might have been between 27 and 30 m long and some 1·3 to 1·5 m high. Traces of the net itself of double threaded cord made from the bast of willow bark were preserved under some of the 18 oblong pine-bark floats. The net had evidently been lost or discarded in some depth of water with the sinkstones still attached and its use seems to imply the employment of some kind of boat. None of the sinkstones had been shaped artificially but traces of the thread used to secure them occurred under some of the 31 examples found. On geological and palaeobotanical grounds it is widely agreed that the net should be attributed to a comparatively early phase of the Ancylus Lake and to a time when the pine was beginning to climb to its Boreal peak. In terms of Quaternary research therefore it belongs to the early Boreal and suggests that fishermen were already operating off the coast of Finland at a period equivalent to an early phase in the development of the western Maglemose tradition.

The chronological status of the group of stone and antler artifacts found (Fig. 58) in a nearby patch only some 60 × 75 cm across seems less secure. Certainly if they were deposited on dry land they must be rather younger than the net. The find is nevertheless of key importance if only because it yielded by far the largest quantity of bone and antler artifacts from the first phase in the Stone Age of Finland. Even the stone tools are of the highest interest because they point in two directions, backwards to a source in the east Baltic states and forward to the initial Suomusjärvi settlement of extensive parts of Finland: they include three wood-working tools shaped by flaking and having polished working edges, including a heavy adze with tapered neck or pointed butt, a smaller one with broad neck and a small narrow chisel having its working edge hollowed by grinding and polishing to a gouge-like form. The artifacts of antler and bone owe not a little of their interest to the fact that conditions in Finland were generally exceptionally unfavourable to the survival of these materials. Where identified, the animal concerned was elk which was to remain the most important source of animal protein over much the greater part of the country down to the end of the Stone Age. Among the most notable pieces was a knife handle (no. 6) made from a pointed piece of elk shin-bone slotted along the middle of one edge to receive a sharp cutting edge made of inset flakes of the kind made of quartz and recovered from the site; a hollow chisel or scraper (no. 4) made from part of a substantial tubular long bone and having its concave working edge carefully polished; a stout chisel (no. 2) with bevelled end made from a narrow splinter taken from a substantial tubular bone; a short, stout point

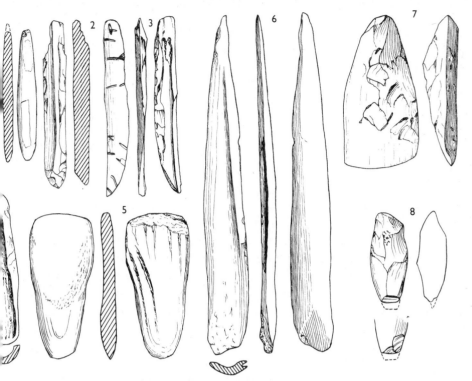

Fig. 58. Objects of antler, bone and stone from the Antrea find.
(*National Museum, Helsingfors.*) (1/3)

with the tip missing (no. 1); a knife-like tool (no. 3) with traces of engraved lines made before detachment from the parent long bone and possibly forming part of a geometric design; and a portion of elk antler resembling a stone adze in outline (no. 5), but which may well have served as some kind of scraping tool.

The obvious immediate source for the earliest settlement of Finland, Esthonia and proximate areas, lies within the territory of what is often conventionally termed the 'eastern Maglemose' or Kunda culture. Until comparatively recently this comprised mainly stray finds of antler or bone artifacts used in hunting and fishing and preserved in old lake beds or swamps, some of which compared with similar objects found stray or in settlement sites in the west Baltic area and even as far away as England. Yet there were always sufficient differences, for example in the lanceolate and conical tipped arrowheads and flat-shanked fish-hooks, to indicate that the territory extending from the Vistula to

Table 18. *Radiocarbon dates from the older Stone Age of Esthonia*

	cm	B.C.
Kunda. Charcoal from the lower level gave		TA 14: 6390 ± 280
Narva III. Three dates are available:	212–23	TA 25: 5630 ± 300
	300–10	TA 41: 5140 ± 230
	313–18	TA 53: 5639 ± 180
Narva II. A sample from the lower level:	212–17	TA 52: 5365 ± 190
Younger samples:		TA 40: 4790 ± 250
		TA 17: 4070 ± 120
Narva I. Only one determination:		TA 7: 3350 ± 250

Latvia and Esthonia across to Vologda and sporadically as far east as the mid-Urals, formed a distinct province. The full nature of the difference on the other hand only became apparent first with the excavation of the settlement of Lammasmägi adjacent to the ancient lake-bed at Kunda and later with the exploration of pre-ceramic levels at Narva. These showed among other things that the lithic artifacts associated with the antler and bone objects from the two finds differed markedly from those on sites in the west Baltic area. The Kunda and Narva excavations also showed in their uppermost levels that the appearance of pottery marked an enrichment of the old culture rather than its displacement by a new population. As we shall see similar evidence of continuity appears in Finland as a whole. Radiocarbon analysis has shown (Table 18) that Esthonian settlements having equipment of Kunda type spanned a period from the seventh to the fourth millennium B.C.

Each of the main components of the Antrea assemblage can be paralleled from Esthonia and Latvia. The correspondence is so complete indeed as to suggest that the pioneer settlers of Finland came from the south. The net from Antrea may be compared with one found not far east of Kunda at Siivertsi: although in this case no trace of the actual net survived the thread found encircling a sinkstone was similarly made of two-threaded bast cord and the pine bark float was elongated though in this case having smoothly convex sides (Indreko 1948, Abb. 79, nos. 1 and 6). Plenty of parallels can be cited for the two most diagnostic bone forms. Knives armed with flakes inset in the edges like that from Antrea had, as we have already mentioned (p. 175), come into use as long ago as the Late-glacial period in south Russia, and examples nearer at hand may be cited from Lammasmägi, Kunda (Indreko 1948, Abb. 74, no. 2). Analogies for the so-called chisel with hollow edge (*Höhlmeissel*) made from a split long bone are numerous: Lammasmägi itself yielded examples (Indreko 1948, Abb. 51, nos. 2, 5, 6) and others may be cited from Pernau (Indreko, 1948, 173), Rinnukalns (Briussov 1957, fig. 48, no. 8), from Narva (Site I) and from Lubans Lake, Latvia (Šturms 1970, Taf. 18, 6). Although termed 'chisels' in the literature, closely similar tools of aurochs bone from Star Carr were compared (Clark *et al.* 1954, 161–3) with ones made of caribou bone used by the Copper Eskimo for working skins, a function of widespread relevance to hunting peoples living in a temperate or arctic climate.

The stone implements from Antrea also compare closely with ones from Esthonia, notably from Lammasmägi and from Voisiku. Since flint was absent from Finland and scarce in Esthonia it is not perhaps surprising to find quartz used for small tools just as no doubt it explains why stone was used for the blades of wood-working tools. As Indreko already observed (1948, 152), blades flaked into a more or less triangular form with tapered butt and polished working edge were also part of the inventory from pre-ceramic deposits in Esthonia, like Lammasmägi, Narva and Voisiku. It is also of interest that a chisel with hollow-ground edge (*Höhlmeissel*) was also present at Lammasmägi (Indreko 1948, Abb. 44, 5), a form doubtless suggested by the use of tools made from large long-bones, whose concave edge was formed by part of the medullary cavity.

The Suomusjärvi phase

The earliest widespread indications of settlement in Finland comprise assemblages of artifacts from dwelling sites adhering to strand-lines relating to some stage in the history of the Ancylus Lake and the earlier phases of the Litorina Sea. The idea put forward by Luho (1956a) that certain assemblages of quartz tools, mainly from the parishes of Askola and Saarijärvi, go back to the Yoldia Sea phase of the Baltic has since been discarded as a result of Siiriäinen's demonstration (1969) of the real complexity of the process of land-emergence during early Post-glacial times. It now appears likely that the Askola sites relate to the Suomusjärvi phase in the human settlement of Finland.

Technology. The type fossil by which this phase was first identified is the stone axe of oval or elliptical section and pointed butt of the kind

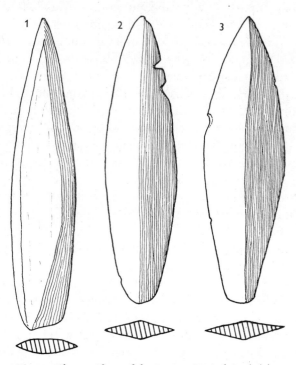

Fig. 59. Slate artifacts of the Suomusjärvi phase (1/2).

already encountered in the Antrea find, a type differentiated from the stump-butted axe of Middle Sweden not merely by its form but also by its technique of production. Again, as at Antrea, we find the hollow-edged, polished stone chisel as a key form. Although, as these forms and the bone equipment from Antrea show, the source of the earlier settlers of Finland lay south of the Gulf, this is by no means to say that Suomusjärvi technology was introduced ready-made from Esthonia. Signs of local development can be seen in the stone equipment itself. For instance, although the concept of perforating stone from two directions was certainly known in Esthonia (Indreko 1948, Abb. 44, 5), it is only in Finland that we find round flattish bun-shaped or deeper beehive-shaped mace heads or weight-stones (Fig. 62).

A new development of some importance for the future was the use of slate for artifacts, a technique without much doubt taken over from bone work and applied to a kind of stone peculiarly amenable to polishing. The material was used for blades, either spearheads or two-

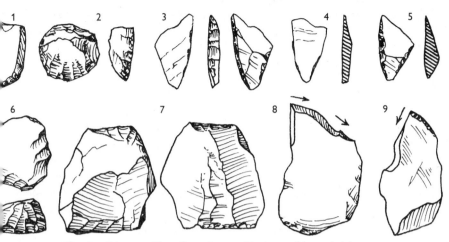

Fig. 60. Quartz artifacts from Suomusjärvi assemblages (2/3).

edged knives (Fig. 59). Quartz was used as at Antrea for making a variety of small artifacts. Although the nature of the material often makes it difficult to detect and interpret secondary flaking, it is evident (Fig. 60) that it was used for scrapers, some button-shaped, others on the ends of flakes or blades as well as burins, *lames écaillés* and arrowheads of oblique cutting form, a type which first appeared in Denmark during mid-Atlantic times.

An innovation which supervened without apparently interrupting either the technology or the economy of the older Stone Age inhabitants of Finland was the practice of potting. The earliest pottery of Finland like that of the Russian taiga was built by the coil process. In this it resembled the Ertebølle ware of southern Scandinavia with which to judge by radiocarbon dating (Meinander 1971) it was broadly contemporary. On the other hand it differed both in form, taking the shape of the lower two-thirds of an egg, and in decoration. Whereas this was normally confined to the rim of Ertebølle pots, in the early Finnish and taiga pottery it tended to be arranged in horizontal bands and to include pit and comb impressions. Historically, on the other hand, the context of the two classes of pottery was broadly analogous. Both reflect the acquisition by peoples living beyond the contemporary margin of cultivation of an art invariably associated further south with peoples whose economy was based on farming.

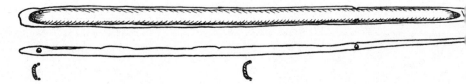

Fig. 61. Early sledge runner from Heinola, Finland (1/20). (*After Itkonen*)

Subsistence. The extreme rarity of organic traces from Suomusjärvi sites limits rather narrowly the possibility of gaining an insight into the basic economy of the earliest inhabitants of Finland. Information about actual dwellings is extremely slight. Fire-places, sometimes with stone settings, have often been observed, but little else is known. One of the few plans published with any detail, that at Mullyluoma, Honkajoki (Luho 1967, Taf. xxv), shows an oval setting of post-holes with another two outside that may indicate a porch and a rectangular setting inside that might have been used to contrive a smoke vent: if the oval of uprights was lintelled it may have supported a conical roof of pine stems.

The position of sites can tell us something. The great majority were found adhering more or less closely to the former shores of the late Ancylus Lake and early Litorina Sea from the Gulf of Finland more or less half-way up Ostrobothnia. The main emphasis undoubtedly rested on coastal settlement and the breadth of the zone occupied by sites argues that this lasted a long time, probably some three millennia. There is evidence on the other hand for settlement at this time in the interior, for instance at Moilanen on the island of Summasaari in Lake Saarijärvi. On the other hand the scarcity and extremely fragmentary nature of the animal remains makes it impossible to decide on the status of the inland and coastal sites and in particular the extent to which they reflected seasonal settlement. There is evidence in the form of a pine-wood runner, recovered by chance lying on necron mud under a metre of clay and coarse sand at Heinola, for the use of snow transport at a time indicated by pollen analysis (Aario 1934) to have been more or less contemporary with Antrea. The runner is 2·46 m in length (Fig. 61). One face has been largely hollowed out and pairs of holes have been drilled through the walls of the hollow. Two alternative explanations have been offered for runners of this type: one that they formed the keels of sledges like those drawn by a man on skis among the Lapps

FINLAND

Table 19. *Identifications by Dr Ann Forstén of animal remains from Suomusjärvi sites, in the National Museum*

	Vasikkahaka, Alavus	Kurejoki, Alajärvi	Pisinmaki, Kerava*	Lanhala, Honkajoki	Moilanen, Saarijärvi
Elk	×	.	.	.	×
Reindeer	.	.	.	.	×
Seal	×	.	×	×	.
Bear	×	×	.	.	×
Fox	.	.	×	×	×
Beaver	.	.	× (?)	×	×
Dog	×	.	×	.	×
Fish	.	×†	.	×†	×
Birds	.	.	.	.	×

* This site yielded some *Ovis capra* but also sherds of boat-axe pottery.
† Identified by Luho 1967, p. 92 and 77.

(Berg 1935, ch. 1), the other that they formed parts of sledges with built up platforms (Itkonen 1938). Since there is no evidence that skis were used at the time of the Heinola runner, the latter interpretation is to be preferred. In either case the runner suggests journeys during the long season of snow cover that would have the effect of opening up the interior at the time of the year when animal furs were in best condition. The size of the sledge suggests the use of animal traction, and it is significant that the remains of dog were identified on three out of the five sites from which bones have been determined.

Thanks to Professor Meinander, a table (Table 19) can be shown of the largest assemblages of animal bones from Suomusjärvi sites available in the National Museum.

It will be noted that seals occurred on three of the four coastal sites, but that these sites on the other hand frequently also yielded remains of forest species. Elk was evidently the main food mammal, though reindeer was apparently available in the interior to judge from the Moilanen find. Bear, fox and beaver were primarily significant for their furs, but also contributed to the supply of meat. Fish remained a significant source of protein. To judge from the wealth and diversity of catching equipment made of antler and bone from Kunda and Narva, including barbed spear- and harpoon-heads, fish-hooks, arrow-heads and the like, the absence or at least the very great rarity of artifacts made from organic materials on sites in most of Finland has deprived us of much detailed information about the precise manner in which the Suomusjärvi people supported life. As it is we have to remain content for direct evidence with the seine-net from Antrea and for the indications for the use of the bow and the spear provided by cutting arrowheads of quartz and by slate spearheads.

Psychic needs. The best evidence that psychic as well as alimentary needs were met is provided by the geometric designs more or less deeply engraved on the surface of the stone clubs that were an important component of material equipment. These included chevrons and metopic patterns formed by opposed sets of parallel lines made up of short strokes (Fig. 62). If we except the few lines incised on a bone knife from Antrea, these provide the sole documentation of symbolic art surviving from the pre-ceramic stage of settlement in Finland. The sources of this art, like the sources of the rest of the cultural endowment of the earliest settlers, lie south of the Gulf of Finland. Studies of representations on bone and antler surviving in the river-beds, lake-beds and lakeside settlements of Esthonia by Indreko (1948, Abb. 84) and of Latvia by Loze (1968, table 1*a* and 5) and Šturms (1970, Taf. 48) show that, although the repertoire is at present more restricted, most of the categories known to the Maglemosian art of the west Baltic are present. Human and animal sculptures abound in the later Stone Age of the East Baltic region, but engravings of either are absent or extremely rare in the Kunda repertoire, although a cervid, optimistically identified as a reindeer by Loze (1968, table 1), is engraved on a bone dagger from the Uzava river in western Latvia. Geometric designs are plentiful and include such familiar patterns as barbed lines, criss-cross shading, obliquely and transversely shaded bands, lozenges and a variety of chevrons and zig-zags. As a rule these have been executed by simple engraved lines, but small pits drilled into the surface, the *Bohrornament* of the Maglemosian tradition, were used to carry out a relatively complex design on a bone plaque from the Pernau river in western Esthonia as well as to decorate the flattened shanks of fish-hooks from the same locality. It is interesting to note that designs of parallel lines traversed by zig-zags and tied together at the ends by short oblique strokes recurs in almost identical form, again made by drilled pits, at Silkeborg Sø, Jutland, nearly a thousand km to the west. Of the more complex designs the chequer-board appears on a bone arrowhead from the

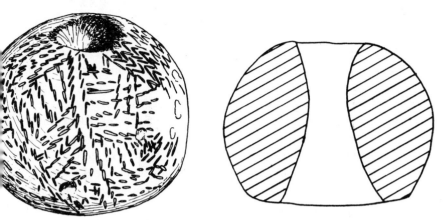

Fig. 62. Perforated stone macehead with engraved design: Suomusjärvi phase (1/2).

Lubans Lake (Loze 1968, table 3, 3). No clear-cut net-pattern appears on objects of certainly pre-ceramic context, but the well-investigated third-millennium site of Sarnate, Latvia, has yielded fine examples both on wood and pottery (Vankina 1970, pls. XL and XLI, 1).

MIDDLE AND NORTH SWEDEN

Geographical background

Whereas much of south Sweden was open to human settlement during the Late-glacial period as a peninsula of the north European plain, the northern and much of the central part of the country was buried under the Scandinavian ice-sheet of this time. Moreover the isostatic recovery which proceeded as the ice-sheet contracted was not fast enough during the earlier phases of the Post-glacial period for the land to gain very rapidly on the rising melt-waters. As a result much of middle Sweden was submerged. During the period of the Ancylus Lake overland access from the south could only be obtained by passing in a north-easterly direction either side of a much enlarged Lake Vänern on the west to Värmland and to the east to Närke and thence into Dalarna and Jämtland: almost the whole of Södermanland, Västmanland and Uppland, at the present time one of the most densely settled zones of Sweden, was still submerged. From the east access could only have been obtained overland by passing round the head of the gulf of

Bothnia from Finnish to Swedish Lappland. On the other hand movements may well have taken place across the Ancylus Lake on a broad front as they certainly did later. The known importance of seal-hunting during the Litorina phase provides a setting in which movements of this kind can readily be visualised in either direction. There remains the possibility that northern Sweden could have been colonised in part from the coastal zone of north-west Norway. As the shape of Lapp territories and their seasonal movements still remind us, the rivers which flow down from the Caledonian mountains provide natural routes to the Bothnian Gulf and Ohthere's reference to the exploits of the Finns in harrying the Northmen reminds us that light skin boats could easily have been carried over portages (Clark 1948*b*, 227). Again, further south links between Jämtland and the Trøndelag can be documented at least as far back as the younger Stone Age (ibid. 227–8).

A fact about the archaeology of middle and north Sweden all the more striking from the presence of reindeer herds and their Lapp proprietors at the present day is the complete absence of any trace of reindeer from early Stone Age sites. The explanation for this is ecological. As indicated in an earlier chapter (p. 53), the open *fjäll* country is a comparatively recent phenomenon, an outcome of the lowering of the tree-level that accompanied the decline of temperature during the first millennium B.C. Until this time the forests of north Sweden seem to have extended high up on the Caledonian mountains. In early times the principal food resource of Norrland was elk, but game birds, fish and fur-bearing animals were also of importance in the interior. Another major source of protein in this region was and still is seal catching on the Bothnian coast. These resources could be cropped most effectively by adopting a seasonal strategy, shifting the focus of activity from the coast to the interior in an annual cycle. Early spring was the best time for seal-hunting. The season for hair or ringed seal extended from February into April. Adults could be taken by the *maupoq* method through holes in the fast ice on which in due season the females gave birth to the young, which were most desirable and still vulnerable when they had reached a peak of fatness immediately before taking to the water. The grey Atlantic seal was likewise most easily taken while the young were still resting on the ice-floes in February/March. The harp or Greenland seal is similarly found on drift ice or on the margins of fast ice. The approach of summer brought renewed sources of protein in the form first of salmon which congregated near the mouths of the main rivers preparatory to moving upstream to spawn and slightly later of whitefish which likewise moved upstream, though not so far as salmon, to breed mostly in late July and August. By following these major food fish upstream bands or microbands put themselves in a position for the final harvests of the year. Winter was the best time for hunting elk and it was at this time of the year also that the pelts of fur-bearing animals were at their best. Skis, when these came into use, provided the readiest means for approaching elk close enough to secure them readily with primitive equipment, just as deep snow cover impeded their movements; and sledges made it possible to transport heavy loads of meat to home bases. The winter was also the best season for snaring and catching game birds like the blackcock, capercailze, hazel-hen and ptarmigan that featured so prominently in Stockholm trade conducted by Jämtland peasants during recent historical times.

Archaeological clues to early settlement

Pending definitive publication of the results of research projects stimulated by hydro-electric works on the rivers of northern Sweden only a few clues can yet be cited as to the nature of the earliest human settlement of this region. A hint that the Caledonian range may have been traversed by groups from the coastal zone of Norway, possibly during the summer expeditions into the interior, is provided by a find at Järnasjön not far over the Swedish side of the border and *c.* 130 km south of the Arctic circle. A patch of worked quartz some three to four square metres in extent on a rocky islet in the southern part of the lake included specimens with steep retouch and among these were micro- liths and an oblique chisel-ended arrowhead resembling those found in Fosna assemblages, notably in the interior of south Norway on the Hardangervidda (Westerlund 1970).

Early settlement of the interior of Norrland is frequently marked by no more than artifacts and traces of fire exposed by surface erosion, frequently on the shores of rivers or lakes. On the other hand particular interest attaches to the mounds or rings of heat-splintered stones (*skärvsten*) situated close to water, sometimes on a tongue of land projecting into a lake, features which presumably represent accumula- tions of stones heated in the fire and used for boiling water perhaps in bark containers. These were first recognised on the Hoting lake on a tributary of the Ångerman river, where the site of Bellsås yielded radiocarbon dates in the fourth millennium B.C. (Janson and Hvarfner 1960, 32 ff. and 53–6). Others have since been recognised further north in the valley of the Ume river, notably at Tjikkiträsk in the parish of Stensele (Meschke 1967) and as far south as the Storsjön in Jämtland where some ten sites have been noted (ibid. 1). The radiocarbon dates obtained from settlement layers at Bellsås (3795±110; 3475±140; and 3150±100 B.C.) show that cooking mounds go back at least to the fourth millennium B.C. (Baudou 1970a) and a hollow cut into the sand underlying the *skärvsten* mound of Tjikkiträsk is claimed to date from around 5000 B.C. (Meschke 1967, 51). In both cases the dominant animal bones refer to elk and it is of particular interest that the elk skulls from Bellsås had lost their antlers indicating that the animals were killed during the winter. The animal material comprising some 30,000 bone fragments from the Tjikkiträsk site analysed by H. Sellstedt and N.-G. Gejvall (in Meschke 1967, 61–2) is composed predominantly of elk. In the case of the early cooking-pit for example elk accounted for *c.* 91% of the identifiable bones. It is no less interesting that beaver accounted for another 7% with fish and seal at 1% each. In this last connection Bo Gräslund, noting that the last species is represented only by two toe-bones, has remarked on the added fact that these are the only toe-bones of any species from the site. In accounting for this he further notes that at the present day where seal skins are taken into use toe bones are often still attached. This strongly suggests that already at this early date the people who hunted elk during the winter in the interior spent part of the year on the coast hunting seals whose skins they brought back the following winter. If this is so it looks as though the kind of seasonal pattern of exploitation adumbrated earlier in this chapter was already being practised at this time. Information about the artifacts from the older Stone Age sites in Norrland is complicated by the fact that many sites were occupied successively over long periods of time, and definitive publication is still lacking or inadequate. What does seem sure is that the earliest settlers of Norrland depended to a significant degree on the utilisation of quartz. It would be premature to speculate on the source of the earliest settlers of Lappland, Norrbotten, Västerbotten or Ångermanland.

In middle Sweden and in the southern zone of Norrland, more especially Dalarna and even Härjedalen in southern Jämtland, such indications as we have point unequivocally to the south and specifically the south-west for the source of early population. In the case of the antler and bone objects sometimes cited, it has to be noted that few come from dated deposits and that many forms had a long life. Thus none of the elk antler mattock-heads from Jämtland can be securely dated. Some of them, nòtably the specimens from Görvik and Singsån (see Appendix A), closely resemble examples of pre-Boreal age from Scania, but an equally 'primitive' example came from phase III at Hälla in the parish of Åsele, Lappland, dated by Baudou to c. 1600 B.C. Again this form can hardly of itself point to a southern rather than an eastern origin since it was equally at home in Esthonia and the presumption is a strong one that, though none have survived in Finland, they were nevertheless used in that country. Again, caution is needed in dealing with stray finds of barbed bone points since these had a long life in the Fennoscandian Stone Age as we know from dated finds in west Sweden and either side of the Gulf of Bothnia, not to mention the Russian taiga. Nevertheless, there are certain pieces which whatever their precise age point rather plainly to a southern source. The most significant of these is the spatulate tool with incised decoration from Agnmyren, Sollerön, Dalarna, illustrated by Fig. 63. The combination of barbed lines and a linear chevron is closely matched on a bone object from the early Boreal site of Mullerup in Zealand (Sarauw 1903, 275). The object itself is most closely matched by the piece with a fine mesh engraving unfortunately from an unknown site in Bohuslän. This provides a clear hint of a northward expansion of settlement or at least of exploration while the 'Maglemosian' style was still practised in its original form and the parallel just cited suggests that the line of movement reached the Siljan area by way of a route either side of Lake Vänern. The well-known stray find of part of a flat bone spearhead with slots on either edge for flint insets from Offerdals in Jämtland on the other hand finds its best parallels in the south from Atlantic time and could well be younger. Apart from the great intrinsic interest of its engravings, this piece is interesting whatever its precise age as a pointer to a northward extension of cultural influence from the south.

The evidence from lithic artifacts is much more abundant. Particular interest attaches to an assemblage made from a variety of raw materials, including jaspis, porphyry and quartzite, as well as occasionally slate and south Scandinavian flint, recovered by Bo Gräslund (1970) from the southern part of Ransjön in the parish of Linsells in Härjedalen, the southern zone Jämtland. These include as their discoverer was quick to

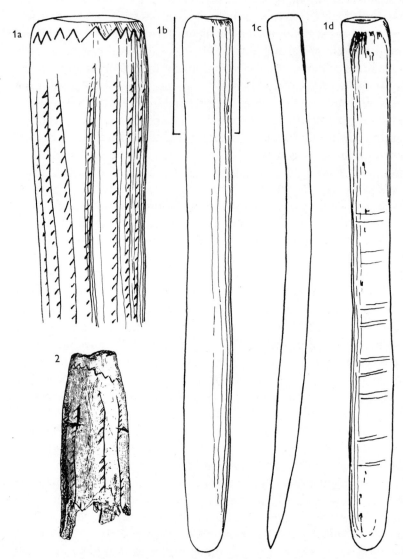

Fig. 63. Spatulate bone tool engraved with barbed lines (motif e) and chevrons (motive q1) from Agnmyren, Sollerön, Dalarna, Sweden (*SHM Stockholm*). With (*bottom left*) engraved bone from Mullerup, Zealand, Denmark. (*After Sarauw*). (1/2, except for 1a 5/4)

point out a number of forms, including handle cores, micro-flakes, long keeled scrapers and small round scrapers, which occur in late Boreal and early Atlantic contexts not merely in Scania, but probably more significantly in the west Swedish coastal zone. Moreover stray finds cited by Gräslund suggest that the Ransjön discovery related to a widespread phenomenon, the spread of lithic techniques from the west coast to the southern borders of Norrland, probably as early as the sixth millennium B.C.

Much more abundant evidence is provided by the spread of stone axes, both flaked and polished examples of the Lihult type and stump-butted ones pecked into shape with their working edges at least ground smooth. As already noted the axes named after the locality of Lihult in the parish of Skee between the west Swedish coast and the Norwegian frontier are not to be distinguished from the Nøstvet axe of Norwegian prehistorians. Their geographical distribution is highly suggestive. Outside the coastal zone of west Sweden they are found in quantity on the sand and silt extending from Göteborg across Västergötland on the eastern side of Lake Vänern; and further north-east they appear as the earliest stone tools recovered from Västmanland from the time when strand-lines with part of Sweden were still around 70 m above present sea level. Here again there is a strong suggestion of movement from west to middle and even the southern marches of north Sweden. Lihult axes accompanied by stump-butted ones, were assigned by Ekholm (1915, 16) to the earliest phase of occupation in Uppland, equivalent in age to a period when sea-level was some 64 m higher. Further north the same two forms, accompanied by polishing stones and quartzite flakes, appeared in the find at Tyllehagen, Torsångs parish, Dalarna. Still further north an axe of Lihult type may be cited from Rörösjön in the Storsjön district of central Jämtland (Janson, Biörnstad and Hvarfner 1962, Bild. 4l). As we have seen, stump-butted axes, which in south Scandinavia appeared as early as the late Boreal–early Atlantic transition, frequently accompanied ones of Lihult–Nøstvet form in Fennoscandia. On the other hand the stump-butted axe had a long life in Sweden and it is hardly possible by plotting individual finds to define the area of settlement during the last stages of the earlier Stone Age. What remains sure is that the widespread occurrence of this type of axe, which in Finland is a comparative rarity, points to the colonisation of the middle and the southern parts of northern Sweden from the south rather than the east.

APPENDIX A

List of elk antler mattock-heads shown on Map 10

Abbreviations: L.U.H.M. Lunds universitets historika museum; N.M. Nationalmuseet, Copenhagen; S.H.M. Statens historika museet, Stockholm

Nos.	Sites	Form	Age	Source
1	Vattabakkjen, Stenkjær Trøndelag, Norway	A	Sub-B	Gjessing, G. 1945, 206, 255
2	Hälla, Åsele, VB, Sweden		Sub-B	S.H.M. 869. 70
3	Görvik, Hammardals, Jämtland, Sweden	A		Jämtland Mus. 9002
4	Singsån, Ragunda, Jämtland, Sweden	B		Jämtland Mus. 15825
5	Hackås, Storsjön, Jämtland, Sweden	B		Jämtland Mus. 20. 2705
6	Återvall, Ingarö, Uppland, Sweden	A	Sub-B	S.H.M. 15388: 263; Salomonsson 1961, fig. 9
7	Sittesta, Ösmo, Söder-manland, Sweden	A		S.H.M. 1379: I
8	Korsnäs, Grödinge, Södermanland, Sweden	A	Sub-B	S.H.M.; E. Baudou
9	Lammasmägi, Kunda, Esthonia	B	BO2	Indreko 1948, Abb. 47, 3
10	Pernau, Esthonia	A, B		Indreko 1948, Abb. 49, 1, 3
11	Tingelstad, Hadelund, Norway	A		Brøgger, A. W. 1938, XXVII
12	Hurum, Drammen Fjord, Norway	A		Brøgger, A. W. 1938, XXVI
13	Rörvik, Kville, Bohuslän, Sweden		Sub-B	Janson 1936, 77
14	Holmängen, Väster-götland, Sweden	B		Fälkoping Mus. 1780
15	Borre bog, Valla, Tjörn, Bohuslän, Sweden			Montelius 1917, fig. 68
16	Maglekärr, Kristofta, Scania, Sweden	A	PB/ BO1	S.H.M. 20336; Salomonsson 1961, II

Nos.	Sites	Form	Age	Source
17	Harlösa, Scania, Sweden	A	PB	L.U.H.M./29126; Salomonsson 1961, 12; Tilander 1961
18	Sjörup, Scania, Sweden	B		L.U.H.M. 5037; Salmonsson 1961, 8, 9
19	Mossby, Nöbbelöv, Sweden	A	PB/ BO1	L.U.H.M./15946; Salomonsson 1961, 10–11
20	Hillerød, Zealand, Denmark	A		N.M. A 8525
21	Verup, Åmosen, Zealand, Denmark	A	BO1	Andersen, K. 1960, fig. 3
22	Skellingsted, Zealand, Denmark	A		N.M. A 49860
23	West of Skellingsted	A		N.M. A 39854
24	Gøgsmose, Kongsted, Zealand, Denmark	A		N.M. A 39085
25	Sværdborg, Zealand, Denmark	B	BO2	Friis Johansen 1919, 209, fig. 41
26	Nisted, Lumby, Fünen, Denmark	A		N.M. A 20853
27	Gjersbøl, Jutland, Denmark	A		Thisted M. 3790

Form A made from shed antlers; form B from ones broken out of a slain animal.

APPENDIX B

List of antler or bone points whose barb-spacings
are shown on Fig. 23

Nos.	Sites	Sources	Number of barbs	Mean spacing (mm)
	Finely toothed spearheads			
1	Bothildenslunds mosse, Scania	S.H.M. 13675	46	5·0
2	Vellinge, Scania	S.H.M. 2918	11	6·1
3	Unsted, Jutland	Århus 3097	22	5·1
4	Bog., N. Jutland	Thisted 654 K	22	6·0
5	Madlagelved, Sorlfeldt, Skjoldborg, Jutland	Thisted 3238	8	6·6
6	Hundborg, Jutland	Thisted 3870	12	5·6
7	Mors, Jutland	Nykobing	6	8·0
8	Tidemomsholm mose, Tars, Jutland	Hjørring 14923	14	6·3
9	Fannerup, Jutland	Århus 5551	21	4·7
10	Søbygaard Sø, Søby, Jutland	Århus 5088	19	7·0
11	Sönder Uldum, Hedensted, Jutland	Århus 6735	14	5·6
12	Beder, Jutland	Århus 2816	23	5·3
13	Bölling Sø, Jutland	N.M. A 39486	32	5·0
14	Vandløse, Amosen, Zealand	Brøndsted 1957, 82b	55	4·6
15	Mullerup, Zealand	Sarauw 1903, fig. 30	10	5·2
	Medium-barbed spearheads (Mullerup type)			
1	Sværdborg, Zealand	Friis Johansen 1919, fig. 56	4	15·3
2	Sværdborg, Zealand	ibid. fig. 57	3	11·3
3	Sværdborg, Zealand	Danske Oldsager, I, 173	4	14·0
4	Verup, Zealand	K. Andersen 1960, fig. 6	2	18·1

Nos.	Sites	Sources	Number of barbs	Mean spacing (mm)
5	Holmegaard, Zealand	Broholm 1931 fig. 27	4	13·0
6	Holmegaard IV, Zealand	Becker 1945, fig. 2	3	18·5
7	Holmegaard IV, Zealand	ibid.	3	12·0
8	Mullerup, Zealand	Sarauw 1903, fig. 28	3	19·5
9	Loc.?	N.M. A 39800	3	19·0
10	Mullerup	Danske Olds. I, 169	4	12·3
11	Løjesmølle, Rerslev, Zealand	Clark 1936, pl. v, 3	3	14·6
12	Undlöse Bro, Zealand	Mathiassen 1943, fig. 58, 2	5	16·5
13	Undlöse Bro, Zealand	ibid. fig. 58, 3	3	15·00
14	Undlöse Bro, Zealand	ibid. fig. 58, 2–4	4	12·0
15	Øgaarde	ibid. fig. 41, 8	3	13·5
16	Øgaarde	ibid. fig. 40, 3	3	12·0

Harpoon-heads

Denmark

1	Aggerup, Mertøse, Zealand	DOI, no. 167	5	40·5
2	Bloksbjerg, Zealand	Westerby 1927, fig. 34	2	36·7
3	Flynderhage, Jutland	Århus 3472	3	30·5
4	Løjesmølle, Rerslev, Zealand	Clark 1936, pl. v, 4	3	46·9
5	Overby, Odden, Holbæk, Zealand	DOI, no. 166	7	23·0
6	Sölager, Zealand	N.M. A 337	3	c. 33·0
7	Tjørnelunds Raamose, Finderup, Jutland	N.M. A 22763	4	42·6
8	Tubæk Mølle, Skibbinge, Praestø	N.M. A 34587	2	34·0
9	Vallensgaard mose, Bornholm	Becker 1951a, fig. 33	2	46·0
10	Vallensgaard mose, Bornholm	ibid.	3	33·8
11	Vallensgaard mose, Bornholm	ibid.	3 (biserial)	30·6 28·0

Sweden (mainland)

12	Balsby, Råbelövsjön, Scania	S.H.M. 13900: 291	3	41·0
13	Hästefjorden, Dalsland	Thomasson 1938; S.H.M. 4011	3	55·0
14	Hyltebergen, Skurup, Scania	S.H.M. 12716: 1	5	31·0
15	Klövsjö, Jämtland	Östersund 20. 658	6	22·2
16	Leksand, Jämtland	S.H.M. 19670	9	17·1

Nos.	Sites	Sources	Number of barbs	Mean spacing (mm.)
		Sweden (mainland) (*cont.*)		
17	Mellantorp, Hammerland, Åland 260 Åland I		4	38·3
18	Möllehausen, Gualöv, Scania	L.U.H.M. 28. 570	2	32·5
19	Norrköping, Östergötland	S.H.M. 13467	2	52·0
20	Örnskoldsvik, Ångermanland	S.H.M. 13303	3	35·0
21	Djurnäs, Ösmo, Södermanland	S.H.M. 3940	4	33·6
22	Marietorp, Smedstorp, Scania	S.H.M. 9822: 672	2	22·0
23	Åmosen, Slågarp, Scania	S.H.M. 3400: 44	4	44·6
		Gotland*		
24	Hemmor	Nihlén 1927, fig. 64	2	29·0
25	Stora Forvar, Karlsø	Schnittger and Rydh 1940, pl. 1, 3	3	23·3
26	Västerbjers cemetery	Stenberger 1943, fig. 58	2	30·0
		ibid.	2	31·0
		ibid.	2	38·0
		ibid. fig. 38	2	38·0
		ibid. fig. 29	2	46·0
		ibid. fig. 37	2	60·0
		Finland		
27	Närpes, Österbotten	Sauramo 1938, 28	4	30·3
28	Oulu, Österbotten	N.M.F. 10310: 1	5	26·5

* Specimens illustrated in the literature are taken as a sample of the extremely abundant material from Gotland.

APPENDIX C

Faunal assemblages of early Post-glacial (Pre-boreal, early Boreal, late Boreal) age from northern Europe

	Star Carr	Hohen Viecheln	Hesselbjerggaard	Holmegaard	Mullerup	Sværdborg	Vinde-Helsinge	Øgaarde
Mammals								
Roe deer (*Capreolus capreolus* L.)	×	×	×	×	×	×	×	×
Red deer (*Cervus elephas* L.)	×	×	×	×	×	×	×	×
Elk (*Alces alces* L.)	×	×	×	×	×	×	×	×
Aurochs (*Bos primigenius* L.)	×	×	×	×	×	×	×	×
Wild pig (*Sus scrof. ferus* Gmelin)	×	×	×	×	×	×	×	×
Wild horse (*Equus ferus* Pall.)	.	×	.	.	.	.	.	.
Beaver (*Castor fiber* L.)	×	×	×	×	×	×	×	×
Wild cat (*Felis silvestris* Schreber)	.	×	.	×	×	×	.	×
Lynx (*Lynx lynx* L.)	.	×	.	×	×	×	.	×
Brown bear (*Ursus arctos* L.)	.	×	.	.	×	×	.	×
Pine marten (*Martes martes* L.)	×	×	×	×	×	×	×	×
Badger (*Meles meles* L.)	×	×	.	×	×	×	×	×
Otter (*Lutra lutra* L).	.	×	.	×	.	.	×	×
Fox (*Vulpes vulpes* L.)	×	×	.	×	×	×	×	×
Wolf (*Canis lupus* L.)	×	×	.	.	.	×	.	×
Dog (*Canis familiaris* L.)	×	×	×	×	×	×	.	×
Polecat (*Putorius putorius* L.)	.	×	.	.	.	.	.	.
Squirrel (*Sciurus vulgaris* L.)	.	.	.	.	.	×	×	.
Field hare (*Lepus europaeus* Pall.)	×	×	.	.	×	.	.	.
Grey seal (*Halichoerus grypus*)	.	.	.	.	.	×	.	×
Hedgehog (*Erinaceus europaeus*)	×	.	.	×	.	.	.	×
Birds								
Grey lag-goose (*Anser anser* L.)	.	×	.	.	.	×	.	.
Bean-goose (*A. fabalis* (Lath.))	.	×	.	.	.	.	.	.

245

Birds (cont.)

	Star Carr	Hohen Viecheln	Hesselbjerggaard	Holmegaard	Mullerup	Svaerdborg	Vinde-Helsinge	Øgaarde
White-fronted goose (*A. albifrons* Scop.)	.	×	.	.	.	.	.	.
Whooper swan (*Cygnus cygnus* L.)	.	×	.	.	.	.	.	.
Mute-swan (*Cygnus olor* Gmelin)	.	.	.	.	×	×	.	.
Swan (*Cygnus* sp.)	.	.	.	.	.	.	.	×
Mallard (*Anas platyrhynchos* L.)	.	×	.	.	×	.	.	×
Wigeon (*A. (Mareca) penelope* L.)	.	×	.	.	.	.	.	.
Shoveler (*A. clypeata* L.)	.	.	.	×	.	.	.	.
Pintail (*A. acuta* L.)	× ?	×	.	.	.	×	.	.
Tufted duck (*Nyroca fuligula* L.)	.	×	.	.	.	×	.	.
Long-tailed duck (*Pagonetta glacialis*) or ?(*Clangula hymenalis* L.)	.	.	.	.	×	.	.	.
Goosander (*Mergus merganser* L.)	.	×	.	.	.	×	.	.
Red-breasted merganser (*M. serrator* L.)	×	×	.	.	.	×	.	.
Smew (*Mergellus albellus* L.)	.	.	.	.	.	.	.	×
Heron (*Ardea cinerea* L.)	.	.	.	.	×	×	.	.
Bittern (*Botaurus stellaris* L.)	.	.	.	.	×	×	.	.
White stork (*Ciconia ciconia* L.)	× ?	.	.	.	.	.	.	.
Black stork (*C. nigra* L.)	.	.	.	×	.	.	.	.
Grey crane (*Grus grus* L.)	×	×	.	.	.	.	.	×
(*G. antigone* L.)	.	×	.	.	.	.	.	.
(*G. cinerea* L.)	.	.	.	×	×	×	.	.
Great black-backed gull (*Larus marinus*)	.	.	.	.	.	×	.	.
Black-headed gull (*L. ribibundus*)	.	.	.	.	×	.	.	.
Black-throated diver (*Colymbus articus* L.)	.	×	.	.	×	.	.	.
Red-throated diver (*C. stellatus*)	×	×	.	.	.	.	.	.
Great crested grebe (*Podiceps cristatus* L.)	×	×	.	×	×	×	×	×
Little grebe (*P. ruficollis* Pallas)	×	.	.	.	.	.	.	.
Coot (*Fulica atra* L.)	.	×	.	×	.	.	.	.
Capercaillie (*Tetrao urogallus* L.)	.	×	.	.	.	×	.	×
Grouse (*Lyrurus tetrix* L.)	.	×	.	.	.	.	.	.
Cormorant (*Phalacrocorax carbo* L.)	.	.	×	×	×	×	.	.
Lapwing (*Vanellus vanellus* L.)	×	.	.	.	.	.	.	.
Buzzard (*Buteo buteo* L.)	×	.	.	.	.	.	.	.
Great black woodpecker (*Picus martius*)	.	.	.	.	.	×	.	.
Jay (*Garrullus glandarius*)	.	.	.	.	.	×	.	.
Kite (*Milvus ictinus*)	.	.	.	.	.	×	.	.

	Star Carr	Hohen Viecheln	Hesselbjerggaard	Holmegaard	Mullerup	Sværdborg	Vinde-Helsinge	Øgaarde
Birds (*cont.*)								
Osprey (*Pandion haliaëtus*)	.	.	.	.	.	×	.	.
White-tailed eagle (*Haliaëtus albicilla* L.)	.	×	.	×	×	×	.	×
Reptiles								
Tortoise (*Emys obicularis* L.)	.	×	.	×	×	×	.	.
Toad								
Toad (*Bufo* sp.)	.	.	.	.	.	.	.	×
Fish								
Pike (*Esox lucius* L.)	.	×	.	×	×	×	×	×
Perch (*Perca fluviatilis* L.)	.	×	.	.	.	.	.	.
Bream (*Abramis brama* L.)	.	×	.	.	.	.	.	.
Sheat fish (*Silurus glanis* L.)	.	.	.	×	.	.	.	×

SOURCES: Star Carr: Fraser in Clark *et al.* 1954. Hohen Viecheln: Gehl in Schuldt 1961. Mullerup: Winge in Sarauw 1903. Sværdborg: Winge in Friis Johansen 1919 and Broholm 1931. Holmegaard: Winge in Broholm 1931. Hesselbjerggaard, Vinde-Helsinge and Øgaarde: Degerbøl in Mathiassen 1943.

APPENDIX D

List of objects from the west Baltic area engraved with designs
of 'Maglemose' character

Locations	Objects Author refers to red deer unless otherwise stated	Motifs Engraved unless defined by pits (B: *Bohr-ornament*) or dots (P: *pointillé*)	References Figure references to the present book shown in heavy type
	Jutland		
1. Horsens Fjord	Antler	Mesh, α1	**Fig. 30**; Broholm 1931, fig. 28
2–4. Koldingfjord	Antler	Mesh (B)	Müller, S. 1986, fig. 14–16
5. Monbjerg	Bone, 2-edged knife, flint insets	p	Vebæk 1939, fig. 1
6. Resen mose	Amber figurine	K, y2	**Fig. 36**; Müller, S. 1918, fig. 24
7. Resen mose	Amber figurine	n	Müller, S. 1918, fig. 29
8. Ringkjøbing	Amber pendant	a (B)	Müller, S. 1918, fig. 38
9. Ryomaa, Randers	Bone pick	t	Brøndsted 1957, 79a
10. Silkeborg	Perforated antler	Mesh, o, u (B)	Müller, S. 1896, fig. 12
11. Sørkel	Slate	Row. (B)	Mathiassen 1937, pl. III, 2
12. Ø. Jolby	Perforated antler	Curvilinear (B)	Liversage 1966, fig. 1 and 2
	Fünen		
13. Langø	Antler base mattock	Haphazard (B)	Broholm 1928, fig. 15

248

Locations	Objects Author refers to red deer unless otherwise stated	Motifs Engraved unless defined by pits (B: *Bohr- ornament*) or dots (P: *pointillé*)	References Figure references to the present book shown in heavy type
14. Refsvindinge	Bone handle	Anthr., e (P)	**Fig. 34, 4**; Müller, S. 1918, figs. 18, 27
15. No loc.	Bone knife	Anthr. (B)	**Fig. 34, 6**; ibid. fig. 35
	Langeland 1		
16. No loc.	Bone, 2-edged knife, flint insets	Therio., y4	Madsen 1868, pl. 40, 1a–b; Clark 1936, fig. 59, 1
17. Illebølle	Bone	e	Müller, S. 1918, fig. 19
	Zealand		
18. Bjernede, Søro	Perforated antler	1, s	Mathiassen 1943, fig. 37
19. Copenhagen	Finely toothed barbed point	straight lines (P)	Müller, S. 1918 fig. 23
20. Holmegaard (BO2)	Bone handle	q1	Broholm 1931, fig. 29
21. Holmegaard (BO2)	Perforated antler tine	i1	ibid. fig. 23.
22. Horsø, Mariager	Antler base mattock	y2	Broholm 1931, 102
23. ibid.	Antler	b2	ibid. 101–2
24. Jordløse, Aamosen	Antler base mattock	Anthr. bi, r, y3	**Fig. 34, 2**; Mathias- sen 1943, fig. 37
25. Kalundborg	Perforated antler	Chequer, c, d, h	**Fig. 33**; Friis- Johansen 1919, fig. 51
26. Kongemose (BO2/AT)	Slotted bone point	Mesh	**Fig. 31, 4**; Jørgen- sen 1956, fig. 8
27. ibid. (BO2/AT)	Antler base mattock	q2, y2, α	Jørgensen 1956, fig. 7
28. Køge Sønakke, Stevns	Slotted, 2-edged knife	Anthr., r	**Fig. 34, 7**; Mathias- sen 1943, fig. 72
29. Magleø, Aamosen	Antler base mattock	b2, α, B2	Mathiassen 1943, fig. 50
30. Mullerup (BO1)	Bone	q1	Sarauw 1903, fig. 45
31.　　(BO1)	Bone handle	e, q1	ibid. fig. 44
32.　　(BO1)	Bone	Mesh	**Fig. 31, 3**; Sarauw 1903, fig. 37

Locations	Objects Author refers to red deer unless otherwise stated	Motifs Engraved unless defined by pits (B: *Bohr-* *ornament*) or dots (P: *pointillé*)	References Figure references to the present book shown in heavy type
	Zealand (*cont.*)		
33. Mullerup (BO1)	Slotted bone point	k, q1, x2	**Fig. 43**; Sarauw 1903, fig. 31
34. Ringsted	Bone	q1	Müller, S. 1918, fig. 1
35. Ryemarksgaard (BO2)	Bone (aurochs metapodial)	Anthr., r	**Fig. 35, 1**; *DOI* 188
36. Skalstrup	Antler base mattock	Therio., chequer	**Fig. 33**; Broholm 1931, figs. 14, 15
37. Stensby	Bone	Anthr., j1	**Fig. 35, 5**; Müller, S. 1918, figs. 22, 26
38. Sværdborg (BO2)	Antler base mattock	a(B)	**Fig. 16, 6**; Friis-Johansen 1919, fig. 35.
39. (BO2)	Bone handle	Haphazard (B)	ibid. fig. 61
40. (BO2)	Antler base mattock	x1	Broholm 1931, fig. 49
41. (BO2)	Perforated antler	g	ibid. fig. 51
42. (BO2)	Perforated antler	e	ibid. fig. 54
43. (BO2)	Antler handle	s	ibid. fig. 61
44. (BO2)	Pointed bone	a, s(P)	ibid. fig. 55
45. (BO2)	Slotted bone point	Haphazard	ibid. fig. 59
46. Svinninge Vejle	Antler base mattock	τ, y2	Vebæk 1939, fig. 15
47. Søborg	Slotted bone point	c	Müller, S. 1918, fig. 9
48. Søholm	Slotted bone point	e	Westerby 1927, fig. 45
49. Taarbæk	Antler	b2	Müller, S. 1918, fig. 6
50. Uggerløse, Aamosen	Perforated tip elk antler	b2, f, g, q, z	Mathiassen 1943, fig. 73
51. Veksø mose	Perforated antler	Anthr., 1	**Fig. 34, 3**; Liversage 1966, fig. 5
52. Vinde-Helsinge, Aamosen (BO1)	Bone	e	Mathiassen 1943, fig. 5, 3
53. Øgaarde, Aamosen	Various	b1, b2, c, d, f, g	Mathiassen 1943, fig. 44
54. Øgaarde, Aamosen	Perforated antler	m	ibid. fig. 35

Locations	Objects Author refers to red deer unless otherwise stated	Motifs Engraved unless defined by pits (B: *Bohr- ornament*) or dots (P: *pointillé*)	References Figure references to the present book shown in heavy type
55. Øgaarde, Aamosen	Perforated antler	n	ibid. fig. 36
55A. Øgaarde, Aamosen	Perforated antler	l	ibid. fig. 37
56. Ølby Lyng	Perforated antler	b2, i1, q2, x2	Liversage 1966, fig. 1, 2
57. No loc.	Amber pendant	Anthr. (B)	**Fig. 35, 8**; Müller, S. 1918, fig. 36
58. No loc.	Amber pendant	Anthr. (B)	**Fig. 35, 9**; Müller, S. 1918, fig. 37
59. No loc.	Amber pendant	Haphazard (B)	ibid. fig. 39
	Sweden		
60. Bohuslän	Socketed spatulate bone tool	Mesh, v	**Pl. V**; S.H.M. 2898
61. Bråttjar, Orust, Bohuslän	Perforated star- shaped stone object	Mesh, b2, e, f, q1, r	Montelius 1917, Abb. 341
62. Flackarp, Scania	Amber	a(B)	L.U.H.M. 16119
63. Höganäs, Scania	Antler base mattock	f, g, y1, y3	Rydbeck and von Post 1929, fig. 2
64. Limhamn, Scania	Spatulate bone tool	a(B)	**Fig. 18, 2**; L.U.H.M. 14175
65. Lybymose, Scania (BO)	Bone (ulna)	e, q1	Malmer and Mag- nusson 1955, Abb. 2
66. Sjöholmen, Scania	Perforated antler	Mesh, g, i1, i2, j2 q1, y2, x2	L.U.H.M.
67. Sollerön, Dalarne	Socketed spatulate bone tool	e, qi	**Fig. 63, 1**; Stjerna 1911, fig. 24
68. Ystad, Scania	Antler base mattock	Therio., b2, B1	**Pl. VI** and **Fig. 34**; S.H.M. 3437
	Germany		
69. Havel lakes	Bone disc	Starfish pattern (B)	Stimming 1925, fig. 165a
70. Havel lakes	Stout bone needle	Irregular (B)	ibid. fig. 141a
71. Hohen Viecheln (BO2)	Perforated bone mattock	a(B), e	**Fig. 17, 3**; Schuldt 1961, Taf. 51
72. (BO2)	Perforated bone mattock	b2	ibid. Taf. 52

Locations	Objects Author refers to red deer unless otherwise stated	Motifs Engraved unless defined by pits (B: *Bohr-* *ornament*) or dots (P: *pointillé*)	References Figure references to the present book shown in heavy type
	Germany (*cont.*)		
73. (BO2)	Bone (pig tibia)	b2	ibid. Taf. 55
74. Hohen Viecheln	Perforated antler	q1, x1, y1	ibid. Taf. 60
75. (BO2)	Perforated antler	e, g	ibid. Taf. 61
(BO2)			
76. (BO2)	Perforated antler	j1	ibid. Taf. 62
77. Klein-Machnow, nr. Berlin	Perforated antler	g, h	Kossinna 1921, fig. 28
78. Mendrienen, Kr. Allenstein	Stout bone needle	Linear (B)	Ebert, *Reallexikon* IX, Taf. 207, c, d
79. Trave canal, Schl.-Holstein	Perforated antler	b1, q1, x1	Schwantes 1939, Taf. 4
80. Travenort, Schl.-Holstein	Stout bone needle	Chequer, x2	**Fig. 18, 4;** Schwantes 1939, Abb. 104
	Poland (1918–39)		
81. Biskupin	Pointed bone	j1, k	Rajewski 1958
82. Grabowo, Szczecin	Perforated antler	Therio., g, x2	Kozłowski, S. K. 1972, pl. xxxv
83. Nitki	Perforated antler	r, y3	ibid.
84. Ostrołeka	Perforated antler	c, q, x2	ibid.
85. Podjuchy, Szczecin	Perforated antler	Anthr., e, k	ibid.
86. Wozniki, Biala Podlaska	Perforated antler	e, q	ibid.

APPENDIX E

Faunal assemblages of Atlantic age from Denmark

	Jutland							Zealand				
	Norslund	Kolind I, II	Dyrholm	Aamølle	Brabrand	Ertebølle	Havnø	Villingebæk	Vedbæk	Klintesø	Ølby-Lyng	Occurrences
Mammals												
Roe deer (*Capreolus capreolus*)	×	×	×	×	×	×	×	×	×	×	×	11
Red deer (*Cervus elephas*)	×	×	×	×	×	×	×	×	×	×	×	11
Elk (*Alces alces*)	×	.	×	.	.	×	.	.	.	.	.	3
Aurochs (*Bos primigenius*)	×	×	×	×	×	×	×	×	.	.	.	8
Wild pig (*Sus scrof. ferus*)	×	×	×	×	×	×	×	×	×	×	×	11
Beaver (*Castor fiber*)	.	.	×	.	.	.	.	.	×	×	×	4
Wild cat (*Felis sylvestris*)	×	.	×	×	×	×	×	.	×	×	×	9
Lynx (*Lynx lynx*)	.	.	×	.	.	×	.	.	.	.	.	2
Brown bear (*Ursus arctos*)	.	.	×	.	×	.	.	.	.	.	.	2
Pine marten (*Martes martes*)	×	×	×	.	×	×	×	.	×	.	.	7
Badger (*Meles meles*)	×	.	×	×	.	×	.	.	.	.	.	4
Otter (*Lutra lutra*)	×	.	×	.	.	.	.	.	.	.	×	3
Fox (*Vulpes vulpes*)	×	×	×	.	.	.	.	×	×	.	×	6
Wolf (*Canis lupus*)	×	.	×	×	.	×	.	.	.	.	.	4
Dog (*Canis familiaris*)	×	×	×	.	.	.	.	×	×	.	×	6
Squirrel (*Sciurus vulgaris*)	×	.	×	.	.	×	.	.	.	×	.	4
Hedgehog (*Eriaceus europaeus*)	.	.	.	.	.	×	.	.	.	×	.	2
Common seal (*Phoca vitulina*)	.	.	.	.	.	.	.	.	.	×	.	1
Ringed seal (*P. foetida*)	.	.	.	.	.	×	.	×	.	.	.	2
Greenland seal (*P. groenlandica*)	.	.	×	.	.	.	.	.	.	.	×	2
Grey seal (*Halichoerus grypus*)	×	×	.	×	×	×	×	×	×	×	×	10
Dolphin (*Lagenorhynchus albirostris*)	.	.	.	×	.	.	.	.	.	.	.	1
Killer whale (*Orca gladiator*)	.	.	.	.	.	×	.	.	.	.	.	1
Porpoise (*Phocaena communis*)	×	.	×	.	.	×	.	×	×	×	×	7
Dolphin (*Delphinus delphis*)	.	.	×	.	.	.	.	.	.	.	.	1

APPENDICES

		Jutland							Zealand				
	Norslund	Kolind I, II	Dyrholm	Aamølle	Brabrand	Ertebølle	Havnø	Villingebæk	Vedbæk	Klinteso	Ølby-Lyng	Occurrences
Fish												
Cod (*Gadus morrhua*)	×	×	.	.	.	×	.	×	×	×	×	7
Flounder (*Pleuronectes* ap.)	×	.	.	.	×	×	×	.	★	×	×	6

★ Occasional occurrences of 8 other species.

Birds

c. 35 species represented

SOURCES: Aamølle, Ertebølle, Havnø and Klinteso: Winge in Madsen *et al.* 1900. Brabrand: Winge in Thomsen 1907. *et al.* Dyrholm II: Degerbøl in Mathiassen *et al.* 1942. Vedbæk: Degerbøl in Mathiassen 1946b. Norslund: Møhl in Andersen S. and Malmros 1965. Villingebæk: Møhl in Kapel 1969. Ølby Lyng: Møhl 1970.

WORKS CITED IN THE TEXT

ABBREVIATIONS

Aarbøger	*Aarbøger for Nordisk Oldkyndighed og Historie.* Copenhagen.
Acta Arch.	*Acta Archaeologica.* Copenhagen.
Ant. J.	*The Antiquaries Journal.* Oxford University Press.
DGF	*Meddelelser fra Dansk Geologisk Forening.* Copenhagen.
DGU	Danmarks Geologiske Undersøgelse. Copenhagen.
DOI	*Danske Oldsager 1: Ældre Stenalder.* Copenhagen.
FFT	*Finska Fornminnesforeningens Tidskrift.* Helsingfors.
GFF	*Geologiska Foreningens i Stockholm Forhandlingar.*
KDVS	*Det Kongelige Danske Videnskabesnes Selskab.* Copenhagen.
KVAH	*Kungl. Svenska Vetenskapsakademiens Handlingar.* Stockholm.
KVHAA	*Kungl. Vitterhets Historie och Antikvitets Akademien.* Stockholm.
Med. LUHM	*Meddelanden fran Lunds universitets historiska museums.*
MIA	*Materialy i Issledovaniya po Arkheologii SSSR.* Moscow and Leningrad.
NM Arbm.	*Fra Nationalmuseets Arbejdsmark.* Copenhagen.
PPS	*Proceedings of the Prehistoric Society.* Cambridge.
SGU	Sveriges Geologiska Undersökning. Stockholm.
SM	*Suomen Museo.* Helsingfors.
SMYA	*Suomen Muinaismuistoyhdidistytksen Aikakauskirja.* Helsingfors.
TOR	*Meddelanden fran institutionen for nordisk fornkunskap vid Uppsala universitet.* Uppsala.

Aario, L. (1934) Heinolan pitäjän Viikinäisistä löydetyn reenjalaksen turve-geologinen iänmääräys. *SM*, **41**, 22–7.

Ailio, J. (1909) *Die steinzeitlichen Wohnplatzfunde in Finland.* 2 vols. Helsingfors.

Alin, J. (1953) *Stenåldersforskningen i Bohuslän.* Göteborg.

Alin, J., Niklasson, N. and Thomasson, H. (1934) *Stenåldersboplatsen vid Sandarna.* Göteborg.

Allibone, T. E. *et al.* (ed.) (1970) *The Impact of the Natural Sciences on Archaeology.* British Academy, Oxford University Press.

Althin, C. A. (1950) *Bäckaskog och Lummelunda. Technica et Humaniora* (A. Nevsten Festschrift,) 13–37. Malmö.

Althin, Carl-Axel (1944) *The Chronology of the Stone Age Settlement of Scania, Sweden*, 1. Acta Ach. Lundensia, Lund.

Althin, C. A., Brorson-Christensen, B. and Berlin, H. (1949) Renfyndet från Nebbe Mosse och Sveriges Senglaciala Bebbyggelse. *Bull. Soc. Roy. des Lettres de Lund*, 1946–49, V, 115–46.

Andersen, A. and Møller, K. (1946) *Fund af Urokse (Bos taurus urus L.) i Grænge Mose paa Lolland*. DGU IV R., Bd. 3, Nr. 1.

Andersen, Björn G. (1965) The Quaternary of Norway. *The Geologic Systems. The Quaternary*, vol. 1 (edt. K. Ramkama), 91–138. Interscience Publishers, London

Andersen, K. (1951) Hytter fra Maglemosetid. Danmarks ældste boliger. *NM Arbm.* 69–76.

Andersen, K. (1960) Verupbopladsen. En Maglemoseboplads i Åmosen. *Aarbøger*, 118–51.

Andersen, Søren H. (1965) Stenalderbopladsen i Hjortmose. *Hardsyssels Årbog*, Bd 60, 252 ff.

Andersen, Søren H. (1969a) Brovst. En Kystboplads fra ældre stenalder. *Kuml*, 67–90.

Andersen, Søren H. (1969b) Flintægdolken fra Flynderhage. *Kuml*, 91–5.

Andersen, Søren H. (1970) Senglaciale bopladser ved Bro. *Fynske Minder*, 85–100.

Andersen, Søren H. (1971) Gudenåkulturen. *Holstebro museums årsskrift 1970–1*, 14–32.

Andersen, Søren H. and Malmros, Claus (1965) Norslund. En Kystbopleds fra ældre stenalder. *Kuml*, 35–114.

Anderson, E. C., Levi, Hilde and Tauber, H. (1953) Copenhagen Natural Radiocarbon Measurements, 1. *Science*, vol. 118, no. 3053, 6–9.

Andersson, G. (1902) *Hasseln i Sverige fordom och nu*. SGU, Ser. C a, Nr. 3. Stockholm.

Andree, J. (1932) *Beiträge zur Kenntnis des norddeutschen Paläolithikums und Mesolithikums*. Mannus – Bibl. no. 52. Berlin.

Auerbach, N. K. and Sosnovskij, G. P. (1932) Materials for the study of the palaeolithic industry and the conditions of discovery of the site of Afontova gora. *Trudy Komisii po Izucheniyn chetvertichnogo Perioda*, No. 1, 45–114. Academy of Sciences of the USSR, Leningrad.

Äyräpää, A. (1927) Stenålderskeramik frå Kustbopladser i Finnland. *FFT* XXXVI: 1, 45–77.

Äyräpää, A. (1950) Die ältesten steinzeitlichen Funde aus Finnland. *Acta Arch.* XXI, 1–43.

Bagge, A. and Kjellmark, K. (1939) *Stenåldersboplatserna vid Siretorp i Blekinge*. Stockholm.

Balodis, F. (1940) *Det äldsta Lettland*. Transl. (Swedish) by W. W. Freij. Almqvist and Wiksell, Uppsala.

Baudou, Evert (1968) *Forntida bebyggelse i Ångermanlands Kustland. Arkeologiska undersökningar av ångermanländska Kuströsen*. Arkiv f. Norrländsk Hembygdsforskning XVII. Härnösand.

WORKS CITED IN THE TEXT

Baudou, Evert (1970a) Forskningsprojektet NTB och Hälla. *Västerbotten,* 5–16.

Baudou, Evert (1970b) Bofast eller icke bofast i Norrlands förhistoria. Lecture (unpublished ts) to the Northern Archaeologists' Congress at Tromsø, June 1970.

Becker, C. J. (1939) En stenalderboplads paa Ordrup Næs i Nordvestsjælland. *Aarbøger,* 199–280.

Becker, C. J. (1945) En 8000-Årig stenalderboplads i Holmegaards Mose. *NM Arbm.* 61–72.

Becker, C. J. (1951a) Maglemosekultur paa Bornholm. *Aarbøger,* 96–177.

Becker, C. J. (1951b) Late-Neolithic Flint Mines at Aalborg. *Acta Arch.* XXII, 135–52.

Becker, C. J. (1951c) Flintgruberne ved Aalborg. En 3500-aarig Dansk Eksportvisksomhed. *NM Arbm.* 107–12.

Becker, C. J. (1953) Die Maglemosekultur in Dänemark. Neue Funde und Ergebnisse. *Actes IIIe Sess. Int. Congr. Pre- and Protohist. Sciences, Zürich,* 180–3.

Becker, C. J. (1954) Stenalderbebyggelsen ved Store Valby i Vestsjælland. Problemer omkring tragtbægerkulturens ældeste og yngste fase. *Aarbøger,* 127–83.

Becker, C. J. (1971a) Late Palaeolithic Finds from Denmark. *PPS* XXXVII, 131–9.

Becker, C. J. (1971b) Istidsmandens Redskaber. *Skalk* nr. **4,** 3–7.

Berg, G. (1935) *Sledges and Wheeled Vehicles, Ethnological Studies from the view-point of Sweden.* Nordiska Museet, Stockholm.

Berglund, B. (1966) *Late-Quaternary vegetation in eastern Blekinge, southeastern Sweden. A pollen-analytical study.* I. *Late-Glacial Time;* II *Postglacial Time. Opera botanica* 12: 1 and 2. Lund.

Berglund, B. (1971) Litorina Transgressions in Blekinge, South Sweden. A preliminary Survey, *GFF* **93,** 625–52.

Berlin, H. (1941) Benfynden från stenåldersboplatsen i Gualöv. *Medd. LUHM,* 151–2.

Berthelsen, W. *Stenalderbopladser i Sønderkær og Vejledalen.* Copenhagen.

Biörnstad, Margareta (1965) Norrland in the Younger Iron Age – as Source of Raw Materials and as Market. *Hunting and Fishing* (ed. H. Hvarfner), 73–82.

Bjørn, A. (1929) Studier over Fosnakulturen. *Bergens Mus. Årb., Hist.-Ant. R.,* no. 2.

Blankholm, Ruth and Ejner, and Andersen, Søren H. (1967) Stallerupholm. Et bidrag til belysning at Maglemosekulturen i Østjylland. *Kuml,* 61–115.

Blytt, A. (1876) *Essay on the immigration of the Norwegian Flora during alternating rainy and dry periods.* Kristiania.

Bøe, Johs. (1942) *Til høgfjellets Forhistorie. Boplassen på Sumtangen ved Finsevatn på Hardangervidda.* Bergens Museums Skr. Nr **21.** Bergen.

Bøe, J. and Nummedal, A. (1936) *Le Finnmarkien. Les origines de la civilisation dans l'extrême-nord de l'Europe.* Oslo.

Bohmers, A. and Wouters, A-Q. (1956) Statistics and graphs in the study of flint assemblages. *Palaeohistoria* V, 1–39. Groningen.

257

Bordes, F. (1950) Principes d'une méthode d'étude des techniques de débitage et de la typologie du Paléolithique ancien et moyen. *L'Anthropologie*, **54**, 393–420. Paris.

Brandt, K. (1933) Die ersten bearbeiteten Rentiergeweihe aus Westfalen. *Mannus Z.* xxv, 325–31. Berlin.

Briussov, A. Ja. (1957) *Geschichte der Neolithischen Stämme im Europäischen Teil der UdSSR*. Akademie-Verlag, Berlin.

Broadbent, N. D. (1971) The Komsa culture and the circumpolar area. Nordisk och Jämförande Fornkunskap Uppsala. (Unpublished.)

Brøgger, A. W. (1908) *Vistefundet. En ældre stenalders kjøkkenmødding fra Jæderen*. Stavanger.

Brøgger, A. W. (1938) Elghornøksen fra Hurumryggen. *Viking*.

Brøgger, W. C. (1905) *Strandliniens beliggenhed under stanalderen*. I. Det sydøstlige Norge, Kristiania.

Broholm, H. C. (1928) Langøfundet. En boplads fra den Ældre Stenalder paa Fyn. *Aarbøger*, 129 ff.

Broholm, H. C. Nouvelles trouvailles du plus ancien âge de la pierre. Les trouvailles de Holmegaard et de Sværdborg. *Mém. d. Antiqu. du Nord 1926–31*, 1–128. Copenhagen.

Brøndsted, J. (1957) *Danmarks Oldtid*: vol. I, 2nd ed. Gyldendal, Copenhagen.

Bucha, V. and Neustupný, E. (1967) Changes of the earth's magnetic field and radiocarbon dating. *Památky archeologické* LVIII, 599–613.

Burch, E. S. (1972) The Caribou/Wild Reindeer as a Human Resource. *American Antiquity* **37**, 339–68.

Chavannes, E. (1941) Written records of forest succession. *Scient. Monthly*, July, 76–80.

Chernysh, A. P. (1961) *Paleolitichna Stoyanka Molodova* v. Ukranian Academy of Sciences, Kiev.

Chmielewska, M. and Chmielewski, W. (1960) Stratigraphie et Chronologie de la dune de Witów, dist. de łęczyca. *Biuletyn Peryglaejalny*, Nr. **8**, 133–41. Łódz.

Clark, J. G. D. (1934) The classification of a microlithic culture. *Archaeological Journal* **90**, 52–77. London.

Clark, J. G. D. (1936) *The Mesolithic Settlement of Northern Europe*. Cambridge Univ. Press.

Clark, J. G. D. (1939; also 1947, 1957, 1960, 1965) *Archaeology and Society*. Methuen, London.

Clark, J. G. D. (1946) Seal-hunting in the Stone Age of North-Western Europe: a study in economic prehistory. *PPS*, 12–48.

Clark, J. G. D. (1947) Whales as an economic factor in prehistoric Europe. *Antiquity* xxi, 84–104.

Clark J. G. D. (1948 a) The development of fishing in prehistoric Europe. *Ant. J.* xxviii, 45–85.

Clark, J. G. D. (1948 b) Objects of South Scandinavian Flint in the northernmost provinces of Norway, Sweden and Finland. *PPS*, 219–32.

Clark, J. G. D. (1948 c) Fowling in Prehistoric Europe. *Antiquity* 22, 116–30.

Clark, J. G. D. (1952) *Prehistoric Europe: the Economic Basis*. Methuen, London.

Clark, J. G. D. (1953) The economic approach to Prehistory. *Proc. Brit. Acad.* 39, 215–38.

Clark, J. G. D. (1963) Neolithic bows from Somerset, England, and the prehistory of archery in North-Western Europe. *PPS* 29, 50–98.

Clark, J. G. D. (1965) Traffic in Stone Axe and Adze Blades. *Economic History Review* 18, 1–28.

Clark, J. G. D. (1966) The Invasion Hypothesis in British Archaeology. *Antiquity* XL, 172–89.

Clark, J. G. D. (1970 and 1974) *Aspects of Prehistory*. Univ. of California Press, Berkeley.

Clark, J. G. D. (1971) A shaped and utilized beaver jaw from Ulrome, Holderness, Yorkshire (E.R.). *Ant. J.* LI, 305–7.

Clark, J. G. D. (1972 a) *Star Carr: a case study in bioarchaeology*. Addison-Wesley Modular Publications, Reading, Mass. Anthropology Module 10.

Clark, J. G. D. (1972 b) The Archaeology of Stone Age Settlement. *Ulster J. of Archaeology* 35, 1 ff. Belfast.

Clark, J. G. D. (1973) Seasonality and the interpretation of lithic assemblages. In *Estudios Dedicados al Professor L. Pericot* (edt. J. Muluquer de Motes), Barcelona.

Clark, J. G. D. and Thompson, M. W. (1953) The Groove and Splinter Technique of working antler in Upper Palaeolithic and Mesolithic Europe. *PPS* 19, 148–60.

Clark, J. G. D. (with D. Walker, H. Godwin, G. F. Fraser and J. E. King) (1954 and 1971) *Excavations at Star Carr, an Early Mesolithic Site at Seamer, near Scarborough, Yorkshire*. Cambridge Univ. Press.

Darling, Fraser (1969) *A Herd of Red Deer*. Oxford Univ. Press.

Degerbøl, M. (1933) Danmarks Pattedyr i Fortiden i Sammenligning med recente Former. I. Rovdyr (*Carnivora*). *Vidensk. Medd. fra Dansk naturh. Foren.* Bd. 96, 357–641. Copenhagen.

Degerbøl, M. (1945) Subfossile Fisk fra Kvartærtiden i Danmark. *Vidensk. Medd. fra Dansk naturh. Foren.* Bd. 108, 103–60. Copenhagen.

Degerbøl, M. (1961) On a find of a Preboreal Domestic Dog (*Canis familiaris* L.) from Star Carr, Yorkshire, with remarks on the other Mesolithic Dogs. *PPS* 27, 35–65.

Degerbøl, M. and Fredskild, B. (1970) The Urus (*Bos primigenius Bojanus*) and Neolithic Domesticated Cattle (*Bos taurus domesticus Linné*) in Denmark. Kongl. Danske Vidensk. Selsk. Biol. Skr. 17, 1. Copenhagen.

Degerbøl, M. and Iversen, J. (1942) On a Find of a Sheat-Fish (*Silurus glanis* L.) from the Ancylus Period in Denmark. *Vidensk. Medd. fra Dansk naturh. Foren.*, Bd. 105. Copenhagen.

WORKS CITED IN THE TEXT

Degerbøl, M. and Iversen, Johs. (1945) *The bison in Denmark. A zoological and geological investigation of the finds in Danish Pleistocene deposits.* DGU II R., nr. 73. Copenhagen.

Degerbøl, M. and Krog, H. (1951) Den europaiske Sumpskildpaddle (*Emys orbicularis* L.) i Danmark. DGU II R., 78. Copenhagen.

Degerbøl, M. and Krog, H. (1959) *The reindeer (Rangifer tarandus* L.) *in Denmark.* Danske Videnskabernes Selskab, Biol. Skr. 10, 4.

Donner, J. J. (1965) The Quaternary of Finland. *The Geological Systems. The Quaternary* I, 199–272. Interscience Publishers, London.

Ekholm, G. (1913) Upplands äldste bebyggelse. *Ymer,* 369–80.

Ekholm, G. (1915) *Studier i Upplands Bebyggelsehistoria.* I. *Stenåldern.* Uppsala.

Ekman, Sven (1910) *Norrlands jakt och fiske.* Norrländskt handbibliotek Nr. IV. Almqvist and Wiksells, Uppsala.

Evans-Pritchard, E. E. (1940) *The Nuer. A description of the modes of livelihood and political institutions of a Nilotic people.* Oxford Univ. Press.

Fægri, K. (1940) *Quartärgeologische Untersuchungen im westlichen Norwegen.* II. *Zur spätquartären Geschichte Jærens.* Bergens Museums Årbok 1939–40 Naturvidensk. r., nr. 7.

Fægri, K. (1943) *Studies on the Pleistocene of Western Norway.* III. Bergens Museums Årbok Naturvidensk. r., nr. 8.

Firbas, F. (1949) *Spät- und nacheiszeitliche Waldgeschichte Mitteleuropas nördlich der Alpen.* Jena.

Flint, F. R. (1947) *Glacial Geology and the Pleistocene Epoch.* John Wiley, New York.

Florin, Sten (1948) *Kustförskjutningen och bebyggelse-utvecklingen i Östra Mellansverige under Senkvartär tid.* I. *Allmän Översikt.* Stockholm, 1948.

Florin, Sten (1959) Hagtorp. En prekeramisk kvartsförande fångstboplats från tidig Litorinatid. *TOR* V, 7–51. Uppsala.

Forssberg, E. (1963) Jämtarnas handelsfärder till Stockholm. *Jämten,* 81–104. Östersund.

Fredsjö, Å. (1953) *Studier i Västsveriges Äldre Stenålder.* Göteborg.

Freundt, E. A. (1948) Komsa–Fosna–Sandarne. *Acta Arch.* XIX, 1–68.

Fries, Magnus (1965 a) The Late-Quaternary Vegetation of Sweden. *Acta Phytogeographica Suecica* 50, 269–84. Uppsala.

Fries, Magnus (1964 b) Outlines of the Late-glacial and Postglacial vegetational and climatic history of Sweden illustrated by three generalized pollen diagrams. *International Studies on the Quaternary* (H. E. Wright and D. G. Frey), VII Congr. Int. Assoc. for Quaternary Research, Boulder, Colorado.

Fries, Magnus (1969) Aspects of floristic changes in connection with the developments of the cultural landscape. *Oikos Suppl.* 12, 29–34. Copenhagen.

Friis Johansen, K. (1919) Une station du plus ancien âge de la pierre dans la tourbierè de Sværdborg. *Mém. d. Antiqu. du Nord 1918–19,* 241–359. Copenhagen.

Gejvall, N.-G. (1970) The Fisherman from Barum – mother of several children! *Fornvännen* **65**, 281–9.

Gimbutas, Marija (1958) Middle Ural Sites and the Chronology of Northern Eurasia. *PPS* xxiv, 120–57.

Gjessing, G. (1932) *Arktiske helleristninger i Nord-Norge.* Oslo.

Gjessing, G. (1936) *Nordenfjelske Ristninger og Malinger an den arktiske gruppe.* Oslo.

Gjessing, G. (1942) *Yngre Steinalder i Nord-Norge.* Oslo.

Gjessing, G. (1943) *Træn-Funnene.* Oslo.

Gjessing, G. (1945) Nøstvet–Ertebølle–Campignien. *FFT*, 1–9.

Glob, P. V. (1939) Der Einfluss der bandkeramischen Kultur in Dänemark. *Acta Arch.* **10**, 131–40.

Glob, P. V. (1949) Barkær, Danmarks ældste landsby. *NM Arbm.* 5–16.

Godwin, H. (1956) *The History of the British Flora.* Cambridge Univ. Press.

Godwin, H. (1962) Half-life of Radiocarbon. *Nature* **195**, no. 4845, 984.

Godwin, H. and Willis, E. H. (1959) Radiocarbon dating of the Late-glacial Period in Britain. *Proc. Roy. Soc. B*, **150**, 199–215.

Gräslund, Bo (1970) En stenåldersboplats vid Nedre Ransjön i Härjedalen. *Jämten*, 141–6. Östersund.

Grewingk, C. (1887) Geologie und Archäologie des Mergellagers von Kunda in Estland. *Arch. Naturk. Liv.-, Esth.- u. Kurlands*, ix. Dorpat.

Gross, H. (1937a) Pollenanalytische Altersbestimmung einer ostpreussischen Lyngbyhacke und das absolute Alter der Lyngbykultur. *Mannus Z.* **29**, 109–13.

Gross, H. (1937b) Der erste sichere Fund eines paläolithische Geräts in Ostpreussen. *Mannus Z.* **29**, 113–18. Berlin.

Gross, H. (1937c) Die ältesten Spuren des Menschen in Nordostdeutschland. *Nachrichtenblatt für Deutsche Vorzeit* **13**, 73–80. Berlin.

Gross, H. (1940) Die Renntierjäger-Kulturen Ostpreussens. *Prähist. Z.* xxx–xxxi, 39–67.

Gurina, N. N. (1967) *On the history of ancient settlement in the western provinces of the SSSR (On the materials from the Narva Expedition).* MIA no. **144**. Leningrad.

Gustawsson, K. A. (1949) Kokstenshögar. *Fornvännen* **44**, 152–65. Stockholm.

Hagen, Anders (1959) Funn fra Fjellvann. *Viking* xxiii, 35–51. Oslo.

Hagen, Anders (1960–1) Mesolittiske jegergrupper i norske høyfjell. *Univ. oldsaks. Årbok*, 109–42. Oslo.

Hagen, Anders (1967) *Norway. Ancient Peoples and Places.* London.

Hägg, R. (1924) Stånganäskraniets skalbank. *GFF*, 443 ff.

Hallström, Gustaf (1938) *Monumental Art of Northern Europe from the Stone Age.* 1. *The Norwegian Localities.* Thule, Stockholm.

Hansen, Sigurd (1965) The Quaternary of Denmark. *The Geologic Systems. The Quaternary*, vol. 1 (edt. K. Rankama), 1–90. Interscience Publishers, London.

Hansson, H. (1944) Den Forntida Bebyggelsen in Lars Dalagren. *Västerviks Historie*, 17–40. Västervik.

WORKS CITED IN THE TEXT

Hartz, N. and Milthers, V. (1901) *Det senglaciale ler i Allerød Teglværksgrav.* *DGF* No. **8**.

Hartz, N. and Winge, H. 1906 Om Uroxen fra Vig. *Aarbøger*, 225 ff.

Hatting, Tove (1969) Er bævrens tænder benyttet som redskaber in Stenalderen i Danmark? *Aarbøger*, 116–26.

Helle, Reijo (1966) An Investigation of Reindeer Husbandry in Finland. *Fennia* **95**, no. 4, 1–65.

Heptner, V. G. and Naumov, N. P. (edt.) (1966) *Die Säugetiere der Sowjetnunion.* Bd. 1: *Paarhufer und Unpaarhufer.* Jena.

Higgs, E. S. (1971) Further information concerning the environment of Palaeolithic man in Epirus. *PPS*, 367–80.

Higgs, E. (edt.) (1972) *Papers in Economic Prehistory.* Cambridge Univ. Press.

Hyyppä, E. (1966) The Late-Quaternary land uplift in the Baltic sphere and the relation diagram of the raised and tilted shore levels. *Proc. Second International Symposium on Recent Crustal Movements, Aulenko, Finland, 1965,* 153–168. Ann. Acad. Scient. Fennicae Ser. A, 111. Geologica-Geographica **90**. Helsinki.

Indreko, R. (1926) Die Rambachsche Sammlung. *Sitzungsberichte der Altertumforschenden Gesellschaft zu Pernau,* Bd. **8** (1914–25), 283–344. Pernau.

Indreko, R. (1934) Vorläufige Bemerkungen über die Kunda-Funde. *Sitz. ber. Gelehrte Estonische Gesellschaft in Tartu,* 225–98. Tartu.

Indreko, R. (1948) Die mittlere Steinzeit in Estland. *KVHAA,* del. **66**. Stockholm.

Ingebrigsten, O. (1924) *Hjortens utbredelse i Norge.* Bergens Museums Aarbok 1922–3. Naturvidensk. r. nr. **6**.

Isberg, O. (1930a) Der Vorkommen des Renntieres (*Rangifer tarandus* L.) in Schweden während der postarktischen Zeit nebst einem Beitrag zur Kenntnis über das dortige erste Auftreten des Menschen. *Ark. f. Zool.* Bd. **21** A. Nr. 12, 1–26. Stockholm.

Isberg, O. (1930b) Till frågan om människans och renens första uppträdande på den skandinaviska halvön under postarktisk tid. *Ymer.* 381–400. Stockholm.

Isberg, O. (1962) Uroxen (*Bos primigenius* L.) i Sverige. *GFF* Bd **84**, H. 4, 416–518.

Itkonen, T. I. (1938) Muinaissuksia jajalaksia. *Suomen Museo* XLV, 13–34.

Iversen, J. (1937) *Undersøgelser over Litorinatransgressioner i Danmark.* DGF, Bd. **9**, Hft. 2.

Iversen, Johs. (1941) *Land occupation in Denmark's Stone Age.* DGU, II R., n. 66.

Iversen, Johs. (1942) *En pollenanalytisk Tidsfæstelse af Ferskrandslagene ved Nørre Lyngby.* DGF, Bd. **10**, H. 2.

Iversen, Johs. (1942) Geologisk Datering af en Senglacial Boplads ved Bromme. *Aarbøger,* 198–231.

Iversen, Johs. (1949) *The influence of prehistoric man on vegetation.* DGU, IV R., Bd. **4**, nr. 6.

Iversen, Johs. (1953) Radiocarbon Dating of the Alleröd Period. *Science* **118**, no. 3053, 9–11.

WORKS CITED IN THE TEXT

Iversen, J. (1954) *The Late-glacial Flora of Denmark and its Relation to Climate and and Soil.* DGU, II R. nr. 80, 87–119.

Iversen, Johs. (1960) *Problems of the Early Post-glacial Forest Development in Denmark,* DGU, IV R., Bd. 4, nr. 3, 1–32.

Jacobsson, U. (1954) Om Härjedalens samfärdsel med Haslingland och Norge på 1800-talet. *Jämten,* 26–34. Östersund.

Janson, S. (1936) En boplats från yngre stenåldern vid Rörvik i Kville sn. *Göteborgs och Bohuslans Fornminnesförenings Tidskrift.*

Janson, S. (1965) Settlement and Hunting Grounds. Settlement culture in the Interior of Norrland; its Distribution and Character. In H. Hvarfner, 339–48.

Janson, S. (1970) Bygd och fångsmark: boplatskultur i det inre av Norrland; dess utbredning och Karaktär. *Norrbotten,* 77–84.

Janson, S., Biörnstad, M. and Hvarfner, H. (1962) *Jämtlands och Härjedalens Historia. Arkeologisk Inledning.* Norstedt, Stockholm.

Janson, S. and Hvarfner, H. (1960) *Från norrlandsälvar och fjällsjöar.* Stockholm.

Jessen, K. (1935a) Archaeological Dating in the History of North Jutland's Vegetation. *Acta Arch.* 5, 185–214.

Jessen, Knud (1935b) *The composition of the forests in northern Europe in Epipalaeolithic time.* Biol. Medd. Danske Videnskab Selsket 12, no. 1.

Jessen, K. (1938) Some West Baltic pollen diagrams. *Quartär* 1, 124–39. Berlin.

Johansen, A. B. (1969) *Høyfjells funn ved Lærdalsvassdraget.* 1. *Den teoretiske Bakgrunn og det første analyseforsøk.* Årbok f. univ. i Bergen: num. ser. no. 4.

Jonsson, A.-B. (1958) Stenåldersboplatsen vid Mårtsbo. *TOR* IV, 26–41.

Jørgensen, Svend (1954) *A Pollen Analytical Dating of Maglemose Finds from the Bog Aamosen, Zealand.* DGU II. R., Nr. 80, 159–87

Jørgensen, Svend (1956) Kongemosen. Endnu en Aamose-Boplads fra Ældre Stenalder, *Kuml,* 23–40. Aarhus.

Jørgensen, Svend (1963) *Early Postglacial in Aamosen,* DGU, II R., nr. 89.

Kapel, H. (1963) En ny boplads fra ældre stenalder i Kongens Mose. *Haderslev Amts Museum.*

Kapel, H. (1969) En boplads fra tidlig-atlantisk tid ved Villengebæk. *NM Arbm.* 85–94.

Kjellmark, K. (1905) *En stenåldersboplats i Järavallen vid Limhamm.* Antiquarisk Tidskrift f. Sverige, 17, nr. 3.

Klima, B. (1957) Übersicht über die jüngsten paläolithischen Forschungen in Mähren. *Quartär* 9, 85–130.

Kolp, O. (1967) Beitrag zur Entwicklungsgeschichte der Bornholm-Mulde. *Petermanns Geographische Mitteilungen,* Jhg. III, 207–13.

Kossinna, G. (1921) *Die Indogermanen.* Mannus Bibl. no. 21. Berlin.

Kozłowski, L. (1926) L'époque mésolithique en Pologne. *L'Anthropologie* 36, 47–74. Paris.

Kozłowski, S. K. *Prehistory of the Polish territories between the 9th and the 15th millennium B.C.* Pánstwowe Wydawnictwo Naukowe, Warsaw.

Krukowski, S. (1922) Importance des zones de recession de la dernière glaciation en Pologne pour la connaissance des plus anciennes industries sur le terrain de cette glaciation. *Wiad. Archeol.* VII, 92 ff.

La Cour, V. (1961) *Næsholm.* Nationalmuseet, Copenhagen.

Larsson, C., Cnattingius, B. and Lindell, T. (1938) Östergötlands äldsta fornfynd, Nätkaveln från Träbo. *Medd. från Östergötlands Fornminnes och Museiförening 1937–8*, 143–50. Linköping.

Lee, Richard B. (1969) !Kung Bushman subsistence: an input-output analysis. A. P. Vayda (edt.), 47–79.

Libby, W. F. (1955) *Radiocarbon Dating.* 2nd edt. Univ. Chicago Press.

Libby, W. F. (1970) Radiocarbon dating. In *The Impact of the Natural Sciences on Archaeology* (edt. T. E. Allibone *et al.*), 1–10. British Academy, Oxford Univ. Press.

Lidén, O. (1938) *Sydsvensk Stenålder belyst av fynden på Boplatserna i Jonstrup.* I. *Skivyxkulturen.* Lund.

Lidén, O. (1942) *De flinteggade benspetsarnas nordiska Kulturfas.* Lund.

Lilljeborg, W. (1874) *Sveriges och Norges Däggdjur.* Uppsala.

Linder, A. (1966) C14-datering av norrländsk abestkeramik. *Fornvännen*, 140–53.

Lithberg, N. (1914) Gotlands stenålder. Stockholm.

Liversage, D. (1966) Ornamented Mesolithic artefacts from Denmark. *Acta Arch.* **37**, 221–37.

Lomborg, E. (1962) Zur Frage der bandkeramischen Einflüsse in Südskandinavien. *Acta Arch.* XXXIII, 1–38.

Loze, I. (1964) Mesolithic discoveries on a low-lying cape in Lake Lubans. *Isvestia Akad. nauk Latviiskoy SSR* No. **3** (200), 7–20.

Loze, I. (1968) Drawing and decoration on Stone Age bone and horn artefacts of Latvia. *Izvestia Akad. Nauk Latvian SSR* II, 24–37.

Loze, I. (n.d.) *Stone Age in Lubāna marshy meadows.* Pub. Madona district museum.

Luho, V. (1956*a*) *Die Askola-Kultur. Die frühmesolithische Steinzeit in Finnland.* Suomen Muinaismuistoyhdistyksen Aikakauskirja, nr. **57**. Helsinki.

Luho, V. (1956*b*) Die Komsa-Kultur. *SMYA* **57**: **2**, 281–301.

Luho, V. (1967) *Die Suomusjärvi-Kultur. Die mittel und spätmesolithische Zeit in Finnland.* Helsingfors.

Lund, H. E. (1951) *Fangst-Boplassen i Vistehulen.* Stavanger.

Lundberg, Erik B. (1942) Undersokningarna på Visbyboplatsen 1936–37. *Fornvännen*, 161–74.

Lundqvist, G. (1959) *Description to accompany the map of the Quaternary Deposits of Sweden.* SGU ser. Ba, no. **17**. Stockholm.

Lundqvist, G. (1962) *Geological Radiocarbon datings from the Stockholm station.* SGU Årsbok **56**, no. **5**. Stockholm.

WORKS CITED IN THE TEXT

Lundqvist, Jan (1965) The Quaternary of Sweden. *The Geological Systems. The Quaternary*, vol. I (edt. K. Rankama), 139–98. Interscience Publishers, London.

Madsen, A. P. (1868) *Afbildninger af danske Oldsager*. Copenhagen.

Madsen, A. P. *et al.* (1900) *Affaldsdynger fra Stenalderen i Danmark*. Copenhagen.

Magnusson, E. (1962) *Lyby Mosse. En vegetationshistorisk och utvecklingshistorisk undersökning*. SGU Årsbok **56**, no. 4. Stockholm.

Magnusson, E. (1964) *Pollen-analytical investigations at Tåkern, Dagsmosse and the Neolithic settlement at Alvastra, Sweden*. SGU Årsbok **58**, no. 4. Stockholm.

Malmer, M. and Magnusson, E. (1955) Mesolithische Harzornamentik, Ein Fund aus dem Lyby-Moor, Schonen. *Medd. LUHM*, 81–104.

Marshack, A. (1972) *The Roots of Civilization*. McGraw-Hill, New York.

Marstrander, S. (1956) Hovedlinjer i Trondelags Forhistorie. *Viking* **20**, 1–69. Oslo.

Mathiassen, T. (1935) Blubber lamps in the Ertbølle culture? *Acta Arch.* VI, 139–51.

Mathiassen, T. (1937) Gudenna-Kulturen. En mesolitisk inlandsbebyggelse i Jylland. *Aarbøger*, 1–186.

Mathiassen, T. (1941 a) Two new Danish implements of reindeer antler. *Acta Arch.* XII, 125–34.

Mathiassen, T. (1941 b) Vore ældste Menneskefremstillinger. *NM Arbm.*

Mathiassen, T. (1943) *Stenalderbopladser i Aamosen*. Copenhagen.

Mathiassen, T. (1946 a) En Senglacial Boplads ved Bromme. *Aarbøger*, 121–231.

Mathiassen, T. (1946 b) *En Boplads fra ældre Stenalder ved Vedbæk Boldbaner*. Søllerød Bogen, Søllerød.

Mathiassen, T. (1948) *Danske Oldsager. I. Ældre Stenalder*. Copenhagen.

Mathiassen, T. (1952) An amber elk head from Zealand. *Acta Arch.* XXIII, 167–9.

Mathiassen, T., Degerbøl. M. and Troels-Smith, J. (1942) *Dyrholmen. En stenalderboplads paa Djursland*. KDVS, Ark.-Kunsthist. Skr. Bd. **I**, nr. 1. Copenhagen.

Meinander, C. F. (1957) Kolsvidja. *SMYA* **58**, 185–213.

Meinander C. F. (1971) Radio Karbondateringar till Finlands Stenålder. *Societas Scientiarum Fennica Årsbok* XLVIII B, No. 5, 1–14.

Meschke, C. (1967) *En Norrländsk Stenåldersboplats med Skärvstensvall. KVHAA* Antikvariskt Arkiv. 31. Stockholm.

Mitchell, F. Studies in Irish Quaternary Deposits: No. 7. *Proc. Roy. Irish Academy*, vol. LIII, Sect. B, 111–206.

Moberg, C.-A. (1955) *Studier i Bottnisk Stenålder*. Almqvist and Wiksell, Stockholm.

Moberg, C.-A. (1965) Coastal Regions and River Country in the North and South-West. In H. Hvarfner (edt.), 363–76.

Møhl, U. (1954) Første sikre spor af mennesker fra interglacialtid i Danmark: marvspaltet Knogler fra diatoméjorden ved Hollerup. *Aarbøger*, 101–26.

Møhl, U. (1970) Fangstdyrene ved de danske strande, *Kuml*, 297–329.

WORKS CITED IN THE TEXT

Møhl, U. (1971) Oversigt over dyreknoglerne fra Ølby Lyng. En østjællandsk kystoboplads med Ertebøllekultur. *Aarbøger* 1970. 43–77.

Mongait, Alexander (1959) *Archaeology in the USSR*. Foreign Languages Publishing House, Moscow.

Montelius, O. (1917) *Minnen från vår Forntid*. Bd. I. *Stenåldern och Bronsåldern*. Norstedt, Stockholm.

Mörner, N-A. (1969) *The Late Quaternary History of the Kattegatt Sea and the Swedish West Coast. Deglaciation, shorelevel displacement, chronology, isostasy and eustasy*. SGU Ser. C. Nr. 640. Årsbok **63**, Nr. 3, Stockholm.

Müller, S. (1896) Nye Stenalders Former. *Aarbøger*, 303–419.

Müller, S. (1918) *Stenalderens Kunst i Danmark*. Copenhagen.

Munthe, H. (1940) *Om Nordens, Främst Baltikums, Senkvartära utreckling och Stenåldersbebyggelse*. KVAH 3 ser., Bd. **19**, no. 1. Stockholm.

Nathorst, A. G. (1871) Om några arktiska växtlemningar i en sötvattenslera vid Alnarp i Skåne. *Lunds Univ. Årsskrift*, v. 7.

Nihlén, J. (1927) *Gotlands stenåldersboplatser*. Stockholm.

Niklasson, N. (1936) Rengeweihhacken aus Mitteldeutschland. *Jahresschr. f. d. Vorgeschichte d. sächsischthüringischen Länder*. Bd. XXIV, 44–56.

Niklasson, N. (1965) *Hensbacka. En mesolitisk boplats i Fossn, Bohuslän*. Studier i nordisk arkeologi, no. 6. Göteborg, 1965.

Nilsson, Erik (1968) *The Late-quaternary History of Southern Sweden. Geochronology, Ice-lakes, land-uplift*. KVAH 4th Ser., Bd. **12**, nr. 1.

Nilsson, T. Die pollenanalytische Zonengliederung der spät- und postglazialen Bildungen Schonens. GFF **57**, 385–562.

Nilsson, T. (1948) *On the application of the Scanian Post-glacial Zone system to Danish pollen-diagrams*. KDVS Biol. Skr. Bd. v, nr. 5. Copenhagen.

Nillsson, T. (1964a) *Standardpollendiagramme und C14 Datierungen aus der Ageröds Mosse im mittleren Schonen*. Lunds Univ. Årsskr., N.F., Avd. 2, Bd. **59**, no. 7.

Nilsson, T. (1964b) *Entwicklungsgeschichtliche Studien im Ageröds Mosse, Schonen*. Lunds Univ. Årsskr., N.F., Avd. 2, Bd. **59**, no. 8.

Nilsson, T. (1967a) *Geologische Datierung einer mesolithischen Küstensiedlung in Häljarp, Schonen*. Acta Univ. Lund, Sec. 2, No. 14.

Nilsson, T. (1967b) *Pollenanalytische Datierung mesolithischer Siedlungen im Randgebiet des Ageröds Mosse im mittleren Schonen*. Acta Univ. Lund., Sect. 2, No. 16.

Nilsson, T. (1968) Pollenanalytische Datierung der Pfeilfunde aus Loshult im nördlichsten Schonen. GFF Bd. **90**, H. 4. Stockholm.

Nœ-Nygaard, N. (1967) Recent "Kokkenmøddinger" i Ghana. *Geografisk Tidsskrift* **66**, 179–97.

Nordenskiöld, A. E. (1881) *The Voyage of the Vega round Asia and Europe*. London.

Nordhagen, Rolf (1933) *De Senkvartære Klimavekslinger i Nordeuropa og deres Betydning for Kulturforskningen*. Oslo.

Nordmann, V. (1936) *Menneskets Invandring til Norden* (English summary). DGU r. III, nr. 27.

Norling-Christensen, H. and Brøste, K. (1945) Skeletagraven fra Korsør Nor. *NM Arbm.* 5–17.

Nougier, L.-R. (1972) La genèse de la 'Grecque' à Mezin (Ukraine). *Préhistoire Ariégeoise* XXVII, 83–101. Tarascon-sur-Ariège.

Nummedal, A. (1921) Nogen primitive stenaldersformer i Norge. *Oldtiden* IX, 145 ff. Oslo.

Nybelin, O. (1943) Västsvenska subfossilfynd av ren, kronhjort och urox. *Göteborgs Musei Årstryck*, 99–116.

Oakley, K. P. (1969) *Frameworks for Dating Fossil Man.* 3rd edt. London.

Odner, Knut (1966) *Komsakulturen i Nesseby og Sør-Varanger.* Tromsø Univ. Skr. vol. XII.

Olsen, H. (1967) *Varanger-Funnene* IV. *Osteologisk Materiale.* Tromsø Museums Skrifter vol. VII, Hft. IV.

Osgood, C. (1940) *Ingalik Material Culture.* Yale Univ. Publ. in Anthropology, no. 22.

Ozols, J. (1971) Zum schamanismus der Jungpaläolithischen Rentierjäger von Mal'ta. *Kölner Jhb.* 12, 27–49. Köln.

Petersen, E. B. (1966) Klosterlund-Sønder Hadsund-Bøllund. *Acta Arch.* XXXVII, 77–185.

Petersen, E. B. (1970) Ølby Lyng. En Østsjællandsk Kystboplads med Ertebølle-kultur. *Aarbøger*, 5–42. See also U. Møhl.

Petersen, E. B. (1972) A Maglemose hut from Sværdborg Bog, Zealand, Denmark. *Acta Arch.* XLII, 43–77.

Petersson, M. (1951) Microlithen als Pfeilspitzen. Ein Fund aus dem Lilla Loshult Moor, Ksp. Loshult, Skåne. *Medd. LUHM,* 123–37.

Pidoplichko, I. G. (1969) *Late Palaeolithic dwellings of Mammoth bones in the Ukraine.* Kiev.

Pope, Saxton (1925) *Hunting with the bow and arrow.* New York.

Popping, H. J. (1931) *Een Magdalénien Station op de Veluwe.* De levende Natur 35.

Post, L. von (1916) Om skogsträdspollen i sydsvenska torfmosselagerföljder. *GFF* 38, 384 ff.

Post, L. von (1925) Gotlands-agen (*Cladium mariscus* R. Br.) i Sveriges post-arktikum. *Ymer* 45, 295 ff. Stockholm.

Rajewski, Zdzisław (1958) New Discoveries in Western Poland. *Archaeology* 11, 40 ff.

Rankama, K. (ed.) (1965) *The Geologic Systems. The Quaternary,* vol. I. Inter-science Publishers, London.

Rawitschur, F. (1945) The Hazel Period in the Post-glacial Development of Forests. *Nature* 156, 302–3.

Reinbacher, E. (1956) Eine vorgeschichtliche Hirschmaske aus Berlin-Biesdorf. *Ausgrabungen und Funde* 1, 147 ff. Berlin.

Rust, A. (1937) *Das altsteinzeitliche rentierjägerlager Meiendorf.* Neumünster.

Rust, A. (1943) *Die alt- und mittelsteinzeitlichen funde von Stellmoor.* Neumünster.

Rust, A. (1958a) *Die Funde von Pinnberg.* Karl Wachholz, Neumünster.

Rust, A. (1958b) *Die jungpaläolithischen Zeltanlagen von Ahrensburg.* Karl Wachholz, Neumünster.

Rydbeck, O. (1930) The earliest settling of man in Scandinavia. *Acta Arch.* **1**, 55–86.

Rydbeck, O. (1945) Skelettgraven i Bäckaskog (sittande hukläge) och dess ålder. *Medd. LUHM.* 1–44.

Rydbeck, O. and Post, L. von (1929) Ornerad skafthålsyxa av hjorthorn funnen i Höganäs. *Fornvännen* **24**, 129–154.

Salomonsson, B. (1960) Eine neuentdeckte Steinzeitliche Siedlung auf der Bjäre-Halbinsel. *Medd. LUHM,* 5–33.

Salomonsson, B. (1961) Some early Mesolithic artefacts from Scania, Sweden. *Medd. LUHM,* 5–26.

Salomonsson, B. (1962) Sveriges äldsta kontakt med Västeuropa. En boplats vid Segebro i Skåne, pp. 1–25. Off-printed from: *Proxima Thule, Sweden in prehistoric and Medieval Times,* a volume in homage to H.M. the King of Sweden. Stockholm.

Sandegren, R. (1920) *Najas flexilis* i Fennoskandia under postglacialtiden. *Svensk bot., Tidskr.* **14**, 147 ff.

Sarauw, G. F. L. (1903) En Stenalders Boplads i Maglemose ved Mullerup sammenholdt med beslægtede Fund. *Aarbøger,* 148–315.

Sauramo, M. (1938) Ein harpunierter Seehund aus dem Litorina-ton Nordfinnlands. *Quartär* I, 26–35. Berlin.

Sawicki, L. (1936) Das Alter der Swiderien–Industrie im Lichte der Geomorphologie des Weichselurstromtales der Ungebung von Warschau. *Festschr. zur Hundertjahrfeier des Mus vorgesch. Altertümer in Kiel,* 18–42. Neuminster.

Scheffer, J. (1674) *The History of Lappland.* London.

Schindler, R. (1960) *Die Bodenaltertümer der Freien und Hansestadt Hamburg.* Hamburg.

Schnittger, B. and Rydh, H. (1940) *Grottan Stora Förvar på Stora Karlsö.* Stockholm.

Schuldt, E. (1961) *Hohen Viecheln. Ein mittel-steinzeitlicher Wohnplatz in Mecklenburg.* Deutsche Akad. d. Wissen. zu Berlin Schr. d. Sect. für Vor und Frühgeschichte, Bd. **10**.

Schwabedissen, H. (1944) *Die mittlere steinzeit im westlichen Norddeutschland.* Neumünster.

Schwabedissen, H. (1953) Fruchtschalen aus Schleswig-Holstein und ihre Zeit. *Offa* Bd. **12**, 14–66.

Schwabedissen, H. (1954) *Die Federmesser-Gruppen des nordwesteuropäischen Flachlandes.* Neumünster.

Schwabedissen, H. (1958) Die Ausgrabungen im Satruper Moor. *Offa* Bd. **16**, 5–28.

Schwabedissen, H. (1956) Ein horizontierter 'Breitkeil' aus Satrup und die mannigfachen Kulturverbindungen des beginnenden Neolithikums im Norden und Nordwesten. *Palaeohistoria* XII, 409–68.

Schwantes, G. (1923) Das Beil als Scheide zwischen Paläolithikum u. Neolithikum. *Archiv. f. Anthropologie*, N.F. Bd. **20**. Heft, 13 f.

Schwantes, G. (1928) Nordisches Paläolithikum und Mesolithikum. *Mitt. aus dem Mus. f. Volkerkunde in Hamburg*, XIII, 159–252.

Schwantes, G. (1939) *Die Vorgeschichte Schleswig-Holsteins (Stein- und Bronzeseit)*. Neumünster, 1939.

Semenov, S. A. (1964) *Prehistoric Technology* (trans. M. W. Thompson). Cory, Adams and Mackay, London.

Shawcross, W. (1967) An investigation of prehistoric diet and economy on a coastal site at Galatea Bay, New Zealand. *PPS*, 107–31.

Shetelig, H. and Falk, H. (1937) *Scandinavian Archaeology*. Oxford Univ. Press.

Siiriäinen, A. (1969) Über die Chronologie der Steinzeitlichen Küstenwohnplätze Finnlands im Lichte der Uferverschiebung. *SM*, 40–73.

Siiriäinen, A. (1971) Shoreline Dating of the Säräisniemi I – Ceramics in Finland. *SM*, 9–19.

Siiriäinen, A. (1972) A gradient/time curve for dating Stone Age shorelines in Finland. *SM*, 5–18.

Simonsen, P. (1951) Nye fund fra Himmerlands Ertebølle-kultur. *Aarbøger*, 199–226.

Simonsen, P. (1958) Recent research on East Finnmark's Stone Age. *Rivista di Scienze Preistoriche* XIII, 131–50.

Simonsen, P. (1961) *Varanger-Funnene* II. *Fund og udgravninger på fjordens Sydkyst*. Tromsø Museum.

Smith, A. G. (1970) The influence of Mesolithic and Neolithic man on British vegetation: a discussion. In D. Walker and R. B. West (eds.), 81–96.

Stenberger, M. (1943) *Das Gräberfeld von Västerbjers auf Gotland*. Stockholm.

Stenberger, M. (1964) *Det forntida Sverige*. Almqvist and Wicksells, Uppsala.

Stimming, R. (1917) Die Renntierzeit in der märkischen Havelgegend. *Mannus Z.* **8**, 233–40. Berlin.

Stimming, R. (1925) Die Ancyluszeit in der markischen Havelgegend. *Archiv für Anthropologie* N.F. XXI, 109–21. Brunswick.

Stjerna, Knut (1911) Före Hällkistiden. *Antikvarisk Tidskrift* **19**, 2, 1–64. Stockholm.

Sturdy, D. (1972) Reindeer economics in Late Ice Age Europe. Cambridge Ph.D. dissertation.

Šturms, E. (1970) *Die Steinzeitlichen Kulturen des Baltikums*. Bonn.

Suess, H. E. (1970) Discussion. In T. E. Allibone *et al.* 54–5.

Sulimirski, Tadeusz (1970) *Prehistoric Russia. An Outline*. John Baker, London.

Tansley, A. G. (ed.) (1911) *Types of British Vegetation*. Cambridge Univ. Press.

Tauber, H. (1960) Danske Kulstof-14 dateringer af arkæologiske prøver I. *Aarbøger*, 243–59.

Tauber, H. (1965) *Differential pollen dispersion and the interpretation of pollen diagrams.* DGU, II R. Nr. **89.**

Tauber, H (1967) Danske Kulstof-14 dateringer of Arkæologiske prøver II. *Aarbøger* 1966, 102–30.

Tauber, H. (1971) Danske Kulstof-14 dateringer of Arkæologiske prøver III. *Aarbøger* 1970, 120–42.

Taute, W. (1968) *Die Stielspitzen-Gruppen im Nordlichen Mitteleuropa.* Böhlan, Köln.

Tegner, H. S. (1951) *The roe deer, their history, habits and pursuit.* London.

Thomas, S. E. (1954) Sjöholmen, site 179. Appendix I in Althin, 1954, 169–87.

Thomasson, H. (1937) Harpunfyndet från Hästefjorden. *Göteborgs och Bohusläns Fornminnesforenings Tidskr.* 32–56.

Thomasson, H. (1938) Harpunfyndet från Hästefjorden. *Göteborgs och Bohusläns fornminnesförenings Tidskrift.* (1937), 32–56.

Thompson, M. W. (1961) Foreword to translation of A. L. Mongait's *Archaeology in the USSR.* Penguin Books, London.

Thomsen, T.(1907) Une trouvaille de l'ancien âge de la pierre. La trouvaille de Braband. *Mém. d. Ant. du Nord,* 1902–7, 161–232.

Thomson, D. F. (1939) The Seasonal Factor in Human Culture. *PPS,* 209–21.

Thomson, P. W. (1926) Pollenanalytische Untersuchungen von Mooren und lakustrinen Ablagerungen in Estland. *GFF* **48,** 489–97.

Tilander, I. (1961) Pollen-analytical dating of the Elk Antler Mattock-head from Harlösa, Skåne. *Medd. LUHM,* 27 ff.

Troels-Smith, J. (1941) Pollenanalytisk Tidsbestemmelse af Urokseknoglen med Menneske fremstillinger fra Ryemarksgaard. *NM Arbm.*

Troels-Smith, J. (1943) Geologisk Datering af Koelbjerg-skeletettet. *Aarbøger,* 232–8.

Troels-Smith, J. (1946) Stammebaade fra Aamosen. *NM Arbm.* 15–23.

Troels-Smith, J. (1953) Ertbøllekultur–Bondekultur. *Aarbøger,* 5–62.

Troels-Smith, J. (1955) Senglacialtidens Jægere. *NM Arbm.* 129–53.

Troels-Smith, J. (1957) Maglemosetidens jægere og fiskere. *NM Arbm.* 101–33.

Troels-Smith, J. (1959) En Elmetræs–Bue fra Aamosen og andre træsager fra tidlig–neolitisk tid. *Aarbøger,* 91–145.

Troels-Smith, J. (1960) *Ivy, Mistletoe and Elm. Climate indicators – Fodder Plants. A Contribution to the Interpretation of the Pollen Zone Border VII–VIII.* DGU, IV. R., Nr. **4.**

Troels-Smith, J. (1967) The Ertebølle Culture and its Background. *Palaeohistoria* XII, 505–25. Groningen.

Vankina, L. (1970) *Sārnates Purva Apmetne.* (German summary) (*Торфяниковая стоянка Сарнате*). Riga.

Vayda, A. P. (ed.) (1965) *Man, culture and animals.* Washington.

WORKS CITED IN THE TEXT

Vayda, A. P. (ed.) (1969) *Environment and Cultural Behaviour*. The Natural History Press, New York.

Vebæk, C. L. (1939) New finds of Mesolithic ornamented bone and antler artefacts in Denmark. *Acta Arch.* **9**, 205–23.

Vebæk, C. L. (1940) Bøllund, en Boplads fra den ældre Stenalder i Vestjylland. From *Fra Danmarks Ungtid* (Brønsted Festschrift: edt. H. Norling-Christensen and P. V. Glob), 21–41.

Vita-Finzi, C. and Higgs, E. S. (1970) Prehistoric Economy in the Mount Carmel area of Palestine: Site Catchment Analysis. *PPS*, 1–37.

Vogt, E. (1937) *Geflechte und gewebe der steinzeit*. Basel.

Walker, D. and West, R. G. (1970) *Studies in the Vegetational History of the British Isles*. Cambridge Univ. Press.

Welinder, S. (1971) *Tidigpostglacialt Mesolithicum i Skåne*. Acta Arch. Lundensia. Ser. in 8° Minore. No. 1.

Werner, Margit (1970) Flintfynd efter svenska Västkusten. *Ymer*, 227–42.

West, R. G. and McBurney, C. B. M. (1954) The Quaternary Deposits at Hoxne, Suffolk, and their Archaeology. *PPS*, 131–54.

Westerby, E. (1927) *Stenalderbopladser ved Klampenborg*. Copenhagen.

Westerlund, Ernst (1970) Stenåldersverkstad vid Tärnasjön. *Västerbotten*, 20–1. Umeå.

Zeist, W. van (1957) De mesolithische boot van Pesse. *Nieuwe Drentsche Volksalmanak*, 4–11.

Zemljakof, B. F. (1940) Arkticheskii paleolit na severe SSSR. *Sovetskaya Arkheologiya* **5**. Moscow.

Zeuner, F. E. (1950) *Dating the Past. An Introduction to Geochronology*. 2nd edt. Methuen, London.

INDEX

INDEX

colonisation 26, 29, 68, 79, 99 f., 200–9, 219–27, 233–9
continuity 25 f., 29, 106, 128, 148–51, 158 f., 161, 163–8, 171–83, 237, 239
cooking (skärvsten) mounds 235 f.
Copenhagen, Denmark 80, 85, 161
cormorant (Phalacrocorax carbo) 142, 246
crane (Grus sp.) 139, 142, 246
cultural idioms see: Ahrensburg; Bloksbjerg; Ertebølle; Fosna-Komsa; Gudenaa; Hamburg; Kongemose; Kunda; Lihult; Lyngby–Bromme–Segebro; Magdalenian; Maglemose; Nøstvet; Rössen; Suomusjärvi; Swidry–Chwalibogowice; Vedbæk
culture 12; see also: change; continuity; cultural idioms; culture contact; social groups and systems; psychic needs; technology; territories (social)
culture contact 183–9, 229
Czechoslovakia 79, 81

Darling, F. 64
Degerbøl, M. 48, 50, 55, 58 ff., 63 f., 85, 91 ff., 137, 140 f., 144, 147, 196
Deimern, Germany 96 f.
Denmark 33–6, 38 f., 43, 58 f., 66, 69 ff., 73, 79–87, 91, 93 f., 110 ff., 116, 118, 121 f., 126 f., 130–7, 142–7, 149–52, 155, 158–74, 176 ff., 180–99, 205, 207, 229, 232, 237, 245 ff.
digging sticks 146
divers (Colymbus sp.) 142, 246
Djupedal, Sweden 208
dog (Canis familiaris) 65, 121, 140, 195, 198, 231, 245, 253
dolomitic flint 211
dolphin (Delphinus delphis) 192, 253
domestic animals: dog (Canis familiaris) 17, 140, 195, 231; sheep/goat (Ovis aries/ Capra hirca) 17, 65, 196; horse (Equus caballus) 17, 65; ox (Bos taurus domesticus) 17, 65, 196; pig (Sus scrofa domesticus) 17, 65
domestication see: domestic animals; cereals
Dordogne, France 95
drills 108
Dryas 46 ff., 71–5, 77, 81 f., 84, 87, 90 f., 94 f., 98 f.
duck (Anas sp.) 142, 246
Duvensee, Germany 100, 102, ff., 109, 112, 144, 146
dwellings 19 f., 96 f., 104 f., 203, 212, 230
Dyrholm, Denmark 137, 163 f., 167, 170, 181, 197 f.

'Early Coastal Culture' 190 ff.
Eckertsdorf, Germany 72 f.
ecology 2 ff., 7, 10 ff., 27 f., 70, passim; see also: environment
economy 4, 9 ff.; see also: redistribution; seasonality; sub-division of labour; subsistence; technology
Edgren T. xxii
Eemian 66
Egemarke, Denmark 158
Ekholm, G. xxii 239
Elinelund, Denmark 169
Elisavichi, USSR 148, 151
elk (Alces alces) 49, 59, 62 ff., 84, 114 ff., 119 ff., 133, 136 f., 142, 158, 191, 224 f., 231, 234 ff., 245, 253
elm (Ulmus) 53, 56, 124, 127
Emmersboek, Denmark 135
Engesvang, Denmark 158
England 3 f., 43, 53, 100 f., 106 ff., 112 ff., 122 f., 127, 130, 134 ff., 139 f., 142, 145, 175, 227, 245 ff.
environment 4, 9, 11; see also: climate; fauna; glaciation; land/sea; soils; vegetation
Ephedra distachya 48
erämaanomistukset 17 f.
Ertebølle Phase, Denmark 137, 160 f., 163 f., 166 ff., 171 f., 176 ff., 180–98, 205, 207, 229
Eskimos 89 f., 94 ff., 123, 126, 216 f., 227
Esthonia, USSR 22, 42, 101, 115, 134 f., 144, 175, 225 ff., 231 f., 237
ethnographic data, European: xix, 142 f., 145, 216; see also: Algonquin Indians; Bushmen; Eskimos; Maori; Nuer; Torres Straits; Wik-Monkan
eustacy 28, 42, 180
Evans-Pritchard, E. 3, 24
Evenus, Norway 216
exchange see: redistribution

Faareveille, Denmark 197
fabod 18
Faegri, K. xx f., 46, 53
Falbygden, Sweden xxiii, 33
farming see: agriculture
fauna see: birds; fish; mammals; reptiles
Fennoscandian moraines 38 ff., 50, 90, 99
Finiglacial 39
Finland 33, 38, 42 ff., 98, 149, 219–33, 239
Finnmark 211 ff., 213
Finseøya, Norway 204, 209
Firbas, F. 124
fire, use of 53

275